TRAVELS IN AN AMBASSADOR

MICHAEL TOBERT

Travels in an Ambassador

Published by Ormolu Publishing, Fife, Scotland

ISBN 9798323296507

The author's photo is by Caroline Trotter
The cover art is by Jurek Pütter
Typesetting by www.bookstyle.co.uk

to Shunryu Suzuki

ABOUT THE AUTHOR

Travels in an Ambassador is an account of Michael Tobert's first visit to India. Many visits have followed since, as have two novels with a very Indian flavour: *The Mating Call of the Racket-tailed Drongo* and *Karna's Wheel*. He is also the author of *Pilgrims in the Rough* and *Cryptogram*.

For more about the author, please visit
www.michaeltobertbooks.com.

INTRODUCTION

One of the pleasures of being a solo tourist with notebook in hand is that the evenings are reliably enjoyable. Over supper, with a smile on your face, you note down all those little details that made the day delightful or, indeed, not so delightful. But even if not delightful, you have come through. Whatever misadventures may have occurred, here you are; you're alive, you're able to eat, another eventful day lies ahead.

This book is primarily an account of my first visit to this extraordinary country. First visits are the best visits. Nothing quite matches the excitement, the open-mouthed wonder, those moments when you think to yourself, 'Really?'

If there is one thing, however, which does add to the experience of the first-time visitor (or any visitor for that matter), it's a smattering of history. India is so vast, so ancient, so teeming with different cultures and religions that travelling across it without any history is like being in a bath without any water. It's just not the full monty.

So, by way of supplement, you'll discover as you go along sundry bath-filling footnotes and, at the end, the shortest history of India ever written.

But that's for later. Now it's time to get travelling.

THE STOPS (IN STARTING ORDER)

PART ONE

Delhi (1)

Delhi (2)

Delhi (3)

Varanasi

Khajuraho

The Jungle (Madhya Pradesh)

Agra

Pushkar

Jodhpur

Jaisalmer

Luni

Udaipur

Jaipur

Back to Delhi

PART TWO

Calcutta / Kolkata

Kaziranga

Kalimpong

Gangtok

Pemayangtse

Darjeeling

Chandigarh

Shimla

Back to Delhi (again)

And (to conclude) An Extremely Brief History of India.

PART ONE

1. DELHI (1)

… arrival, survival.

India, so I thought then (and still think), is a country like no other. It isn't Europe. It isn't America. It isn't a place to which you just slip across. Going to India, is an expedition, an adventure, a journey into the unknown.

By way of preparation, I sought advice from a doctor friend who has family in India. He sucked his teeth and muttered about food hygiene. 'How strong is your stomach?' he asked. 'Probably best to steer clear of street food, roadside cafés, that sort of thing, until you're hardened up. And don't drink unbottled water. Don't drink it and don't dream of eating anything that's been washed in it … like a tomato. Oh, and watch out for the mosquitoes. Drainage, you know, not always what it should be.' Then, smiling broadly, he added by way of encouragement, 'Still, if you're not ravaged by dysentery and diarrhoea, mugged and left for dead in a back alley, seduced by a water-injected water melon, eaten by a giant bug or bitten by a rabid rat, you may discover that, for all its faults, India is the greatest country on earth.'

'Can't wait,' I said.

And here I was. The cabin doors had been thrown open and, moments later, I was hit by a wall of heat and a sweet, pungent aroma somewhere between incense and red-hot peppers. I had arrived in Delhi.

The airport emptied fast and, before long and to my considerable surprise, I found myself more or less alone. This was not as advertised. Alone in India! Had I come to the right place? The scene reminded me somewhat of the airport at Edinburgh, except for a comforting difference of about 30° Celsius. I took stock. I took a taxi.

The driver proudly announced that he was 'very experienced. I driving 10 years.' Which was just as well because I spent most of the journey with my mouth hanging open in disbelief. Was I on my way from the airport to my hotel or had we taken a wrong turning and were now making our way through the inner suburbs of insanity? Cars were buzzing around us as furiously as if we had stolen honey from the hive. An ancient bus, which was so far beyond 'rusty' as to have become just 'rust', was jinking between lanes like a rugby three-quarter, with young men hanging on to its external surfaces like human earrings. What if it stopped suddenly? What if the passengers lost their grip or were swung out and, then, on the way back, came crashing through its sides like a troupe of Indian Arnold Schwarzeneggers? The whole contraption would probably disintegrate into a heap of jagged iron filings, into which we would, unhappily, plough.

It didn't bear thinking about. I didn't. I was too busy

worrying about terminal carbon monoxide poisoning. Had nobody heard of catalytic converters, or at the very least engines that burnt fuel rather than emit it in the form of noxious gas? This was traffic beyond the imagining of this western European. When exhaust clouds weren't being fired at me like floaty black cannonballs, my eardrums were being battered by the incessant hooting. Either Delhi drivers were deaf, or they had expired from too much CO and were slumped, asphyxiated, over their car horns.

I reached for my seat belt (how naïve can you get?) and cowered in the back seat gibbering quietly as we swerved past an ox-cart that had lumbered out of a side street. In so doing, we cut in front of a family of four on a scooter. Dad braked sharply. Mum, who was sitting side-saddle carrying a baby in her arms, wobbled alarmingly. And do you know what? They didn't mouth obscene imprecations at us. They didn't flick V-signs. They didn't even look round. They took this narrowest of escapes with complete calm and composure – which was more than could be said for myself.

The road narrowed as we reached Old Delhi, and the traffic congealed. Nothing I had read or heard about India had prepared me for this. I had expected a slightly decayed grandeur. Mughal temples frayed at the edges. Elegant edifices in need of a lick of paint. I hadn't expected a war zone. The buildings looked as if a squadron of bombers had seen fit to unload their cargo overhead, and nobody had bothered with repairs since.

Around this bombsite, a destitute crowd the size of Manchester drifted past the car windows. For some reason, the business of the city seemed exclusively given over to selling tyres, probably retreads. Probably retreads of retreads. If there were other 'shops', and I suppose there must have been, I didn't notice them. And woven through this human tapestry were cows, which grazed contentedly on mounds of abandoned litter, meandered down the street or simply slept, reassured by the certain knowledge that even if they happened to become cataleptic while ruminating between the bumpers of rush-hour traffic, no harm would come to them. Cows in India are sacred, and any Hindu who accidentally kills one is encouraged to go to the Ganges – the sort of diversion that can take quite a chunk out of your weekend.

We made it to the Hotel. Check-in was leisurely, but I didn't mind a bit. I was still alive. Small mercies like this tend to put a spring in my step. I felt perky and ready to see the town. I splashed water on my face, taking great care not to swallow a drop, bounced out of the hotel and took a cab down to the nearest monument: the Red Fort.

The taxi was an Ambassador, the old Morris Oxford, the sort of vehicle that was obsolete in Britain after the 1950s. The engine went nicely enough, but I realised as soon as I sat down that the upholstery was going to be a problem. It was entirely without backbone. If I sat upright, the back seat stayed in place but, as I leant against it, it flattened out, like a recliner. Every time we hit a bump, I was thrown against the back seat – which gave way beneath me and had me stretched out staring up at the roof. It was amusing the first time. 'Whoops, how funny, my seat has collapsed, ha ha.' However, it was the kind of joke that became less uproarious with every crater – and Old Delhi roads are full of them – so that after a while I wasn't laughing at all. I stretched myself out as lightly as I could and was carried to the Red Fort as if on one of those racing toboggans, where you lie on your back, and try to look at the world through your knees. In this sporting position, I was just about able to see out of the window, skyward.

The Red Fort was massive, red (like boiled lobster), imposing and closed. I wandered around the outside for half an hour or so, surprised, impressed and amazed at how huge it was. Shah Jehan, the last but one of the Great Mughals (more later), built this enormous pile in 1648. Inside he kept his considerable harem and indulged himself on a scale that would take a fevered imagination even to dream about. In his spare moments, he also sat on the most splendid treasure of all, the Peacock Throne, which was so over the top that the world was said to have run short of gold in building it.[1]

I'd have liked to have gone in and nosed about and gawped, but it was getting late and, as I said, the fort was shut. Not that I would have seen the Peacock Throne in any event. The Persians nicked it when they sacked Delhi in 1739 and took away enough loot to remit all taxes in Persia for three years[2].

Anyway, I was strolling around looking at those vast walls positively dripping with history, and vaguely wondering what to do next, when a young, thin, moustachioed Indian lad invited me to step aboard his bicycle rickshaw. He proposed to pedal me across an enormous junction and then, if we made it through, onto a major thoroughfare called Chandi Chowk and around the old market lanes nearby.

This was about the hundredth such proposition I'd received in the last fifteen minutes, but what the hell. Off we started into a torrent of oncoming traffic. Now a bicycle rickshaw is like a pony and trap without the pony. It's a very outdoors experience.

I hadn't fully appreciated this until that moment but sitting in nothing more than a waist-high sheet of the thinnest metal ever milled, while surrounded by substantial vehicles which didn't look as if they regarded you as an object worth going out of their way to avoid, was a bit like slicing a baguette with no clothes on. Your imagination gets to work and comes up with plenty of possibilities you'd rather not dwell on.

I started to chatter inanely – it's a nervous reaction – but, from these random scatterings of verbiage, Shibu, the young cyclist, and I managed to progress to conversation. We talked about his bicycle. It looked shiny and new. Compared to the others on the road, this was not saying a great deal, but it was definitely a cut above. Shibu was proud of it. It cost him 50 rupees (70p) a day to rent, and anything he made over and above that was his. A new rickshaw, I discovered, cost 4,000 rupees (under £60), a distant fortune for the rickshaw drivers. I did the sums. 50 rupees a day for the rickshaw owner. Say 300 days a year. That's 15,000 rupees a year for a layout of 4,000. The capitalist gets all his money back in three months. So it goes. As the Dundee jute workers in the 1900s were prone to lament; '*Oh dear me, the world is ill-divided / Them that works the most are aye wi least provided.*'

The Chandi Chowk was magical. This was November and the time of Diwali, the festival of lights. The traffic was at a standstill. The chowk was choked: choc-a-bloc. It was party time. The people were out celebrating and we were tugged along by the happy current. I sat back in the warm evening air watching Shibu weave through the milling thousands taking their gentle pleasures, and thought that I had come a long way in the last 24 hours.

We drifted past a bicycle whose back wheel had collapsed under the strain of carrying an enormous sack of grain, and turned off into an indoor warren of narrow lanes. Cut into the walls of these lanes were arched openings stuffed with people sleeping and selling. They were no doubt aching with poverty, but all I can say is that they didn't look unhappy. In fact, they looked a good deal happier than, let's say, 90% of the people on the London Underground or just about everybody in Paris. And considering that we were in back alleys of the type that any self-respecting Victorian cutpurse would have considered home, I never felt in the slightest danger.

Shibu wanted to show me a temple. He parked the rickshaw by abandoning it where it stood, unlocked. We took off our shoes, climbed some steep steps and were guided around by a boy at the door. Twenty minutes later we came back. Nobody had stolen my shoes. Nobody had stolen Shibu's bicycle. This was impressive. Where else in the world (apart from Switzerland) can a man leave valuable possessions – in Shibu's case, his entire source of income – lying unguarded in the street in the sure and certain knowledge that, when he returned, it would still be there?

Shibu took me back to the Fort. Who should be waiting for me there, like an expectant father, but the taxi driver who had brought me? I can't think what had possessed me, unless I'd struck my head harder than I remembered on the way here but, apparently, I'd asked him to hang on. The big vein in my neck started to throb in anticipation. There was nothing for it but to step aboard, lie back like Count Dracula in his coffin and be tobogganed back to the hotel. But at least it was cheap. For 30 rupees (45p), a taxi will wait an hour. For 100 rupees, he'll sit it out until the last trumpet. Can't grumble at that.

It was, by now, late and I was weary. Bed beckoned, and, as I lost consciousness somewhere in the airspace above my sheets, my last recollection was that, should I make it through until morning, I would have negotiated Act 1, Scene 1 of the Indian adventure. That would be a start.

On the importance of timing and the Peacock Throne (which I didn't get to sit on).

It doesn't matter whether you're boiling an egg or invading India, timing is everything. This was clearly understood by the Persian, Nadir Shah, who picked 1739 to loot Delhi. No better year than that. India was between empires. The last of the Great Mughal emperors, Aurangzeb, died in 1707 and, by 1739, his successors were emperors in name only. The British, who were to fill the imperial gap, were still carving out a presence in Bengal. (More on all this later.) The doors to India were open.

Before Nadir Shah got his hands on all that loot, India was rich. In 1600, a quarter of everything made in the world was made in India. (England at that time – good Queen Bess, Shakespeare and all that – contributed less than a measly 3%.) Much of the profit found its way into the Mughal treasury, giving the Emperor an income of some £10,000 million in today's money. No other monarch came remotely close[3].

Besides the Peacock throne, which by the way included the Koh-i-Noor diamond, Nadir Shah made off with 700 elephants, 4000 camels and 12,000 horses carrying wagons overflowing with gold and precious stones. The only things he left behind were Delhi's uncountable dead. 200 years of Mughal accumulation went up the swanee and the power of the Mughal elite with it. That's what comes of hoarding!

Now, should you be wondering who on earth are these Mughal people, don't worry. All – or at least some – will shortly be revealed.

2. DELHI (2)

… how I received valuable advice, saw 15.7%
of the ancient cities of Delhi, and lost my hat.

I woke up next day and, for the first time, took a deep and relaxing breath. I was just starting to count my blessings – being alive and kicking was high on the list – when the phone rang. It was not bad news. On the contrary. People can be very kind. I had, before setting out, written to an Indian gentleman with whom I had only a slight acquaintance. There he was, on the phone, inviting me for a round at Delhi Golf Club and to a party afterwards.

Golf courses are good places to get confirmation from your companions of those things you believe to be true but for which you'd welcome a nod of agreement. One thing I confirmed – though I was pretty certain about this beforehand – was that if a course is surrounded by jungle, it's not a good idea to go in there looking for your ball. Snakes! They don't enjoy being trodden on. (Who does?) The other thing I managed to road test, at least in a fragmentary way between shots, was a few ideas about Indian history. This has since solidified into my Five-Clump summary. Since you can't go anywhere in India without bumping into its history, I offer this as a route map[A]. (I'll plump up the clumps as we go along but, for a little more, you might also like to turn to the Appendix; *An Extremely Brief History of India).*

That evening I smoothed out the creases in my jacket, dug into my holdall for a token of my appreciation (a pot of Dundee marmalade) and went to the party. There, a man who worked for the Indian railways filled me in on its mysteries. It has plenty of track (40,000 miles of it, apparently), plenty of stations (7,000) and plenty of journeys each day (12m). 'Isn't it a wonder,' he asked, 'with all that going on, that it works as well as it does?' He looked at me for confirmation. I confirmed. Though completely ignorant on the subject, it did feel rather wonderful: all that track and all those journeys.

Somehow thereafter I found myself blended into a group of young and articulate mothers who were talking about babies. Their own. This was at a level of detail that left me wishing I'd paid more attention, when my kids were younger, to the finer points of pureed beans and mashed vegetable stew with chocolate sauce.

I listened intently, doing my best to retrieve some nugget which might allow me to include myself in the conversation.

A *Clump One, the Hindu Age,* c.1500BCE - 1001CE: Buddha, Ashoka, good times relatively speaking, 8/10. *Clump Two, the Muslim invasions,* 1001 - 1526: Buckets of blood, 2/10. *Clump Three, the Great Mughals,* 1526 - 1707: a mixed bag but with an impressive building programme (remember the Taj Mahal?) 6/10. *Clump Four, the British,* early 18th century – 1947: (hmm, also a mixed bag; we'll get to them). *Clump Five, Independence,* from 1947 onwards.

Finally, feeling that I could stand there no longer without saying something, I blurted out, like the idiot I am, 'There seem to be a lot of them about... babies... in India.' The conversation stopped abruptly. There was a pause, a group recalibration, a silent fall-back into private thoughts. Then, one very kind woman, who I will always remember with gratitude, smiled and said, 'Yes. 15 million a year, one baby every 29 seconds, enough to populate Chile. There was a new Chile this year. There will be another one next year, and the year after, and the year after that.' I had been rescued. Conversation resumed.

Population, I discovered, had the same resonance for educated Indians as the iceberg had to passengers on the Titanic. It worried them. It was what was going to sink them all, if nothing changed. The conversation moved on naturally to disease. Malaria was back. 'Watch out for the mosquitoes.' Dengue fever was back too. 'A friend of a friend had died of it.' A collective thought then dawned on them, and they turned to look at me. Written all over their faces were the words: 'and we all know which pink-skinned visitor will make the best eating round here.' 'By the way', said one, picking up the unspoken theme of *things which might finish me off*, 'be careful about the water, even if it is bottled. Check the seal. Check for tampering. And if I were you, I wouldn't drink ...' – and here, in a whisper, she divulged the name of the *Forbidden Brand*. I thanked her for her advice and assured her I wouldn't forget. Certainly not.

Next morning, I felt like seeing ruins. Delhi has plenty. It must be one of the most invaded and destroyed cities in the world. In the days when Delhi was being regularly ravaged, conquerors weren't always satisfied with the keys to the city, and a note pinned to the taps in the palace bathroom saying that they could do with a squirt of WD-40. They wanted blood and guts. When Timur the Lame (Tamburlaine) conquered Delhi in 1398, he slaughtered 50,000 prisoners (in an hour) – and he was only passing through.[4] Those that stayed around longer usually decided to obliterate the existing city and build a new one. That's why there are seven former cities in Delhi.

I thought I would spend the day looking round them. I needed a guide and the hotel lined me up with a chubby, smiling, utterly charming gentleman called Satya Gupta. One of the first things I discovered about Satya was that he was not a great believer in the virtues of stopping. Once he had locked onto a target, that was it. No diversions were tolerated.

We decided to make Tughluqabad, the third city of Delhi and the furthest away, our first port of call. We headed south. After about five minutes, I happened to notice an ancient fort about 200 yards to our left, which I thought might be worth a look. Satya didn't. A brief discussion ensued. Satya pointed out how difficult it would be to stop. There would be nowhere to park. We wouldn't be allowed in. It would take too much time. And then, before the 'but' that was forming on my lips could see the light of day, he cut me short with the sort of look mothers give their children when they are being difficult. It was the ultimate raised eyebrow, the penetrating stare over the half-moon glasses, the one that says, 'I said no, darling, and no means no.' That always did for me as a child. Somehow, I could never find the right reply. So we drove on to Tughluqabad while I sat in the back, muttering.

When we arrived, we stopped by the side of the road and got out. Satya pointed at some old City-like ruins on the far side of an unpromising area of scrubland and then scrambled down a sparse embankment to relieve himself. A few goats were grazing among the battered walls, boys were playing an impromptu game of cricket and, apart from an indication that new concrete foundations had been put down close to the road, not a great deal else was to be seen.

If this was as close as I could get (as Satya said – and which I seriously doubted), the Tughluqs deserved better. Few dynasties have produced a more charismatic figure than the demented and patricidal genius, Mohammed Tughluq, a Sultan who, able and generous as he may have been, spilt blood with an abandon rarely seen even in the annals of India's gory and ensanguined history[B].

Mohammed Tughluq was completely barking, no two ways about it. If you incurred his displeasure, you were lucky if you were merely invited to join the happy band queuing at the city gates for their turn to be executed. Otherwise, you were likely to have your skin stripped from your body, stuffed with straw and sent on tour round the Provinces. Alternatively, you could end up being casseroled (with rice) and served to your own children. Charming. Leftovers were thrown to the elephants.'[5]

Then there was the famous occasion when he took the maniacal decision to force all the citizens of Delhi to abandon their homes and march 1400 kilometres south to Daulatabad (only to march them back again a few years later). By way of persuasion, he fired one of the reluctant from a medieval catapult, and ordered a blind man who hadn't shown much enthusiasm for the move to be dragged for 40 consecutive days all the way to his new abode. Unfortunately, 'he fell to pieces on the road',

B   Mohammed Tughluq, Sultan of Delhi 1325-1351, Clump Two.

23

and the only thing that reached its destination was his leg.'[6]

None of this was of any interest to Satya. Well, we didn't actually discuss it but, being sensitive to the little nuances of life, I could detect from the way that he was holding the back door of the car open and looking at his watch that idle chit-chat would not be allowed to compromise his schedule. We hurried back.

The first and, as it turned out, his only scheduled stop was Lal Kot, the site of the first city of Delhi. The thing about Lal Kot – the awful thing if you happened to be a Hindu (as more or less everybody was back then, give or take the Buddhists and Jains that is) – was that, once it was captured by Mohammed of Ghor in 1194, the Hindus of Delhi were never again governed by people of their own religion. Not until Independence in 1947. That, I couldn't help but reflect, was a long time to be under the cosh. When the good citizens finally thought they'd seen the back of a succession of alien Muslim dynasties[c], along came the even more alien British.

Satya wanted me to see the Qutb Minar or, as we would say, Minar(et), built by those same victorious Afghans out of the ruins of 27 demolished Hindu temples. Demolishing temples was how they liked to say hello. The Qutb was a splendid sight. Wide enough for an elephant to walk up[7] and tall enough

---

c   I should point out that Nehru, India's first Prime Minister at Independence in 1947, would not have described the Muslim invasions as alien. For Nehru, there was no *us* and *them*. In his book, *The Discovery of India,* written while under somewhat gentlemanly detention by the British, Nehru saw all the different races and religions of India as absorbed in India's 'depth of soul', all part of a composite whole. The Afghans, he thought, should be considered 'a border Indian group, hardly strangers to India'. (From Patrick French, *India*, [Penguin, 2012], p.11). Nehru was a good and generous man.

to serve as a lightning conductor. It was, however, closed to climbers. The authorities didn't wish to see a repeat of that moment in 1831 when a man jumped from the top, stayed perfectly vertical for half his descent, and then offered his audience a repertoire of tightly tucked somersaults, until striking the ground like a shot from a gun. You could see their point.

Much more fascinating, in its own way, was the small iron pillar that stood nearby. This was 5th century and it hadn't rusted, which singular fact has prompted suggestions that it had been left behind by visiting spacemen.[8] It's not every day you come across something that might be extra-terrestrial, so I gave it my undivided attention. I walked round the thing a few times and made a brave attempt to recall some relevant science – which, since I don't know any science, was an endeavour always doomed to failure.

I was thus engaged in trying to dredge something from the depths, when I found myself approached by an Indian lady with an engaging smile, who asked if I would be photographed with her family. I thought initially she wanted me to take the photo, but no, she wanted me in it. This was a world first. I agreed of course. They stuck me next to her brother, Prakash, who didn't look at all pleased by the turn of events. His face was a picture. Every irate crease was spewing forth expletives, whose general drift might be summarised as 'what the *!*! has my sister done now, inviting this plonker who we've never seen before in our lives, and if I have anything to do with it will never see again, to step into our family album.' The photograph was duly taken and Shanti, for that was the lady's name, promised to send me a copy. She did. I cherish it still for the sight of Prakash doing his best to smile.

Satya had, by this time, become extremely agitated and was fluttering around in the background, anxious to transport me to what turned out to be the arms of a carpet salesman, from whom Satya would have pocketed a decent rake-off had I succumbed (which I didn't). Thence to the main business of the day, lunch. As far as Satya was concerned, this was the nub of the proceedings. Before you could say 'chicken vindaloo', I found myself sitting down in a smart restaurant, ordering myself a coke, and watching my guide tuck into a gargantuan mound of curry which I knew I would end up paying for. Curiously enough, I didn't mind. I couldn't help liking the fellow.

We chatted amiably, mainly about where Scotland actually was and, in the way these things do, the conversation drifted to my elegant St Andrews[D] golf cap. He wanted it. So did I. It was an old friend. We had travelled many miles together in victory and defeat. Besides which, it kept out the sun. I resisted his advances for as long as I could, which was about as long as a lady of the court would hold out against the advances of Shah Jehan (he, of Clump Three). Satya tried the cap on – just to see how it looked. How proud his wife would be, and how jealous his friends, were he ever to possess such magnificent headgear as this. Of course, I gave it to him, with as much grace as I could muster, and he sat through lunch with it on, squeezing the peak occasionally with both hands, as if firming up a pat of butter. After lunch, he shook my hand warmly, asked me to give his sweet regards to my wife and, with a cheery wave and

D   St Andrews is a medieval town on the East Coast of Scotland, somewhat north of Edinburgh. It is well known to golfers and students of the University, and largely unknown by everyone else.

a broad infectious grin, disappeared into the afternoon sun. So ended my guided tour of the seven cities of Delhi.

I hung around for a while outside the restaurant, read the Lonely Planet Guide and regretted that my dear old cap was now departed. Still, what was done was done. No point in brooding. I decided to see another of Delhi's magnificent sights, Humayun's tomb[E]. A taxi deposited me outside the main gate and I managed about two paces forward before being over-whelmed by kids, who gathered around me like flies around a freshly-laid dropping. Well, I was lunch to them, I suppose, and why not? They offered to sell me just about everything known to man – I went for the wooden snake (50 rupees) – but what they didn't have for sale was the one thing I really wanted. It didn't even have to be that slightly faded blue with the tastefully muted St Andrews label. I eased through, bought my ticket and walked in.

Blow me down if Satya, flaunting his new headgear, wasn't standing there with a couple of tourists. We both did a double-take simultaneously and then, with a smile that stretched from one side of my old companion to the other, he introduced his new friends. It turned out they were from Kinross, in Fife, of all places.

As we talked, I began to feel that, given we were neighbours more or less, I should warn them to keep any prized possessions hidden from Satya's acquisitive glances. This wasn't going to be

---

E   Humayun was the second of the Great Mughals. The list of Great Mughals reads like this; Babur, Humayun, Akbar, Jahangir, Shah Jehan, Aurangzeb. Of these, Humayun was the least great. He lost the kingdom his Dad (Babur) had left him and only got it back a year before he died. A bit too fond of opium was Humayun.

easy with Satya standing there. I looked the husband straight in the eye and, like a hostage who has a kidnapper with a gun in his back and wants to tell the postman to fetch the police, inclined my head ever so slightly in Satya's direction, and, out of the corner of my mouth, rasped the words 'watch out.' But there's no helping some people. The man put a protective arm around his wife and shuffled backwards, as if suspecting dengue fever.

It was probably too late anyway. The pair of them were smiling inanely, which suggested to me that they were in that euphoric, isn't the world wonderful, state that immediately follows an act of selfless generosity. Remorse would come later. Besides which, it wasn't my business. Why try to interfere with the laws of nature? The tiger eats the buck. That's how it is. I said my goodbyes, told Satya that the cap really suited him and left him to feed.

3. DELHI (3)

... Food, and other small matters of life and death

That evening, I transferred, courtesy of my kind friend, from my hotel in old Delhi to a club that occupied extensive, and probably priceless, acres of New Delhi. It had been built during the British Raj and gave every impression that not much had changed since. As soon as I arrived, I asked directions for the dining room[F]. It was cavernous. It would not have looked out of place on one of those ocean liners of old, except that it was empty apart from three minuscule waiters standing at the far

---

[F] Back home, as you may recall, my doctor friend had advised caution when eating in India; but, as I remembered, he hadn't advised equal caution everywhere. There would be places – and this Delhi club was clearly one of those – where I could eat to my heart's content without worrying about his wagging finger. There would be others where, if I chose sensibly – nothing too microbially compromised, nothing lounging seductively at just the right temperature for incubation – I'd probably be alright. And then there would be those eateries above whose entrances would be engraved the subliminal (and much suppressed) thought of every belea-guered tourist: '*abandon hope, all ye who enter here.*' I just had to steer clear of those ... and eat bananas. You can't go wrong with bananas.

end. One of them, seeing me take a seat, started on the long trek towards me and when, eventually, he arrived, I could see he was a smiling man with short grey hair, who was a good deal taller than I had initially supposed.

We began the usual ritualistic dance to establish what I might like to eat. 'You want soup?' he asked.

'No soup, thank you.' 'You want no soup?' 'Yes, no soup, thank you.'

He brought soup. I lapped it up. For the next course, I ordered from the menu. He smiled, bobbing up and down, a form of behaviour I deludedly took for comprehension. The resulting dishes, whatever they may have been (certainly nothing close to what I believed I had ordered), were delicious and I realised that there are moments when waiters really do know best. I had a tea-bag with boiled water to follow and the bill came to 83 rupees, about £1.10p.

I offered to settle in the traditional manner, with coin of the realm, but this was refused. The spirit of Queen Victoria lived on. I was asked to go to an office outside the dining room and purchase a book of tickets worth 100 rupees which could be torn out and used as currency[G]. I paid up and, clutching my 17 rupees of remaining bearer bonds, moved next door. This

G   This was a British idea which, clearly, had lived on after Independence. One thing to say for the practice is that it avoids putting temptation in the way of people with very little material wealth – and there are plenty of those in India. In spite of having one of the world's fastest growing economies, some 365 million people in India still live below the international poverty line of $1.90 a day. (Chowdhury and Keane, *To Kill a Democracy*, Oxford 2021, p. 73). While estimates on poverty vary, this 365m would make the poor of India the third largest country by population in the world, ahead of the current number 3: the USA. That's a very large number of very poor people.

happened to be the bar, which contained a welcoming and generous bunch of complete strangers. I retired some hours later, considerably the worse for wear, my 17 rupees still intact.

Something was biting my leg. It certainly wasn't a mosquito. It didn't make a stalling noise before putting its nose cone down and accelerating home like a kamikaze pilot in a Mitsubishi Zero. If it wasn't a mosquito, what was it? Whatever it may have been, it had sharp little teeth, was chomping at my nether regions and was highly resistant to my attempts to swat it off. Perhaps it was one of those Dengue-carrying insects. Don't panic. There are one billion people in India. How many die of Dengue fever? It can't be that many or I would have had inoculations. That's if they knew about Dengue fever in St Andrews. Did they know? They must have… They wouldn't … I drifted back to the land of nod.

The layout of the club was curious. Magnificent, but odd. I thought so anyway. It had gardens, lawns (some for croquet, I think), a library, a swimming pool, a ballroom and, quite probably, a host of other things I failed to discover. It also had plenty of buildings dotted about, but the problem was that most of them were identical. There was nothing distinctive, no large central building, visible from anywhere, around which a compass-deficient person like me could navigate. As a result, getting from bedroom to breakfast became a humiliating reminder of my own incompetence.

The nice man sweeping the leaves outside my bedroom would smile at me as I passed by, acknowledge my cheery 'good morning', and a few minutes later, as I reappeared from a different angle, would smile again, lean on his broom and watch me cut behind a hedge before marching off purposefully in entirely the wrong direction. Eventually, I'd bump into a door that looked as if it might be the right one, push it open, insert my bewildered head, and exclaim involuntarily to anyone who happened to be inside, 'Ah, sorry, I thought this was the dining room.' It all serves to give you an appetite though.

Over breakfast, I discovered the name of a travel agent. It must have found its way into my pocket the night before. I decided to pay a visit. The time had come to move on. The Club called a taxi for me, which whisked me away from the broad boulevards of New Delhi and into a tangle of back streets, crumbled houses and knee-deep rubbish that would have done 1945 Berlin proud. In the midst of this carnage was the office of Creative Travel ND. It was indubitably, and courageously (given its surroundings), an office: the kind of place you would walk into and say to yourself, 'this is an office.' It had fax machines, computers, photocopiers, e-mail. We were in the twenty-first century. Deepak Modgill – a name I unhesitatingly recommend – effortlessly secured a next-day ticket to Varanasi, and we sat down to plan the days ahead.

Having booked a flight out, I thought I would spend my last afternoon at the Lodi[H] Gardens, a favourite public park for Delhi-ites. The gardens were a haven of peace and tranquillity, jogging and picnics, and inescapably mammarial fifteenth century tombs, in which nobody except me seemed to be taking the slightest interest. I found myself inspecting the Shish Gumbad and the Bara Gumbad, the resting places of two Lodi nobles, each tomb with its own fulsome boob on top.

H   The Lodis were the last in the line of all those *Clump Two* dynasties. They ruled Delhi and its environs from 1451-1520 until sent packing by Babur, the first of the Great Mughals (and of Clump Three).

Seen as a pair, left breast and right, together as nature intended, and surrounded as they were by other similar rounded protuberances exhibited unashamedly across the park, I don't think it is pushing matters too far to conclude that whoever had the building contract in these parts had breasts on the brain. (It could be me of course. I accept that.)

Tearing myself away, I couldn't help noticing that I was now standing in the middle of an abandoned and, I think, impromptu picnic. A party of 16, I guessed, judging by the number of miniature wooden spatulas that were lying around. I investigated further. 'Ice cream', I concluded, having knelt down to examine the spoons closely, 'they have eaten ice cream'. Someone had also drunk *The Forbidden Brand*. A discarded bottle lay among the other pieces of evidence. This was serious. I listened for groans coming from the nearby bushes but whoever it was had obviously crawled off to die further afield.

A used copy of the Times of India rustled listlessly on the ground. If I was a street-dweller, this is where I would come. Here was peace, quiet and plenty of raw materials. I would read the newspaper, make a small fire out of discarded ice cream scoops and then, when ready to call it a day, snuggle up in a stone alcove beneath a monumental mammary and fall sound asleep.

Instead, I walked towards the park gates where I hoped my taxi would be waiting. Dusk was fast approaching. Perhaps, I wouldn't spend the night here after all. I didn't think I'd want to be out here alone as Mr Mosquito rose from his tomb in search of fresh blood. I quickened my step. But was this the exit I had come in through? It looked different... It was different. No sign of my taxi. I retraced my steps. The light was fading. I broke into a trot. A mild current of alarm pulsed through me. I could see the headline: 'Tourist trapped in Gardens. Body picked clean.' I tried another exit. Nothing. I turned around, stumbled through a break in the trees, found another path and followed it out. There, sublimely unconscious of the emotional crisis to which his client had been subjected, was my taxi. I acted, of course, as if nothing untoward had occurred, and it wasn't long before I was at the Club, exploring its vast acreage in search of a light supper, and packing my bags for Varanasi.

4. VARANASI

… hats, maps, ghats and stupas

To a westerner, not yet acclimatised to the rigours of India, Varanasi is – how shall I put it? – somewhat daunting. Driving in from the airport was a bit like Old Delhi, only more so: the uncountable multitude lining the streets, the roads choked with cows, scooters, dogs, bikes, beggars and knee-deep rubbish – it all takes a bit of getting used to.

I checked in to a hotel that Deepak had booked, and had my bags taken up to a clean, tidy, but not very restful bedroom. Coming through the walls, was the arousing call of a woman emphatically rejecting her last meal. Then, in case, I hadn't heard the first time, she gave me an encore. Ah, if only she'd stuck to bananas, I couldn't help thinking. Or was it something she'd drunk; like water? – at which point in my reflections, the power failed, and I ventured forth.

The day was hot and the first order of business was to buy a cap. Well, actually, the first order of business was to communicate to the driver that this is what I wanted to do – something that was achieved by means of arm gestures of the sort that a traffic cop would have employed if he wished to invite oncoming cars to park on his head. It seemed to work in that the driver drew to a halt alongside an appropriate-looking cluster of kiosks. There I found a stripy, peaked cap, the sort of jaunty number you could comfortably get away with at a rowing regatta. It had an Adidas motif on the front and a Nike one on the clasp but, at the price I paid, I rather doubt whether either company was receiving its usual mark-up. Indians are very creative when it comes to brand labelling. The most hopeful sticker I saw was on the door of an ancient and decrepit repair garage. It read, 'In collaboration with Mercedes-Benz AG.'

We drove on to the Bharat Mata temple, which I had read about in my illustrated Varanasi guide book. 'Bharat' is 'India'[i]. 'Mata' is 'mother' – which, like other Sanskrit words, has enough similarity to Latin and other European languages to prompt those who know about these things to suggest that both have derived from a common Indo-European tongue.[j]

Bharat Mata was a temple dedicated to Mother India, and

[i]   'Bharat' is a Sanskrit word which goes back to India's early Aryan origins. 'India' was the name used by the British, but it's not as venerable. It suggests a reference to the Indus valley which, following Partition in 1947, is now largely in Pakistan.

[j]   Sir William Jones, who was both a judge and a prodigious linguist (a useful combination if you're on the Supreme Court in Calcutta) was the first Brit to make the suggestion and one of the first Europeans to take a scholarly interest in Indian culture. In 1784, he founded the Asiatic Society in Calcutta. This was in the early days of Clump Four. *'The Sanskrit language,'* he wrote, *'is of a wonderful structure; more perfect than the Greek, more copious than the Latin, and more exquisitely refined than either.'*

its big feature was a relief map in marble of the whole country. My kind of map, in fact. Not one of those totally inadequate fold-away things, which has squiggly lines that professional map men look at and immediately recognise as a sheer cliff face, while some of us see only squiggly lines and are surprised when a distance the size of a thumbnail takes eight hours of furious driving round hairpins.

This particular map featured a 3D mountain range rising vertically from the plain, like a thick collar of rough on the edge of a closely cut green – a sort of ruff of rough. Even I could see that this was the Himalayas, and flowing from it, clear as day, were the great river systems of the Indus and the Ganges, rivers which had sustained the early Aryan settlers in northern India. It was a stirring sight.

Forbears of these Aryans spoke the common Indo-European language, so who they were and where they came from has been much debated. Hitler, you may remember, had rather particular views on the subject. For one thing, he thought they were blond and blue-eyed, which from my experience of Indians thus far was curious to say the least. The Führer's other inspired contribution was to suggest that the Aryans came from the legendary island of Thule, in the North Sea. This, so he believed, was where Aryans, fleeing from the lost continent of Atlantis, sought refuge before setting forth to seed the Master Race.[9] (Support for this view faded at much the same speed as support for the Führer himself.)

The latest thinking seems to be that, from wherever they may have started, the Aryans were in northern India between 1500 BCE and 1300 BCE[10] and, sometime thereafter, gave birth to the mystic *Vedas,* to perhaps the world's greatest epic,

The Mahabharata, and to much else besides.

The marble map was endlessly fascinating and I remained for some time slumped over the rail that protected it, with phrases of assorted comprehensibility dropping from my mouth like unwanted spaghetti. This tends to happen to me when I forget that people are watching. 'Oh, look, the Khyber Pass', I heard myself saying to absolutely no-one at all, picking out a slit in the mountains which may well have been the Khyber Pass, if it wasn't something else altogether. 'Sri Lanka', I shouted excitedly, pointing at the far end of India with the enthusiasm of a hapless navigator catching, on the distant horizon, a glimpse of what he imagines to be the first sighting of an undiscovered continent. Spasmodic utterances of similar eloquence continued to be coughed up for a while, until an old man, who was probably too deaf to be alarmed, bumped into me. This was a timely reminder that I was not alone and should leave before they started selling tickets.

I suddenly realised I was hungry. The time had come to top up that meagre slice of toast at breakfast and those two nourishing but not very filling bananas I'd had for lunch. I went back to the hotel, located its restaurant and gorged myself on black bean stew, curried cauliflower, rice, a roti and two bottles of beer. It came to an outrageous 390 rupees. I staggered out of the restaurant aghast at my extravagance. I had just spent over £5 on a meal. In St Andrews, this might have covered the cost of sitting down but, here, it felt like a King's ransom – thus confirming the general proposition that the cheaper things are, the meaner people become. Nobody goes to expensive department stores and haggles, but watch them in the Pushkar market (more anon) beating down some poor trader over the price of a bangle.

After dinner, I felt like a stroll, a quiet promenade, perhaps doffing my smart new Adidas/Nike bunnet to the ladies, perhaps taking in a quiet roadside café and watching the world go by. But not in Varanasi. That's one of the pleasures you forego. The idea of battling through all the animate and inanimate obstacles that Varanasi strews in front of you made me weary just to think of it. I went up to my room instead, listened out for gagging noises coming from the woman in the next room (all seemed quiet), and turned on the TV.

A Bollywood musical was showing. The lead role was played by a gentleman who would have given Silvester Stallone a run for his money in the 'narrowest expressive range' category, and I never thought to see that day dawn. I jumped between channels for about half an hour and was forced to the dispiriting conclusion that Indian films are not for the uninitiated. The actors don't talk. They sing, or they dance. Sometimes they gyrate their eyebrows. Flick channels as much as you like and that's all you see. Well, that's not quite true. A sports channel was showing a racing programme, fronted by an American who called himself, as far as I could make out, Randy Boss, though I suppose that could have been his job description.

Randy was a deeply worrying sight, let me tell you. It wasn't just that his eyes opened wider than anyone's you ever seen, but that they never blinked. Not once. I imagine his mother must have horse-whipped him every time a childish eyelid was batted. 'If I've told you once, Randolph,' *thwack*, 'I've told you a thousand times', *thwack*, 'DO', *thwack*, 'NOT', *thwack*, 'BLINK', *thwack*, *thwack*. (Collapse of mother into armchair, exhausted.) But it seemed to have done the trick.

Randy had eyes as motionless as those that stare back at you from fish tanks. His mouth was going nineteen to the dozen underneath, of course – he was a sports presenter after all – but, above the moving parts, his unflinching globes remained inert like a couple of frying pans waiting to receive their bacon. I wouldn't say it was entirely un-watchable. It was just that you didn't feel good when you caught yourself doing it.

Not that there was much choice. Channel 8 was showing endless pictures of models parading up and down a catwalk. Without commentary. Without so much as a whisper. It was utterly mute. So was Channel 5, which had managed to procure ten second clips of old Hollywood movies and was showing them one after the other in an order decided by a random number generator. We were treated to ten seconds of sound-less Cary Grant on a roof, then a micro clip from Abbot and Costello, then over to Gary Cooper being shot, noiselessly. After a while I began to feel I was in someone else's dream, probably an aspiring film director's who, tossing and turning in his sleep, is tantalized with all those epic moments he fears he'll never emulate. I did my best to stay with it but there's only so much of this second-hand somnolence anyone can take – so I switched off the TV and tuned into dreams of my own.

I was collected at five o'clock the next morning by Dhanajay Singh, who was to be my guide for the day. By five thirty, we were on a rowing boat on the Ganges waiting for the sun to rise over the ancient stone steps (ghats) that lined the shore. It was as calm and as colourful a scene as you could wish for: pilgrims about their early morning devotions, meditating, praying or bathing; smoke from cremation fires wafting across the river; cows and goats wandering unhindered; monkeys scampering on the ancient walls. It was a scene that might have been repeated every day for the last 3,000 years, and perhaps longer. Varanasi, which used to be called Banares, and before that, Kashi, is a city almost as old as time itself. It was around in 1100 BCE and, in spite of the fact that Muslim rulers and Hindu temples haven't always coexisted amiably, it has rebuilt itself generation after generation as the holiest of Hindu cities, on the bank of the holiest of Indian rivers, the Ganges. There is no better place in India for a Hindu to pray, or to die.

Death, of course, was not part of my plans. Nor was prayer, although I have to admit that, bobbing up and down on the lapping waters, with the chaos of Varanasi a million miles away, I did feel a slight spiritual tingle at the end of my toes. At which point, on cue, a small wiry man with dark spiky hair clambered aboard and offered his services as a masseur. Well, he didn't so much offer, as take my arm and start to manipulate it – but since I didn't physically remove it or tell him to take his ministrations elsewhere, the contract between us was, I suppose, agreed.

We paddled out into mid-stream and I lay on my stomach with my chin on my arms, while he pummelled my back, pulled my fingers out of their sockets and pushed my legs into positions they haven't been in since a couple of lads on a rugby pitch many years ago mistook me for a wishbone. No part was left unattended, including my head. He scooped up some Ganges water, which – as I was thankfully unaware at the time – has a faecal coliform count 250,000 times higher than the permitted World Health Organisation maximum[11], and poured it over my hair. He then proceeded to karate chop my scalp. If you are not expecting it – and I wasn't – this comes as a shock. It's not every day that a complete stranger sees fit to rattle your fillings and generally treat you like a piece of steak in need of tenderising. However, I came through and hardly flinched when he began his final coup de theatre. He took my eyebrow between his finger and thumb, and squeezed. Whether there were chemicals in the water that had numbed the nerves in my face, I don't know, but I have to admit I found the experience pleasurable. At least it was when he stopped. In fact, I felt a new man, ready to appreciate the stunning beauty of the sun rising suddenly and casting its golden shafts across the rippling water and onto the ghats, bringing colour to the cheeks of the stone steps and attendant pilgrims alike.

As the sun rose, Dhanajay put his hands together with his fingers pointing upwards in the position of greeting (namasté), and bowed towards it. 'We worship the sun,' he told me, which is the kind of remark that has had generations of poke-your-nose-in-other-peoples-business Christians believing that Hindus are idolatrous heathens and in urgent need of the salvation of Christ. Which they are not. They must be among the most spiritual people on earth, as you can't help but notice nearly every time you talk to a Hindu for more than five minutes. Besides which, while the religions of revelation – Christianity and Islam – have, for centuries, been bent on blood and conquest in the name of their God, the Hindus have, generally speaking, not been much inclined to impose their beliefs on foreigners. This has to count for something.

The sun sat quietly in the sky, uninterrupted by even the vaguest suggestion of a cloud. India is predictable like that. We drifted downstream, out of reach of the crowd on shore, and feasted quietly on the extraordinary medley of life paraded before us. Women, wearing saris of every colour, were knee-deep in the water, cupping it in their hands and then pouring it back as an offering. Men were bathing, washing themselves or simply standing in prayer. On the bank, sadhus (holy men) were sitting cross-legged staring into space, while monkeys looked down from the walls impassively, and dead bodies were burnt prior to their ashes being cast into the holy Ganges. Babies, apparently, (and animals) are thrown into the waters un-cremated but, fortunately, – or I might have screamed – none washed up against the side of our boat.

I asked Dhanajay if he ever swam in the river. He did, regularly. 'The water is dirty outside' – he was right about that – 'but it cleans the spirit.' He then went on to say that he drank it frequently and had suffered no ill effect. Akbar, the greatest of the Mughal emperors (Clump Three), only ever consumed Ganges water, but I daresay it contained a few less additives 500 years ago.

Dhanajay told me the names of the ghats as we floated past and, true to form, they went in one ear and out of the other. All except one, the Dasashvamedha, whose name refers back to an ancient Aryan custom which must have made young women of the day think at least twice before accepting the hand of their king in marriage. The custom in question was the Ashvamedha, the Horse Sacrifice. Now, in those long-gone days, a King would establish his power over his territory by turning loose his finest stallion and letting it roam. Any land it happened to cross would become his[12] unless the current owner felt inclined to take issue – not likely if the king had a large army and he only had 20 acres, a couple of underweight sons and an ageing bulldog for support.

When the horse had finished his year of walkabout, he came home and was suffocated to death. A sad end, you might think, for doing the king's business. Except that this was not the end. Not quite. One further duty awaited. The stallion, you will understand, represented royal power. The King's number one Queen represented fertility. The two had to mate. So the poor Queen lay down beside the still warm animal and inserted its penis between her thighs and, while this was going on, the King and his other wives offered encouragement of a sort that would not have been out of place in the royal barracks[13]. As I said, this extraordinary ritual might not have been every young queen's cup of tea. Now, the Dasashvamedha ghat celebrates ten consecutive horse sacrifices, ('das' means '10') once performed in the mists of time by a king of Banares, Divodasa – but as to the logistics of doing ten at a time, your guess is as good as mine.

The great thing about the river was that you could watch without being accosted, which was more than you could say about the labyrinth of narrow, snaky lanes that run just beyond the ghats. This was the old City of Kashi. It was still early by the time we had clambered out of the boat and made our way there, so the number of people competing for each square inch of occupiable space was slightly less than usual – in other words about as thick on the ground as the weeds in my neglected garden after a wet summer. What the place was like at rush hour, I cannot imagine.

Thank heavens for Dhanajay. He was walking in front. I was zig-zagging behind like a second-rate private detective tailing a co-respondent. Human life, in many of its forms, was ranged about us. There were beggars, some blind, some with grotesque mutilations, some with no legs. There were neatly dressed children off to school, and smartly clothed businessmen going to work. There was the pitiful sight of a girl, who couldn't have been more than ten, carrying a baby, and begging for food by placing one small cupped hand against her lips. And on it went, street vendors, destitute widows waiting to die, all concentrated in an area the size of a relative pinhead, and most of them interposed between myself and Dhanajay.

We emerged onto a wide road and sunlight. As we made our way back to the car we were followed by a man, with two bandaged stumps for legs, sitting on a trolley pushed by his business manager. He tracked us until another tourist, with a scarf wrapped round her nose and mouth, who clearly thought Varanasi was the most appalling spectacle she had ever clapped eyes on, came past the other way. She, he decided, was the better prospect.

Now, a few miles north of Varanasi is Sarnath, a quiet hamlet and a rather special place. For one thing, it has an Ashoka pillar and, since Ashoka was perhaps the finest ruler ever to grace a throne, and definitely in the top five of my all-time list of people I'd like to invite to dinner, it was here that I guided my reverential footsteps.

Ashoka was around a long time ago (269 to 232 BCE[κ]) and came to rule an empire bigger than anything the Mughals managed, stretching from Afghanistan to Nepal, and from Kashmir in the north to Mysore in the south. Like many great men, it took him a while to see the light. He scrambled to the top by reputedly slaughtering his 99 brothers. (What his

κ   Clump One (needless to add).

mum thought of this, I can't imagine.) He then ruled the country with ruthless efficiency[14], until embarking on his defining moment, the bloody conquest of Kalinga (Orissa), in which 100,000 were slain.[15]

Ashoka was so appalled by what he had done that he promptly adopted the Buddhist creed of non-violence and dotted the country with endearingly personal edicts telling his people how deplorable was the carnage in Kalinga, and how he would behave henceforth. He would restrict the slaughter of animals for food. He would give up hunting and visit Buddhist monks instead. He would pardon all offences that were pardonable. He would encourage all religious sects to live together in harmony. His edicts were written in stone, on rock faces or on specially constructed columns. 'The people of the unconquered territories lying beyond the borders of my dominion', it was chiselled, 'should expect of me only happiness.'[16]

Now tell me, how cool is this? 250 years before Christ, here was the ruler of a vast empire denouncing violence. Here was a king, not only preaching the gospel of benevolence and good conduct but, as far as we can tell, practising it. If anyone deserved an invitation to dinner, he did.

So it was that I found myself standing in front of an ancient Ashoka column, the top of which was the most splendid capital of all the Ashoka columns and, incidentally, the emblem of the modern Republic of India. The only problem was that it had fallen off, and I had to go across the road to the museum to see it. I can't say I was surprised that it had failed to stay aloft. Four large and magnificently alert back-to-back lions, who at one time carried a stone wheel on their shoulders, is quite a thing to perch on the top of a narrow 15m high pillar.[17] It did demonstrate one thing though. In days of yore, lions once roamed across India. I never knew that – but, as I subsequently found out, they still cling on; in the Gir Forest, Saurashtra, North West India.

It was a lovely warm day and I was feeling relaxed in a way I hadn't felt since coming to India. I suddenly realised why. I had space. A few people were wandering around but, compared to Varanasi or Old Delhi, the Sarnath Deer Park was as empty as the Scottish Highlands. I could breathe. I could take in air that had not just been expelled from somebody else's wind pipe. It was a good feeling and, in the way that people do when they are loose and not going anywhere in particular, I found myself ambling along, silently humming a happy tune.

I ambled past ruins where the Lord Buddha used to sit in meditation, past a large neem tree, whose twigs, so Dhanajay told me, were good for teeth massage and towards an immense mound, or Stupa, sitting squat on the ground like the Buddha himself. On this spot, in the middle of the 6th century BCE or thereabouts[L], Buddha delivered his first sermon, which makes it, for Buddhists, one of the holiest places in the world. I was at the epicentre. I stopped humming and felt rather humble. It was from this precise spot that Buddhism spread out to Nepal, Tibet, China, Japan and much of South East Asia. The curious thing is, though, that it only survived in India until the end of the twelfth century CE. A succession of Muslim regimes butchered the monks and battered the monasteries so relentlessly that Buddhism virtually disappeared from its place

---

L   Dates have a habit of moving around in this period. There's a respectable case, apparently, for suggesting the middle of the 5th century, BCE.

of birth. It didn't return in any significant numbers until the second half of the twentieth century.[18]

Varanasi airport was basic and overcrowded. It sported one shop and one toilet: the sort of place that, in Europe, is reserved for charter holidays. The plane was three hours late, but I didn't really mind. Perhaps a little, but if this had been Edinburgh I would have been apoplectic. Either I was getting used to IST, otherwise known as Indian Stretchy Time, or that early morning massage on the river had really done the trick. Or, I suppose, both.

I only started to become anxious when a goat wandered into the terminal and headed for the check-in. It turned out that it was going to Kathmandu, so that was OK. No need to worry about whether it had been properly potty trained. Actually, the goat was looking rather pleased with itself, which could only mean it was unaware of the culinary preferences in those parts. When it wandered past, I took the opportunity to lean across and whisper some advice into its rotating ear. 'Pretend to be a cow,' I said, but I don't think it heard.

By the time we boarded the airplane, the captain was anxious to make up for lost time. This was the gist of his brief announcement, and he clearly meant it. No sooner had the flight attendant begun her safety speech, than we started to taxi down the runway. The poor young woman looked rather alarmed and pressed the fast-forward button. She raced through the seat belt and oxygen mask drill and, in a blur of waving arms, was demonstrating the emergency exits, when the plane took off. Whereupon she was tipped down the aisle, and only by hanging on to a chair back and swinging into an empty seat, did she manage to stop herself being catapulted into the rear lavatory. I thought she executed the whole manoeuvre rather professionally. I looked across to check that she hadn't forgotten to fasten her seatbelt and was pleased to notice that she was doing this in the prescribed manner: passing the strap in front of her and clicking it into the buckle provided.

Not long afterwards, the supper trolley came round. I toyed with the boiled goat but, out of deference to absent friends, plumped for the curried chickpeas and lentils in a black sauce. Pretty soon we landed in Khajuraho.

The Mahabharata – a personal note

Attentive readers may remember that a few pages back, when touching on the Aryan invasion of India, I made mention of the Mahabharata. This was, I admit, slightly self-indulgent, but it's just that my interest in India and my interest in the Mbh have gone hand in hand.

I first heard about the Mbh when listening to an Indian friend holding forth on the opening of the well-known spiritual text, the Bhagavad Gita, itself a tiny part of the enormously large Mahabharata. In the BG, Arjuna and his charioteer, Krishna, are surveying the armies of the Pandavas and the Kauravas lined up against each other before the start of the battle of Kurukshetra. Arjuna, the great Pandava warrior, falls to his knees, weeping. 'How can I fight?' he asks. 'On one side are my brothers, on the other are my cousins, my teacher, my grandfather, all the men I hold dear. If I win, I lose. If I lose, I lose.' To which conundrum, Krishna (in his secondary role as God) offers advice. 'Before you fight the war without,' he says, 'you must fight the war within; you must achieve mastery of the Self'... and, to oversimplify grossly, the BG can be seen as a short instruction manual on how to do this.

That's the BG but, surrounding it, is the much more voluminous but, in its own way, equally marvellous, Mahabharata. The Mbh is an epic of myriad nuances, telling the tale of how the two families, the Pandavas and the Kauravas, end up on the battlefield of Kurukshetra and what happens thereafter. It's an inexhaustible text to which the epigram, which the Mbh directs at itself, applies; 'What is here may be found elsewhere, but what is not here is nowhere.'

5. KHAJURAHO

… All is revealed.

I decided to check into the best hotel in town for an interlude of uninterrupted pampering. For one thing I hadn't been lucky with showers thus far. I needed one that worked, as opposed to something that either projected a pathetic pencil-thin dribble of cold water, or didn't dribble at all but came, cold, out of a waist-high tap, under which you had to crouch like Neanderthal-man gathering nuts.

The hotel did not disappoint. In fact, it was magnificent and, as an unexpected bonus, offered guests a tiny pot of talcum powder, which I sprinkled on liberally – or as liberally as a jar the size of a dwarf's little toe would allow. It was then, that I stumbled across – oh joy of joys – two bars of Kit Kat lurking in the mini-bar. Both were unwrapped and down my throat before I had any inkling of what I was doing. The same sort of thing happens to me when I'm driving. I suddenly shake myself back to consciousness and realise that I haven't the foggiest notion about the last couple of miles. Did I stop at traffic lights? Did I overtake? Is there a dead body hooked to my bumper? All I knew now was that, however they got there, two bars of chocolate were nestling happily in my stomach.

Feeling unusually spruced up and untroubled by hunger, I decided to go out and watch a show at the town hall, which I'd seen advertised in the hotel lobby. Well not quite the town hall, but definitely a show: traditional Indian folk dancing put on by a local troupe.

I learnt one thing. Indian women can contort themselves like no other. They manage to contrive angles between waist and hip, and arm and hand, that would send some of us straight to the chiropractor. It was riveting. There were only about three people in the audience, so afterwards, rather than leaving straight away, I thought I would tell them how good the performance was. Not that I know the first thing about Indian Folk dancing but, in my humble opinion, it was excellent entertainment. I unburdened myself to the tabla player, who seemed to be in charge, and who was also, it turned out, the lead dancer's father. He seemed genuinely pleased and he bestowed on me a broad grin coming out of a round and contented face that quite made my evening.

Afterwards, I wandered around the town for a while, experimenting with a new technique for dallying at shop stalls without giving the slightest encouragement to the owner that I might spend money. The secret was in the eyes. You had to think *Randy Boss*. Get those eyelids stretched 50% further than was comfortable and hold the position. It seemed to work. I wasn't approached more than twice.

My guess is that the shopkeeper gene predisposes its holders to steer a wide berth around anybody who walks around looking as if they've just sat on something pointed, and quite possibly hot. I'd need to test the method elsewhere in case results were affected by Khajuraho being, by Indian standards, a ghost town. (Pop: 8,000, compared to Varanasi 2m and Delhi 13m.) There may also be long term implications for the eyeballs. Otherwise, I'd say those days of being bothered by salesmen were over.

I woke up next morning early, put on my swimming trunks and made my way, under the interested gaze of the hotel staff, across the hotel foyer to the outdoor pool. India in November, before the sun is up, can be chilly. Last night there had been a frost. For Indians, this was not swimming weather. I stood on the stone lip above the water, contemplating the likely temperatures below and feeling the gimlet eyes of Reception drilling into my back. Was this moron, they wanted to know, actually going to take the plunge? And, of course, I was.

Having walked out there in full view, I could hardly dip my toe in and limp back. So, reminding my nerve endings that they'd endured worse without getting completely hysterical – in the North Sea off St Andrews – I stoically lowered myself through that moment of truth when ice and sensitive flesh embrace.

After breakfast, I went to see the temples for which Khajuraho is famous. Only about 20 out of the original 80 remain, but they are something special. Given that most of them were built between 950 and 1050,[19] before, during and after one of the most brutally destructive invasions known to man (by the Afghan Muslim, Mahmud of Ghazni[M]), it's a miracle so many are still standing.

The biggest and the best was the Kandariya Mahadeva temple. Conjure up the silhouette of a mountain range against a clear blue sky, one point leading upwards asymmetrically to another, until finally, last in the line, the summit. Now imagine, around each of the major tops, a myriad of smaller ones like steps and, flecking the peaks, what was once a coating of white plaster.[20] This was the snow-covered Himalayas or, to the Hindu perhaps, a representation of the quest after truth: one spiritual rock face followed by another, until finally the pilgrim ascends to the very top, and inhales the rarefied air of understanding. Whatever it was, it stirred the blood and I found a perch on an adjacent building and sat staring at it, until an alarming ache in my lower back told me it was time to climb down before someone had to call the fire brigade.

Now when I said that Khajuraho was famous for its temples, I was being a touch economical with the truth. What it's really famous for are the erotic sandstone carvings that coil gracefully around the temple walls, some of which would, even today, have the censor reaching for his red pencil. So, to make sure I didn't miss any, I secured the services of a guide.

My induction course in erotica was presented by Raj Kashoor. He started me off gently: a young woman languidly twisting to remove a thorn from her upturned foot; another applying

M   As a destroyer of temples, Mahmud of Ghazni (Clump 2) had few equals. In 1018, for example, he stood before the Mathura temple in Uttar Pradesh and calculated that it would take at least 200 years to build anything comparably magnificent. He then extracted the gold, silver and precious stones from its various images and burned the temple to the ground. (John Keay, *India: a history*, Harper Collins, 2000, p 208.)

make-up to her lashes; one playing the flute; one feeding a bird; one using a mirror to inspect the underside of her breast. Here was a dancing elephant man (Ganesha) with an African drummer. There a beguiling girl was throwing a ball, an event which prompted Raj to cast doubt on the fanciful notion that the English had invented cricket. 'Cricket English? Khajuraho say no', was how he put it and, having thus undermined the one unshakeable verity in my life, he eased me towards the hard-core stuff.

Raj was a young man, who expressed his enjoyment, and indeed his various other social observations, in an enunciation that I couldn't help feeling would have been improved by opening his mouth while speaking, and by lingering a little longer on each syllable. It took me a while to get to grips with this but, in the end, I managed to compile a short Raj-English to English-English dictionary. Here is a selected vocabulary. To Raj, earth was 'ert'; eyes was 'ice'; air, 'er'; tortoise, 'turtwise'; lion, 'line'; face (or fish, depending on context), 'fis'; moon, 'mun'; eyebrow, 'ibro'; and so on in like manner.

'What five delights of beautiful womans'? he asked, and fortunately decided to provide the answer himself: 'Werst like line, ice like fis, fis like mun, ibro like rinbo, wok like dir on ert'. This translates, I believe, as a beautiful woman has a 'waist like a lion, eyes like a fish, a face like the moon, eyebrows like the rainbow, and she walks like a deer on the earth.'

Raj paused by an intricate carving showing a woman playing with a man, a servant playing with himself and another woman with her mouth close to the nether regions of a third man. Something was very clearly passing between them.

'Woman drink coke,' said Raj pointing. This surprised me.

It certainly didn't look like coke to me, and I remarked as such:

'You know, Raj, are you sure that's a bottle of coke?' I enquired.

'Not coke, COKE,' he said with emphasis, but without obvious increase in clarification. Since nothing more enlightening was forthcoming, I was forced to conclude, gentle readers, that he meant to imply that the 'o' was short, as in rock.

Raj commented on something that had not altogether escaped my notice: that these young women were remarkably well endowed. 'Big breast good, small breast not good' was his considered opinion. The women were beautiful because, 'They have pleasure. They are cross only when their boyfriend has left them.' So said Raj anyway. But he was picky. 'This one bit fatty,' he opined, and told me he didn't like fatty women. Actually, the young woman in question didn't look fat to me. Cuddly perhaps, but Raj was still a callow youth.

Raj, I quickly discovered, had spent much of his young life amassing an encyclopaedic knowledge of those little details in the carvings that could so easily have escaped less rigorous students. And he was delighted to share. He showed me an elephant laughing at a man and a woman in the '69' position. Not far away, a man was approaching a woman from the rear with his finger pressing on the pleasure point in her back, while an elephant, looking on, was doing his best, with the somewhat blunter digit at his disposal, to follow suit. A young woman was playing with a monkey or, as Raj said proudly, 'a leetle monkey bisnis.'

I was starting to worry about him. A lifetime spent showing people round these temples was a bit like permanent employment as a porno-cinema usherette. I wasn't sure it was healthy, and I did my tactful best to suggest that foreign travel might be instructive. Raj had lived in England, he told me, which frankly, given the way he tortured the language, I found hard to credit. I dread to think what would have happened had he lent across the bar of the Dog and Duck and ordered a coke.

Nobody seems quite sure why the Khajuraho temples (and others elsewhere) came to be adorned by languid young women in compromising positions. It's not the sort of thing you normally associate with places of worship, even in the land that gave the world the Kama Sutra. Except it's interesting to note – I think so anyway – that, inside their temples, Hindus, more than any of the western religions, venerate female energy[N]. What is more, female sexual organs are explicitly symbolised, and revered equally with the male. Keeping things under wraps is besides, or indeed contrary to, the point.

Nothing much, let me assure you, is kept under wraps at Khajuraho. I shall spare you some of the scenes that Raj encouraged me to witness and bring you, as I was brought, to three adjacent carvings. Each showed a man standing and supporting a woman who had wrapped herself around him. Each represented a different stage in the same sexual act, and Raj suggested that, to see the detail as the sculptor intended, I press my face against the wall and look upwards.

This I did, and was just beginning to appreciate the finer points, when Raj indicated to me to keep my mouth shut, or, as he put it, 'drops fall in.' Heavens, I thought, was I really standing there with my mouth wide open, gawping like a schoolboy.

[N]   It is seen as both a force of creation and destruction; the two being inextricably interlinked. Just look at images of Durga – not a goddess you'd want to tangle with.

I was. I shut it quickly, but what flashed before me was that newsagent in Trinity Square, Nottingham, where we used to go after school and furtively leaf through health and energy magazines, which are what passed for porn when I was growing up. Those were the days.

6. THE JUNGLE (MADHYA PRADESH)

... Tiger

I had arranged with Deepak in Delhi to take a car and driver up to the nature reserves of Bandhavgarh and Kanha. In Britain, having your own driver is reserved for lottery winners and drunks with good insurance, but here the cost was so embarrassingly little that I shall refrain from telling you what it was. There was a drawback, however, that only became obvious when the car arrived at my hotel in Khajuraho.

Now, to be fair to Deepak – who will always remain the one person I turn to for travel arrangements in India – he had asked me whether I wanted air conditioning. I'd said no: I like open windows and the *er* in my *fis*. What I hadn't fully come to terms with was that there was likely to be some correlation between air conditioning and the d.o.b. of the vehicle in question. So it proved. The car waiting outside my hotel was an Ambassador and about as old as I was. My heart sunk. Deepak had said the journey to Bandhavgarh would take seven hours.

There are two things to notice before volunteering for a long journey in an Ambassador. First, headrests. There aren't any. The back of the seat finishes below the shoulder so, should you be relaxed enough to dose off, improbable though that may be on Indian roads, your head has nothing to hold it up except your neck muscles. These, however, are useless for support purposes because they, being attached, tend to nod off when you do. Hence, don't kid yourself that, though it's a long journey, you'll sleep happily through most of it. You won't. Second, any suspension that may have once existed on these vehicles gave up the ghost shortly after the Great Flood. The car has no ability to ride bumps. When the road goes up, it goes up, and when down, down. I climbed into my allotted place in the back, determined to put a brave face on things.

The kindest thing I can say about the thoroughfare from Khajuraho is that tarmac was not totally unknown. On occasions, there was even enough of it for two cars travelling in opposite directions to pass comfortably. But the norm was single track. From time to time this degenerated into a black snake-like trickle, which, while it might masquerade as a highway, was, in fact, a signpost. At least you knew if you followed the asphalt traces, you weren't going to end up in some farmer's field. Potholes were everywhere and, on occasions, craters but, generally speaking, few were large enough to disappear into. Apart from the volume of traffic, which was high, it was the sort of track that used to wander across open sheep country in the Scottish Highlands and went largely unused by anyone (except sheep).

My driver for the trip was Rajjan, a decent man not given to conversation. We got on fine. I took his sudden swerving and braking in good heart, and he gave me a crash course in how to drive on Indian roads. Given that the black stuff was in short supply, jungle rules applied: small gives way to large, just as, at the waterhole, the buck gives way to the tiger. We vacated the tarmac when lorries and buses bore down. Bikes and cars with a retail value greater than zero gave way to us.

Jeeps, however, presented Rajjan with a test of manhood. They were bigger and stronger than we were, but the Ambassador, for all its shortcomings, was solid. It was leopard v jackal. Your money is on the leopard but, if the jackal stands firm and looks determined, the leopard will sometimes give ground. So when a jeep came towards us on the central strip, a steely look would come into Rajjan's eye. He would align himself for a head-on collision and accelerate towards it. I sat in the back demonstrating as much backbone as jelly on a plate. When the cars were about twenty yards apart, one of them would weaken (thank heaven), cut off onto the rolled earth that ran alongside and hammer along that before swinging back onto what, in golfing parlance, we would call the mown surface.

Curiously enough, I adjusted quickly to the fact that, like skiers, we were proceeding in a forward direction by means of sharp left right zigzags. What was more difficult was that each pothole jiggled my head up and down like a pea in a pan of boiling water. I suppose it only bumped against the roof about once in twenty jigs when the road was good, and one in ten when bad, but this is the kind of thing that is inclined to give you a headache.

The landscape was dry, flat and vaguely Spanish in appearance. There were villages now and again with dogs lying by the roadside and cows deep in contemplation on the tarmac.

Mainly, though, Rajjan's macho manoeuvrings took place amid tranquil acres of neat farmland. Where, I thought, have all the people gone? When I came to India, I assumed that there couldn't be any countryside. Perhaps the occasional pocket of greenery sandwiched between those teeming millions, but not long stretches of open emptiness. I was wrong. India, let me tell you, has country. Miles upon miles of it.

After a couple of hours, we stopped at a tourist café a few miles before a town called Satna where the owner greeted us with the usual enquiries about whether he could serve up a four-course meal with all the trimmings. This was the sort of enquiry and the sort of eating establishment which couldn't help but call to mind my doctor friend back home, the one whom I'd invested with a wagging finger – one wag no, two wags definitely not are you crazy? This was a one and a half wag place. I declined politely; 'I'm not really hungry, thank you' (I lied), 'a couple of bananas will be more than enough.'

The café owner duly served up the bananas° accompanied by the conversational remark that the road from Khajuraho to Satna, the minefield upon which we had just been travelling, had been good. Good? If that was good, what I wondered, was bad. I was soon to find out. It was much worse, he said, on the next stretch from Satna to Bandhavgarh. This was not music to my ears. (Actually, as it turned out, he was wrong about the road. It wasn't much worse. Much worse would have meant

---

o   Should you be wondering, the Indian banana, as seen in Rajasthan, is more or less the same as the banana you might see in a British supermarket. It's yellow, fat and curved (as opposed to red, fat and stumpy, as some Indian bananas are). More importantly, the Rajasthan banana – or any self-respecting banana, for that matter – doesn't lend itself to weight-enhancing injections. (The same cannot be said of watermelons).

cutting a way through with machetes. It was just worse.)

I was about to avail myself of the café's facilities prior to enduring the five-hour pounding that lay ahead, when an ultra-modern coach, air conditioned, with full working suspension and radial tyres, pulled in, and a party of Americans poured out. The ladies among them immediately made for the one washroom I'd had my eye on, and formed a queue 15 deep outside. This was a set-back, but the thought dawned on me that I might be able to cadge a lift up to Bandhavgarh and let Rajjan rattle himself to death on his own. I therefore decided to engage the friendliest looking of the bunch, who was probably called Abe, in conversation.

'Going to Bandhavgarh,' I proffered. 'Yes', he said, 'you'? 'Yes.'

'Travelling alone'? 'Yes.'

He glanced around. 'In that?' he said pointing at the Ambassador.

'I'm afraid so,' I replied, 'I organised it before I realised what the roads were like.'

'Hey, you're pretty gamey,' he said and I don't think he was referring to the fact that I hadn't made contact with soap and water for some hours.

'Mm, the suspension's gone and I've got a splitting headache. Heaven knows what the next few hours will be like.' And then, chuckling in my most winsome manner, 'How's the coach? Comfortable? Plenty of room?' I enquired, leaning heavily on the last phrase.

'Yea, smooth and spacious,' he replied, smiling.

At this point, when all seemed to be going according to plan, when the happy ending was there for the taking, I ran into the buffers of what you'd have to call a clash of cultures. My expectation of how the conversation would carry on from here went something like this:

Abe, reading the need in my face: 'Hey, I'm sure there's a spare seat. Would you like to hop aboard?'

Me: 'No really, I couldn't impose.'

Abe: 'Don't be ridiculous, we'd love to have you. Hey Chuck, this Limey is looking for a ride to Ban.'

Chuck: 'Sure Abe, the more the merrier. Hop on in.'

That's how I saw it going. What actually happened was rather different. Abe, being American, assumed that if I wanted a lift, I would ask for one. You don't ask, you don't get. So he carried on smiling, waiting for the request, while I carried on smiling, waiting to be asked. We were grinning so fixedly that a hyena could have taken lessons. I, of course, cracked first. 'Well', I said, 'it's back to the old bone-shaker for me. See you in Ban.' I walked back to the car, reached in to my travel bag and made sure he saw me taking a couple of aspirin.

We were soon in Satna, and Rajjan proceeded to push his way through. I now knew why I had seen so few people in the last couple of hours. They had all moved to Satna. The place was heaving. Street after mud street was packed with milling Satnians and dilapidated shacks selling the three essentials of Indian living: food, clothes and car tyres. The town also boasted an extraordinary collection of animal grotesques. Two very peculiar pigs were rooting around by the side of the road. At least I presume they were pigs. They might have been domesticated wart-hogs. A goat, descended from a long line of giraffes, strutted across the street in front of us. On top of its protracted neck perched a tiny head, sandwiched between a Hapsburg chin below and a topknot above. It was probably auditioning for a part in a Star Wars movie, and was off for a quiet cigarette and a stiff one before its big moment.

To cap it all, the place was awash with cows. I know that every Indian city has them, but Satna looked like Dodge City after the boys from the Rusty Nail had brought the Trail Drive into town. There were dogies all over the place and we found ourselves becalmed behind a herd that had decided to pitch camp on the main road out of town. Given that killing a cow is, for a Hindu, absolutely verboten, I thought we would be there all night, but this was to underestimate Rajjan's skill as a motorised cowpoke. He had a method. He stood on the horn, and nudged them up the backside with his bumper. The cows hopped sideways a few paces, thus enabling – if I might borrow from the imagery of Khajuraho – penetration to be achieved.

Once through Satna, Rajjan put his foot down. I think he had noticed my recent attempt to jump ship and wanted to show me what the car could do. Normally I would have been happy to let him blow off steam, except that, as attentive readers may remember, I had earlier been deprived of the relief that roadside cafés traditionally furnish. To say I was now desperate would have been an understatement. However, we carried on into the middle of nowhere for as long as I could bear it, whereupon I asked him to pull over. Actually, I grabbed him by the shoulder and forced him off the road.

I leapt out of the car and, in the best Indian tradition, began to hose down the dry earth. My tank was still some ¾ full, when I heard the purr of 21st century hydraulics, and looked up to see the Americans' coach come round the corner. Abe gave me a friendly wave as he steamed past, while 15 women just stared. I did my best to give them a cheery smile.

The road became, as predicted, narrower. The ratio of pothole to tarmac approached 1:1. Monkeys played by the roadside. We bunny-hopped past some very African looking women walking bolt upright in the direction of Bandhavgarh carrying large loads of straw on their heads. A little later we passed another group carrying identical amounts of straw walking in the opposite direction. Modern technology is a wonderful thing, I couldn't help thinking. If only these women could pick up a telephone and say, 'hey, I'm phoning from Y and am planning to bring a bale of straw to X. Nobody there by any chance bringing a bale in this direction? There is? Good. Why don't we get together on this and save ourselves a bit of lifting?' After this illuminating insight, darkness fell suddenly and thereafter all I could see were trees in the headlights, the whites of the occasional inquisitive eyeball and, now and then a village. When we arrived in Bandhavgarh, my head felt like a cricket ball after a Tendulkar[p] double century.

I was staying in a rather up-market jungle camp. I even had my own hut. A smell of barbecue was coming from somewhere and, having dumped my bags, I went to investigate. The somewhere turned out to be a campfire, around which a group of English people were deeply engrossed in their dinner. The choice was meat, meat or meat, which posed something of a problem. No flesh had passed my lips since coming to India, partly because I don't eat meat and partly because I'd seen a chicken hanging up outside a butcher's in Varanasi, which

---

p   For those not familiar with cricket, Tendulkar is an Indian batsman; perhaps their best ever.

couldn't have been covered in more flies if it had been fly-paper.

However, having had nothing to eat all day except the bananas at the café, I decided to throw caution to the wind. I piled my plate high and asked Ram for forgiveness and a strong stomach. Afterwards, I lounged around, drank a few beers and chatted to my new friends. My headache had cleared. A benevolent mellowness was beginning to wash over me and then someone produced a guitar. Conversation ceased instantly, the first chords were strummed and everyone around me erupted into a reedy rendering of 'Kumbaya', followed by 'Green Grow the Rushes O!' I sunk back into my wicker chair. It is at moments like these that I am proud to be an adopted Scot. You wouldn't catch a coach-load of Scots singing Kumbaya, I can tell you. By this time of the evening, they would all be legless. I sneaked off to bed. A strange creature was hissing on the roof of my jungle hut, but it didn't detain me for long.

The time to see tigers is at some ungodly hour of the morning, don't ask me why. Either tigers are early risers or they party late. Whatever the reason, a few of the crooners from the night before, and myself, were sitting in a jeep at first light, rattling along and freezing to death. It is cold, first thing, and I hadn't thought to pack a coat. Well, you don't, do you, going to India? Various other jeeps, similarly laden, were heading out in front and behind.

The jungle wasn't as I had imagined it. I'd thought we'd have to slash a path through dense tropical vegetation, peer through curtains of hanging creepers and pluck leeches out of our necks. Instead, the trees let in light, a stream meandered gently below us and, from time to time, the canvas opened up across acres of open grassland. It was a bit like Sherwood Forest[Q] except on an infinitely grander scale and with wildlife rather more interesting than field mice and foxes. Bandhavgarh had everything from the big cats to the racket-tailed drongo. It also had a 1000-year-old fort on a sheer escarpment overlooking the forest, and an ancient temple with a 32-foot reclining Shiva, which Sherwood Forest didn't have the last time I checked. (To be fair, though, Robin Hood's old stomping ground does have the Holm Oak where the Merry Men used to frolic, and is a good day out for the whole family.)

By and by, the dappled sunlight worked its way through the patina of ice that had formed around me and I started to enjoy myself. We rooted around some venerable caves, once home to a holy hermit, and now to horseshoe bats. We stopped by a stream, watched the bubbles of invisible fish rise to the surface, and inspected the dry red mud for tiger tracks, as if we had the first clue what we were doing. We even saw a tiger in the distance, by a bush. Well, everybody said it was a tiger. All I could see was a dark impressionistic arboreal-looking blob. But that didn't matter. It was a good day to be out and pootling along in an open-topped jeep with the sun on your back, and exotic animals you have only ever seen in wildlife

---

Q   Now, I appreciate that the reference to Sherwood Forest (Nottinghamshire, England) must seem a bit random, but it was where I grew up (so please forgive.) At least, I grew up where Sherwood Forest used to be before modernity took the axe to much of it. Sherwood Forest, for those of you unfamiliar with the venue, was the home of Robin Hood, Little John, Will Scarlet, Maid Marion and the rest of them, all robbing the rich to give to the poor. And – should you be so inclined – you might wish to view Robin, with bow in hand, as a homespun (or, should we say, threadbare) version of the consummate archer of the *Mahabharata* (Clump One), Arjuna himself.

documentaries doing their thing alongside. A wonderful day in fact, from which I am able to offer you three selected observations on the Indian Jungle at Bandhavgarh.

1. Tigers must have good agents. Star-struck tiger-groupies drool over their droppings and chase in all directions on the off-chance of a sighting. Once rumbled, the Tiger finds a comfortable spot in the sun a couple of miles away and goes to sleep, while the groupies take out their long lenses and go at it like paparazzi who have caught a film star sunbathing topless.

2. Monkeys are very like us. A Langoor (monkey) sits like a human with the weight of the world on his shoulders, fiddling with his whiskers or resting his arms on his knees, wrists limp. The male, when with his mate, will put his arm around her like a young lover gazing at the sunset. The female is never happier than when displaying her new baby to a gaggle of other females, while telling them how hopeless her husband is at getting up nights. After dinner, they all gather around a campfire and sing Kumbaya.

3. Strange things happen as dusk descends. Faces, wondering what's for supper tonight, appear amid the undergrowth and stare. Branches crack. Low growls hover on the stillness. A Tyranosaurus Rex lurches through a clearing pretending to be a tree-trunk. If you go down to the woods tonight, be sure of a big surprise.

I left next morning for Kanha, an even larger tract of jungle.

I don't know where Rajjan had holed up during the last couple of days, but the break seemed to have done him good. His driving was relaxed and leisurely. We meandered past fields of reddish-brown earth, green crops, yellow crops, oxen pulling a plough, trees interspersed like oak in an English landscape, women elegantly and colourfully dressed in their saris carrying pots on their heads, backs ramrod straight, and old men with bow legs walking to heaven knows where. We rattled through villages packed with curious smiling faces looking out as Rajjan went through tooting his horn.

Now that we were no longer travelling at terminal velocity, it was a treat just to look around and watch the sights of rural India unfold – men squatting by the roadside, bottoms not quite touching the ground, knees by their chins; haystacks of the sort they used to have in Europe before the First World War and still have in the Balkans; a man on a bicycle carrying three times his weight and five times his volume in a package balanced precariously over the back wheel; and another, not taking any chances, cycling along under a cloudless sky with a rolled umbrella under his arm.

We stopped at a small village to buy a bunch of bananas (my lunch, 5 rupees). I did momentarily consider other fruit, most of it of the crinkly and brown variety, but the problem was washing it. With what? With water? Are you joking? No, much better to stick with bananas; they're nutritious, filling and they come in their own sealed container.

The village seemed like a well-to-do little place. The houses had clay tiles mostly and occasionally were 2-storey. One of the buildings had a satellite dish, so there must have been TV and electricity. Nobody pestered me. Nobody begged. There wasn't much traffic. This was country life, as it should be, and why anyone would want to swap it for the squalor of the towns, I couldn't imagine.[R] But they do, by the million, though whether they think it is such a smart move when they arrive in the big city is another matter. Rajjan approved of village living. 'Varanasi too much traffic, too many police,' he said, fingering his 3-day stubble and the collar on his designer golf shirt simultaneously. He was a good man. Wiry, unflappable, happy to drive or not to drive.

We stopped by a river for lunch. Rajjan produced a paratha from somewhere and munched on it. Fifty yards away, an old and redundant bridge with pleasant, symmetrical arches sauntered across the water. Trees lined the banks on either side. It was a hot day in an Indian winter, and there was hardly a soul about. Every 15 minutes or so a battered conveyance of one kind or another chugged by. I gazed around in raptures, while Rajjan leant on the car roof picking things out of his hair. A middle-aged man on a scooter drove up, and stopped. He turned his engine off and watched me in silence as I dealt with what remained of my bananas. I thought of nodding to him, but didn't. I watched the river. He watched me. That was fine.

After a while, we set off again for Kanha. With 50 kms to go, the road as good as ceased and the navigable surface became as ruckled as an under-sheet after a night of passion. Rajjan took this as a cue to put his foot on the gas and use my head to flatten out those indentations in his roof that I had put there, involuntarily, two days ago.

R   Dreams of streets lined with gold most likely, though caste might have something to do with it. If you were an untouchable in the sort of village described by Rohinton Mistry in *A Fine Balance*, you might grab at anything that felt like the exit.

At Kanha, I was staying in what you might call a compound, consisting of a dozen well-appointed huts around a central dining area. Behind these flowed a river that, after 5½ hours in the Ambassador, looked irresistible. I needed a swim. The man in charge was a Portuguese Indian from Goa, by the name of Jason, and I asked him if he would be kind enough to give me the inside track on any crocodiles, piranhas or life-destroying bacteria that might be lurking within. He thought the water was safe – a rather more lukewarm assurance than I had been hoping for – but I set off anyway.

The sun was blazing, and I made my way along a sandy beach – which I presume was the river bed in the wet season – to what looked like the best spot 500 yards upstream. Tall birch-like trees lined the banks. The river swirled in an extravagant 'S' around two sharp-edged boulders in midstream. If ever there was a place where a tiger might come down to cast a hungry eye over the buffalo, this was it.

No-one was about. I pondered whether or not bathing trunks were necessary but felt that I couldn't entirely discount the possibility of a lingering piranha or two. If I was going to go 10 rounds with fish that had teeth, I would rather be wearing bathers. I stepped in, lay on my back, paddled my feet against the current and knew I was in heaven. After a while, a gnarled, black terrestrial goatherd brought his flock down to the water's edge, and I took this as an appropriate moment to emerge. We exchanged cursory greetings, mine tentative, his of the 'what in God's name is this!' variety. I withdrew feeling vulnerably pink.

I had time for a quick nap that night, before finding myself once more in an open-sided, unroofed jeep, rattling along a jungle track. It was at that time of day when sane people are still lying on their backs, making snuffly cxhor-pugh noises. In other words, asleep. Considering how early it was, we, that is a local driver, a jungle guide and myself, were remarkably perky.

We stopped to watch three wild dogs chew the remains of what the guide said was a peacock, although so little remained by the time we got up close, that we would have needed dental records to be absolutely sure. We were lucky to see wild dogs, apparently. They are furtive creatures, not dissimilar to the dogs you see in the average Indian village, but these can bring down Sambur. Tigers give them a wide berth. They are Kipling's dhole of the Deccan and, as it happened, Kanha is where the Jungle Book was supposed to have been set. The Waingunga, where Kaa swam and the red dogs plunged to their death, is 50 miles or so south. It was very Jungle Book country, very jungly. Dense vegation, creepers, vines and vast: from the highest point you can look as far as the eye can see and that's only a quarter of the total area of Kanha. Most of the animals in the Jungle Book are to be found at Kanha: tigers, panthers (a.k.a. leopards, but black), snakes, kites, monkeys, the occasional wolf, but no bears – unless Baloo was a sloth bear which he wasn't. Kipling, by the way, took his character names straight from the Hindi. 'Baloo' means Bear, 'bagh' leopard, (hence Bagheera), 'hathi' elephant, and 'bandar' is monkey, (as in *Bandar-log*). But Kaa is not a python.

We drove on into denser stuff and parked in a clearing to watch several barrel-loads of monkeys playing happily in the branches above, swinging lazily to and fro, and trying to make up their mind who should be the one to throw a banana at those stupid idiots in the jeep. This made riveting viewing, until one of them spotted something and gave out an alarm call.

I may not know much about the jungle, but I know an alarm call when I hear one. I was alarmed. So were the monkeys. 'Tiger' whispered the guide, at which point a number of thoughts involuntarily flooded in. First of all, the monkeys were peeing themselves with panic and they were 20 foot up a tree. Shouldn't we be the teeniest bit apprehensive? Second, did the man who removed the sides and top of this vehicle know what he was doing? And third, the fact that no human had been killed by a tiger round here since 1974, probably meant that another one was due anytime now.

I'd seen a tiger at Bandhavgarh, but that was so far away it might as well have been on TV. This felt real. When you know there is a powerful carnivore out there, probably staring at you from the long grass by the side of the road, and that there is no protection between you and it except a tee shirt, your heart does pump a wee bit faster. It would be just my luck to evade malaria, Dengue fever and terminal dysentery, only to be eaten. I was wondering which of us he would go for first. The others were younger and more tender, but there was no doubt about it, if it was a hearty breakfast he was after, I was the logical choice. I was doing my best to look as thin and indigestible as possible when, ten yards in front of us, a large orange and black tiger loomed out of the long grass and, without looking left or right, ambled loose-limbed across the track, and disappeared. I take back everything I may have said about tigers. This was an impressive, not to say heart-stopping sight, and everything after that was anti-climax.

You would have thought that being a tiger was a cushy number. It swaggers around like a mafia boss in a Sicilian village and just about everything it meets either wets its pants or runs away. It would be a great life, except for the fact that in China and Japan nothing is thought to put a spring in the step or a twinkle in the eye quite like a good helping of ground tiger bones. So tigers have been, and are being, poached to the edge of extinction. Kanha was established as a reserve, as part of the Government's Project Tiger, in 1973, but this hasn't put an end to poaching. It was going on extensively in 1995[21] and it still is. But what makes you weep is that even after the criminals are brought to trial – and hundreds have been – convictions for poaching are minimal.[22] Wipe-out is a distinct possibility.

Mind you, for hundreds of years, people have been doing their best to exterminate tigers. The Mughal approach (Clump Three) was characteristically systematic. Soldiers were employed as beaters. They strung out to form a large circle and drove whatever game they came across into an area in which slaughter could conveniently take place. Then the Emperor jumped into the ring, and when he had had his fill, his officers and senior courtiers had a go, after which came lesser men, and finally the troopers and footmen.

On one occasion, in 1567, when Akbar was Emperor, 50,000 beaters were employed to sweep up the wildlife within a 30-mile radius.[23] It took them a month. After that, the 'hunting' began and, according to the chronicler, 'there was pleasure from morning till evening and from evening till morning.'[24] I bet.

Not that the British were any better. They also used beaters, occasionally up to one thousand at a time.[25] And they had the advantage of more recent technology. In 1851, Captain James Forsyth wrote how he mounted sentry over a tiger for nearly a week, 'girding him in a little hill with a belt of fires, and feeding him with a nightly kine (cow), till half a hundred elephants, carrying the cream of a vice-regal camp, swept him out into the plain, where he fell, riddled by a storm of bullets from several hundred virgin rifles.'[26] Well, well.

And then there was the proud moment in 1834 (Clump four) when 118 tigers were killed by luring them into pitfall traps with sharp spikes at the bottom.[27] So it went. As P.G.Wodehouse put it, 'I like a man to be a clean, strong, upstanding Englishman who can look his gnu in the face and put an ounce of lead in it.'[28] The only problem is that if we continue to allow much more lead to be pumped into the few thousand tigers that now remain, there soon won't be any left. Which would be a pity.

7. AGRA

... The Taj, of course, and other matters.

Rajjan drove me to Jabalpur next morning, and insofar as a four-hour journey on Indian roads in an Ambassador can be uneventful, this was. When we arrived, we found that the terminus served as both train station and place of repose for that (substantial) proportion of Jabalpur society which had nowhere else to go. Rajjan's last act was to select a porter from the colourful crew gathered around me expecting employment. Wisely, I thought, he chose the one who had the firmest grip on my holdall.

I showed the porter my ticket and he mowed a path through the crushing throng, across a 'foot-over bridge', down one over-run platform and onto another, with me sticking to him as tightly as a hungry leech. When he turned around unexpectedly, I was concentrating so hard on staying close that we had a slight shunt, which resulted in us rubbing noses, like a pair of Inuit. No damage was done. He put my stuff down, gave me a sign which I took to mean that I should stay where I was, and left.

The platform was mobbed with a million people. I felt like a little boy on his first day at school. Lost, and a long way from home. No friends, and no idea how to find classroom E1. Well, perhaps not quite that bad, but I would definitely have felt better if there'd been a single shred of evidence to confirm I was on the right platform. There was a loudspeaker but, for it to have been of any use, somebody really needed to tell the announcer not to munch digestive biscuits. There didn't seem to be a notice board either, not one that I could see anyway. My options were either to charge off, bags in hand, to make enquiries or, in the best spirit of oriental detachment, to stay put and trust the porter. I plumped for the latter. It would demonstrate spiritual progress if nothing else, but it wasn't easy. Placing your faith in a complete stranger, even one whose nasal hairs have brushed against your own, rarely is. Nevertheless, I remained where I was, went through my deep-breathing exercises and thought calming thoughts, until, by and by, a train with rusty brown carriages and iron bars across the windows pulled in. Was it, I wondered, going to Agra?

At which point, the porter materialised. Faith is a great thing. He checked my ticket once more, just to make doubly sure, and led me to my seat. We looked into each other's eyes for a moment, each wondering whether this Inuit thing between us had further to run. No, I thought, rather than hand over that tin of seal blubber I always keep with me for emergencies, I would pay in simple rupees. Which I did – 70 rupees in fact (£1). Now this may seem mean, but 70R, as I happened to know, would secure a week's supply of bananas, with enough change left over for a candlelit dinner for two.

Inside, the carriage wasn't bad at all. Much better than it looked from the outside. I was travelling 2nd class, so it wasn't the Ritz, but it was clean and functional. The seats, which cleverly folded down to make beds when the time came, were a sturdy blue plastic, and the walls that light grey colour that, to me, will always mean 'formica'. Apart from curtains which could be drawn when a modicum of privacy was required, the carriage was open plan and something of a challenge to the homemaking instincts of those present – a challenge they rose to with aplomb. Little nests of suitcases and blankets sprang up out of nowhere as my fellow travellers pitched camp for a long stay.

I asked the guard what time the train arrived in Agra. He said 6 am, and then gave a left/right shake of the head which meant 'could be 7 though, or perhaps 12.30.' A boy came through the carriage trying to interest us in one of the six cups of coffee, which he was carrying on a tray. As the train moved slowly off, he was still onboard, not looking unduly perturbed. Finally, he went to the door. I watched him jump out and then swivelled round to see how many cups of coffee had remained upright during the descent. All six. The boy was a pro.

I spent the first hour with my nose pressed against a dust covered window peering out absent-mindedly at the scrubby, hard-working landscape I was coming to regard as an old friend. Deep woods went scampering past. Buffalo drank from a sandbank in a winding river. Tall white birds with long beaks followed the plough. Three haystacks glided across a field. (Either their owners were buried within, legs pumping, or something very strange was going on.) Boys played cricket. Elegantly dressed women worked the land, wearing saris that in the west would be classed as evening wear. It was infinitely watchable.

The train was in no great hurry, stopping every now and again like an overweight jogger desperate for a breather. It probably averaged much the same speed as the Ambassador, but at least I wasn't staring up at the grille of an oncoming lorry thinking that Rajjan really had cut it a bit fine this time. I'd given Rajjan a generous tip when we had parted company, and I idly reflected on why. I think it was relief. In spite of having cranial indentations out of which you could serve soup, I'd made it through. He'd delivered me safe and sound and this, trifle though it may have been, was not something I was inclined to undervalue.

An enormous Sikh was sitting on the other side of the compartment, chatting pleasantly to his companion, a little Indian man whose waist was no wider than the Sikh's forearm. They had in front of them a huge mound of peanuts, and they were each consuming amounts proportional to their body weight. The thin man had six.

Unbeknown to them, a mean and ornery insect, of dubious parentage and, if I knew anything, every inch a carrier of Dengue fever, was crawling menacingly along the carriage floor. I kept a close eye on it in case it decided to come my way but, no, it turned towards the Sikh and, before long, was in the shadow of his enormous foot. It paused, contemplating its next move. It decided to attempt the ascent of the toe. In vain. It tried once more and again it slumped back exhausted. It hadn't brought oxygen. I was wondering whether I should say something to warn the man of the danger he was in, when the Sikh, unaware, like Gulliver among the Lilliputians, reached for another bucket of peanuts and, in so doing, adjusted his foot. The little insect was squashed flat, like a pancake, its murderous intentions with it. Awash with deadly diseases it may have been but, in anyone's language, this was a sad end[s].

The Sikh munched on, impervious to the tragedy beneath. Then, tiring of the effort required to down handfuls of nuts, decided to clean out his ear instead. He did this like no one I have ever seen. It may be that the diameter of his forefinger was badly sized in relation to his ear hole, but his method was to force the digit in and twirl it round, while simultaneously trying to rotate his head in the opposite direction. This had a curious effect on his eyes, which began to bulge alarmingly, as if about to pop out. I couldn't watch and I couldn't not watch, knowing what he was doing to himself; so I got up and went for a walk.

I decided to investigate the train's plumbing. Was there a lavatory worthy of the name? There was, and it had a seat (hallelujah). When I lifted the lid, I found an extraordinarily wide chute dropping vertically downwards towards the track. Of course, I had to try it out. Not unpleasant, irrigating Mother India at 40 mph, though it did induce a slight feeling of vertigo. At the same time, it also began to explain a few things.

One of the more macabre happenings in Indian history is that the occasional head has been chopped off and chucked into the medieval privy[29], on one occasion by the emperor Jahangir

---

s   Although was it? Sad, I mean. A swift, and probably painless, departure is not the worst way to go. I rather hope to meet the same immediate fate myself when the time comes though not, perhaps, at the hand of a foot.

himself (Clump Three).[T] Which does, to my mind, raise the question, 'what happened next?' If you were considering this from the comfort of your armchair, your first thought would be that it would get stuck. It would be too big. It would lie there, in the pan, staring upwards through sightless eyes, ready to induce terminal heart failure in the next person who came along to relieve himself. But, now, seeing this wide hole beneath me, I realised that lavatorial expulsion was the obvious solution.

Feeling glad that I could now strike one of life's eternal questions from my list, I returned to my seat, glancing across at the emaciated Indian as I sat down. I sized him up wondering whether his shoulders were narrower than the diameter of the hole. It would be tight, I could see that, but not impossible. When the moment came for him to obey the call of nature, I just hoped he wouldn't stumble.

A man came through the carriage handing out sheets, pillows and blankets. Night had fallen. It was 5.30pm. I finished what remained of my bananas, read for a while and decided it was time to retire for the evening. I assembled my bed, drew my curtains, lay back on my pillow, kissed teddy goodnight and closed my eyes.

The Sikh had also decided to turn in but, for him, getting off to sleep involved switching on the radio. Pretty soon, he started to snore. Well, either he was snoring, or he had a motorcycle stashed and was practising his traffic light getaways. This was accompanied by rather Arabic sounding music, and as I lay there quietly listening to this ghastly cacophony, I came to the

---

[T]   You'd have thought that an Emperor would have someone to do that sort of thing for him, but perhaps he just liked to make sure the job was done properly.

conclusion that there wasn't a hope in hell of ever getting so much as one wink.

I went for a wander instead and found myself in conversation with an Indian ex-army officer who thought that the problem with India was that the big criminals went unpunished. I couldn't think how to reply to this, short of saying that they had also had a job pinning one on Al Capone. However, since I wasn't sure whether American cultural imperialism had spread this far east, I nodded rather feebly and returned to my cubby.

There I spent the rest of the night reading, and listening to the entertainment laid on by my neighbour, for whom I was beginning to conceive an implacable loathing. I came to realise that I had underestimated his repertoire. There was a second, more irregular snore, which accompanied the motorbike. This began with a sudden pause, then a long 'kaaaa' gutturally exhaled, followed by silence. I christened this, somewhat prosaically, snore 2. Snores 1 and 2 took it in turns to vibrate my ear drums, but every so often, like a false dawn, there was silence. So golden was it that I lay in rapture and listened to the small miracle of an entire carriage sleeping happily – everybody that is, except me, of course, who about now was wishing he had taken the plane. 15 hours, 40 minutes after boarding, I crawled out, took a taxi to my hotel, found that my pre-booked room wasn't ready and burst into tears.[U] Actually,

U   This is all very self-indulgent, I appreciate that. I could have – no, I should have – taken such minor inconveniences in my stride, reflected on the fact that I was lucky to have choices (I could have flown), and been aware that a man's honest snoring, his breath rising and falling, is nothing more than a statement of impermanence; the breath comes in, the breath goes out, always changing, changing. I could have used this to advance my own spiritual understanding but, alas, all those priceless lessons which the good Sikh placed before me went disregarded. Typical.

I'm too resolute for that. I went and had breakfast – a big bowl of porridge – instead.

On my way to the hotel, I couldn't help but notice that Agra is a large, smelly city, with pollution that makes your eyes water. That doesn't stop it being very special because, you see, it was for many years the Mughal capital of India, and if there was one thing the Mughals liked – apart, that is, from booze, opium, women and fratricide – it was erecting magnificent buildings. They chucked money into architecture like it was going out of style. Babur[v], the first Mughal emperor, set up shop here after his swoop down from Afghanistan in 1526 and Agra continued as the seat of government (with a few inter-ruptions), through the imperial reigns of his grandson, Akbar and his great-grandson, Jahangir. His great-great-grandson, Shah Jehan upped sticks and moved to Delhi in 1648, but not before he had put in hand the creation of the world's most magnificent building.

There are two things in this life that I have always wanted to see and one is the Taj Mahal. The other is the Hanging Gardens of Babylon. They were both on a jigsaw puzzle called *The Seven Wonders of the World* that I had with me in hospital, aged six. I was imprisoned, if memory serves, for ten days. Nowadays, spending that long in a British hospital would imply something terminal and probably notifiable, like a lingering attack of Dengue fever, but, in the more leisurely years of my

v   Interesting bloodline, Babur. He was descended on his mother's side, from Genghis Khan, who needs no introduction, and, on his father's, from Timur the Lame (Tamburlaine), who, in 1398, had laid Delhi to waste with such aplomb that 'nothing moved, not even a bird, for two months'. Geneticists might not have predicted that he'd turn out to be a tolerant sort of fellow, a patron of the arts and a keen gardener.

youth, that was the sentence handed down for the removal of an appendix. I was recuperating and, since there was nobody of my age to talk to, and because computer games had yet to be invented, I whiled away the endless hours doing this jigsaw. I haven't a clue what the other five wonders were, but the Taj and the Hanging Gardens have been mitred into my memory ever since. And here I was, approaching the former, wondering what on earth had become of the latter.

That was before I came through a gateway, and there stood the Taj Mahal in the distance, carving its familiar silhouette out of surrounding air too reverential to lay a finger on it, and giving no sign whatsoever that all its pieces had come out of a box. The first glimpse was magical. A vast marble structure, but it looked like embroidered white lace, with edges sharp enough to shave by. What can I say? Go and see it. It will take your breath away[w].

If there is a doubt about the Taj, which there probably isn't, it is its symmetry. It is wonderfully perfect. All problems have been solved. Allah has spoken, and the answers to life's eternal questions have been revealed. Anything further away in spirit from those higgledy-piggledy temples in Hindu Khajuraho cannot be imagined. If I hadn't been to Khajuraho, I wouldn't

---

[w]   You may wonder – I did – where the money to build something like the Taj (or any of the other great Mughal edifices) came from. And the answer? … it came from taxes paid by – who else but – the peasants. Mughal taxation was even higher than British taxation, and that's saying something. And while the peasants laboured in abject penury, the Mughals didn't fritter their extracted money away on enterprises that might have increased the nation's wealth. Instead, they hoarded it. It went into chests of bullion, palaces, jewels that took the breath away, peacock thrones which got carted off to Persia … and on ruinous wars, of which they were very fond. (Abraham Eraly, *The Mughal World, India's Tainted Paradise*, [Phoenix 2008], pp 165-190).

have worried, but I had, and as I wandered around one of the world's great wonders, I did feel a slight niggle somewhere. As Captain Corelli put it, while tuning his mandolin, 'the human heart likes a little disorder in its geometry.'[30]

According to the guidebooks, the Taj was fashioned by a grief-stricken Shah Jehan as a memorial to his wife, Mumtaz Mahal, who had died in childbirth. The Emperor was said to have been so distraught at her death that he mourned for two years, 'rejecting all indulgence and going without gorgeous clothes, or rich food, or music.'[31] Well, maybe, but it sounds unlikely. He doesn't seem like the mourning type to me. He'd bumped off his brother, two nephews and two male cousins in case they interfered with his succession, he kept several baskets of poisonous snakes at court and liked to watch his bitten officials expire in convulsions[32] and, in spite of having some 5,000 women in his harem, spent his evenings seducing the wives of his nobles, not excluding his sister-in-law[33] and, gossip had it, his own daughter, Jahanara[34]. Two years in mourning? I doubt it. If you ask me, it was the classic case of the husband who brings home flowers because he's been fooling around with his secretary. The Taj was the imperial equivalent of a dozen roses. Not that it matters much. The whole magnificent structure is a marvel, even if the chap in charge was a murderous, two-timing, old snake-charmer.

Not far away, downriver, is the walled city built by Akbar (known somewhat prosaically as Agra Fort). It was here that Shah Jehan came to an extremely sticky end. His four sons, noticing that the 61-year-old emperor was not the man he was, fought each other for the succession. Of the sons, the two that mattered were Dara Shukoh and Aurangzeb. Dara was tolerant, inquiring, interested in the arts and naïve. Aurangzeb was a bigot, ruthless, treacherous and a skilled general, hardened by years of relentless campaigning in the Deccan. Guess who won? Dara's severed head was brought to Aurangzeb on a dish. Rumour had it that Aurangzeb called for lights so that he could inspect it properly and then stabbed it three times with his sword. It was then put in a box and sent by runners to Agra with orders that it be delivered to Shah Jehan when he was sitting down to dinner.

The eunuch guarding Shah Jehan waited until he had begun to eat, and then brought it in, saying, "King Aurangzeb, your son, sends this dish to your majesty, to let him see that he does not forget him." The old Emperor was overjoyed that his son still remembered him and ordered the box to be opened. 'Suddenly, on withdrawing the lid, he discovered the face of Prince Dara. Horrified, he uttered one cry and fell on his hands and face upon the table, and, striking against the golden vessels, broke his teeth, and lay there apparently lifeless.'[35] A not unreasonable reaction, I'd say. Shah Jehan struggled on for another seven years in captivity, looking across the bend in the River Jumna towards his finest achievement, the Taj, and being nursed by his daughter Jahanara. When he died in 1666, (the same year, incidentally, as the Great Fire of London), he was buried beside his wife and Dara's head.[36]

While Shah Jehan was lingering unhappily, Aurangzeb was doing away with a substantial chunk of his surviving relatives, including his brother, Murad. This poor man was fed poison while in prison, and every month Aurangzeb had his portrait painted so he could monitor the rate of deterioration.[37] Dear me. All I can say is that something must have gone seriously wrong when the Jehan kids were growing up. They probably missed Mum, good old Mumtaz.

Aurangzeb went on to rule until 1707, doing his best to turn the country into a severe Muslim state and draining the exchequer to the last drop by pursuing an unending series of fruitless campaigns, not least against the charismatic Hindu leader of the Marathas, Shivaji. The upshot of nearly fifty years of religious intolerance and incessant war, was that the Mughal Empire never recovered. It broke up into bits and pieces, Clump Three was no more, and the British were to become the major beneficiaries.

♔♔♔♔♔♔♔♔♔

Yes, but what if the British hadn't filled the vacuum left by the collapse of the Mughal Empire? Would anyone else have stepped in?

Answer: almost certainly, since there were powerful states within India just aching to be top dog, not least the Marathas.

Their power base was in the Deccan (southern India). They had survived all that Aurangzeb could throw at them and, from Shivaji's initial leadership in the 1670s, the Marathas power waxed, waned and waxed again over much of the Indian subcontinent. They were Hindu, generally tolerant of other religions and were no slouch when it came to civic improvements: dams, bridges, underground water supplies, that sort of thing. Add to this that they had a capable navy, as well as armies which were well equipped, well trained, well-versed in military tactics and disciplined. They were extremely formidable, as the British quickly discovered.

There was one problem, however, one little drawback to the Marathas; diplomacy wasn't their strong suit. When it came to their enemies, no brutality, and I mean no brutality, was beneath them[38]. All their wanton mass slaughter, rape, looting, burning, despoilation and indescribable other indignities did rather encourage other Indians to give their backing to less threatening alternatives. Step forward those foreign traders mouldering in Calcutta: the British East India Company. All things are relative.

But, if not the Marathas, India was full of other independent-minded States, not least Mysore (under the charismatic Tipu Sultan) and Hyderabad (not that these were particularly generous to their enemies either). If the British hadn't been there, the India of today might well have developed as a patchwork of several independent states. This might have been good, or not so good, but at least it would have been home grown.

And yet, and yet, if the British hadn't been there, India might have been taken over by the other big foreign player in India back then, the French. Now there's a thought. If the French had become numéro un, the Indians might never have taken up cricket! Unthinkable, surely.

Which all points to the problem of 'what-ifs'. Nail one down and, pretty soon, up pops another.

8. PUSHKAR

… Camels to the right of us, camels to the left of us

I decided to go to Rajasthan[39], so I telephoned Deepak and asked him to sort out a car and driver. I just knew what kind of car would show up. It did.

On our way out of Agra, we passed a sign saying 'Clean, green Agra.' I would say this for Agra: they were trying. Visitors to the Taj had to park 200 yards away and take an electric bus the rest of the way. A start, certainly, but clean and green? I didn't think so, particularly after an auto-rickshaw broke wind to the side of us, and dropped a whiffy black one through the car window.

Through this fresh cloud, a horse, colourfully decked out in ceremonial trappings, trotted by, on its way to a wedding. I don't think the bridegroom on board would argue with me if I were to suggest that he had never sat on a saddle before. Well, he wasn't sitting on it now. He was bouncing off it, like a pinball being whacked. That was until the horse swerved suddenly to sidestep a litter of pigs, and the groom lurched forward, as if he had suddenly remembered an urgent message he had to whisper into his charger's ear. In this pose, he careered out of view and towards a lifetime of marital bliss – assuming, that is, that the horse was galloping in the right direction.

Once out of town, we stopped at a stall by the side of the road to stock up on bananas. I prided myself that, by now, I had become something of an expert on banana prices. I conducted the negotiations with the confident air of a man who knows his onions. There was also on display, a knobbly, wrinkled green fruit, about which I made enquiries. The vendor peeled one, washed it in a tin of dubious-looking brown liquid, and handed it to me, obviously expecting me to put it in my mouth. Did I look tired of life? Gastroenteritis was written all over it. I needed a distraction, so I rustled about in my trousers and produced a rupee by way of payment. He wouldn't take it, but he did give me another knobbly green thing and, by the time I had taken out my penknife, peeled it and taken a bite, the fruit seller had forgotten, thank goodness, that his own kind offering was languishing undigested in my pocket.

I chewed on my self-peeled version and made appreciative ummming noises. Whatever this fruit was, it was definitely edible. It had a firm white flesh and tasted not unlike coconut. I asked what it was called, and the man muttered something that sounded like 'Shigarra', though whether that was its name or merely him practising his Sean Connery impersonation, I couldn't be sure.

The road was a national highway, genuine two-lanes – one lane going, one coming back – and relatively few pockmarks. We were on our way to the camel fair at Pushkar (Deepak's recommendation) and, though I didn't know it at the time, the road would stay wide, tarmacked and generally wholesome for most of the next nine hours. Even the Ambassador didn't feel too bad. The seats had been recently upholstered and there was some indication, from the way we glided over indentations, that springs were in place beneath me. I began to have uncharacteristically warm feelings about the old warhorse.

The other thing about this particular highway that I should mention is that bears were standing at regular intervals by the roadside. This is something you notice, particularly since their owners did everything short of flinging themselves beneath the wheels of our car to flag us down. What were we expected to do? Come screeching to a halt, just so we could hand over money? I don't think so. The bears were on two legs, encouraged, if that is the right word, to stand upright by a stick that was either attached to their noses, or sufficiently close to give even the dumbest of animals (which bears are not) the impression that it shortly would be if they didn't perform. They didn't look as if they were having too much fun.

Having swerved through bear country without smearing any owners across our bonnet, we made a small diversion to Fatehpur Sikri, which, of all the Mughal monuments, is my favourite. Fatehpur Sikri was, from 1571-85, the one-time capital of the Mughal Empire under its greatest emperor, Akbar. Before 1571, it was nothing except the home of a Muslim Saint. Fourteen fat years later, and along came its Pompeii moment. One day everybody was busily going about their daily business and then, *boing*, a volcano erupted (or in this case an imperial decision) and everything stopped immediately. It became as deserted as a ghost town in the old west. If tumbleweed were to blow through and an ole timer leaning against an imperial column, were to say, 'nope, the last stage through here was in, now let me see (scratches scrotum, and spits) '49', you wouldn't be the least bit surprised. And that's not just because spitting and scrotum scratching are big here.

Akbar had a perfectly serviceable capital at Agra, but what he didn't have, in spite of 300 wives, was an heir. Then, one day, he visited a holy man who lived at Sikri who told him that it would come to pass that he would have three sons. And he did: Salim, who was to become the Emperor Jahangir, Murad and Daniyal. The last two died of drink, as it happens, and Jahangir came within a whisker of following suit – but all that was later. In the immediate glow of fatherhood, while his boys were still downing nothing stronger than milk, Akbar was so impressed by the seer's prophetic powers that he built a new capital in his honour. Not just any old capital either. One that in its short life was deemed by a traveller from Elizabethan England to be 'much greater than London'[40], than, let me remind you, the city of Shakespeare and Marlowe, Drake and Raleigh.

If your idea of a purpose-built metropolis is Milton Keynes, then you should consider a visit to Fatehpur Sikri. It has palaces, formal courtyards, reflecting pools, harems, tombs and a great mosque, all exquisitely carved out of the local red sandstone, perfectly preserved in the dry heat and with a wonderful view over miles of peaceful farmland. One of the buildings, (the Hujra-I-Anup Talaq if you want to know), has a plaque outside which informed the reader that its 'geometric and floral designs in red sandstone give the impression of timber decoration.' They do. They really look like wooden carvings. In fact, since nobody was watching, I went up to one of the columns and tapped it to see if it gave a wooden clunk or a stone clunk. It was stone, definitely. And much of the rest of the place was the same. Gorgeous wooden creations made of sandstone.

The problem with Fatehpur Sikri was that it wasn't awash with water[41] so, after fourteen years, Akbar said goodbye to all those glorious buildings on which so much effort had been lavished, and moved back to Agra (via Lahore). Nevertheless, good things had happened during Fatehpur Sikri's brief moment in the sun. The Country had become that bit more civilised; less bandits on the road, a decent postal service, less taxes for the peasants, an official frown on child marriages and widow burning (Sati), that sort of thing.[42]

It had also become more tolerant. Akbar let the majority population get on with being Hindu without feeling the need to tax them as unbelievers, to exclude them from the civil service or obliterate their temples. In fact, from his liking for Hindu dress and Hindu wives (including the mother of his sons), to his distaste for orthodox Islam, the Emperor showed every sign of going native.

Of all the Muslim rulers of India – even those few, like his son Jahangir, who were decent, tolerant men – only Akbar was passionate about creating a society in which Hindu and Muslim might live and work together in harmony.[43] Had those who came after him followed his lead, the current history of India and Pakistan might, perhaps, have taken a different turn.

I wandered across to the splendidly endowed mosque, in its day the largest in the Mughal Empire,[44] and found myself attached to a couple of local kids who saw fit to enlighten me as to its exact physical proportions. 'Mosque 5000 metres high, 28 miles wide and weighs 30,000 tons', they told me. In return, I handed over my supply of pens and was then besieged by every child in the neighbourhood, anxious for similar largesse. This was my fault. I had broken the first rule, which is never give money, or anything else, on the way in. Wait until you are safely back in your car or, at the very least, within grabbing range of the door handle. So I had a quick dash round, discovered in the course of my circumnavigation that the mosque had a beehive in it – for which I awarded it a bonus point – and made for the Ambassador with a flotilla of hopeful children in my wake.

Pappu, my driver, was waiting, and a couple of blasts from him was enough to disburse my convoy. 'Pushkar?' he enquired. 'Pushkar,' I replied, settling into the back seat. Pappu was from Haryana, I discovered, where his wife and kids lived, but he worked most of the time in Delhi. 'Work is necessity,' he said, and I must say there was something about his night black eyes deep in their sockets that gave him the look of a man who had done his share. Probably seen a few things too. He was 5' 6", I suppose, lean, probably hungry and altogether spruced up in a smart sweater, neat trousers and slip-on shoes.

We proceeded out of Fatehpur Sikri and straight into the back of a flock of sheep. If it had been Rajjan at the wheel, he would have been up their backsides before you could say hill-farmer, but Pappu decided (uncharacteristically as it turned out) to adopt a more conciliatory approach. We waited until the sea parted of its own volition, and then edged through. Pretty soon, we came to a tax station on the Rajasthan border, and while Pappu sorted out the paperwork, I haggled with a necklace seller and his three brothers. The asking price was 1200 rupees each, which was about £17. This felt like a great deal of money for a few camel bones – who knew that India even had camels? – so, as the rules of the game dictated, I bargained with them unflinchingly until the price came down to 300 rupees each. We drove through into Rajasthan with me tucking away my new acquisitions (presents for my women-folk) and feeling pretty damn smug.

This part of Rajasthan didn't seem to be short of a bob or two. It was crawling with tractors, for one thing, which is a pretty good indicator of whether the locals have the price of a cup of tea. Two tractors, and an area is rich. Ten, and they could almost be part of the CAP.[x] On this basis, the area must have been rich beyond the dreams of avarice, although it was not immediately clear why. Probably from selling camel-bone necklaces to tourists.

Before long, we came to Bharatpur, which, had I but known at the time, has a wonderful bird sanctuary, the Keoladeo National park. I did wonder though why it had hotels called *Nightingale, Pelican, Painted Stork* and *Racket-tailed Drongo*, but before I could draw the sort of conclusions that might have inclined me to say, 'Hey, Pappu, pull in for a moment and let's investigate,' we were on a main trunk road heading west.

The Indian highway is a frightening place. You don't get the impression that MOT tests are an absolute requirement. If a vehicle is capable of forward motion, however temporary that may be, it's OK for driving. And everything, from bicycles to camels, takes to the road. A jeep, whose best days were by now ancient history, clattered past. I counted 12 people, though there may well have been more. Four were hanging on

---

x   It is through the CAP (Common Agricultural Policy) that the EU gives money to European farmers.

the outside as the vehicle weaved in and out of traffic. Motor cycles buzzed about like mosquitoes. We passed two lorries head-to-head by the side of the road, like a pair of bulls that had locked horns. Unless the drivers had leapt free before impact, I imagined that that was that.

Pappu took all this as an invitation to put his foot down. I watched the speedo edge past 80km /hr, felt the drum of the engine reverberate in my head and looked out at the pande-monium going on all around. Pappu took villages at 65 as a cursory acknowledgement that there were people lining either side of the road. My life flashed before me every half hour or so. There were so many repeats, I might have been watching Inspector Morse.

I decided it was time to intervene in this dance of life and death. 'Pappu', I said, leaning forward, 'you have a wife and two children' (appeal to his sense of responsibility), 'safety is most important' (appeal to the universal code of Professional Drivers which I was sure existed), '60 Km/hr MAXIMUM' (tone of command), 'please' (inviting him to buy into this new contract). This masterly sentence seemed to do the trick. 'I driv-ing 10 years, no accident,' he said, but agreed on the new limit. I could see him itching to let her out, to show me what the old girl could do, but he was aware that my beady eye was on him. 60 km/h it was from then on, except immediately after a break when Pappu's mind took a while to withdraw from wherever it was it went to in his off-duty moments. Silverstone probably.

I was in the back. That's how it works in India. The customer sits behind. It's very traditional. It also provides slightly more distance between you and the windscreen should something happen, should the car in front disintegrate into a thousand pieces, or a cow wander into the middle of the road and decide to take a nap. In such small mercies as this, I resolved to take comfort.

We stopped for lunch at a tourist café. Pappu disappeared to get something round the back and I bought three assorted packets to save for later. One was called '*Cashew*' which I thought, not unreasonably under the circumstances, might be a bag of nuts. It turned out to be a biscuit. The next one was '*Fruit Bite*', which was also a biscuit, but one that, at the first touch, crumbled into tiny granules, which immediately escaped out of the packet and bedded themselves into the back seat. It was the most unstable biscuit I have ever come across. At the merest hint of contact, it returned immediately to its granular, pre-biscuit form. I did what I could to gather up enough crumbs to make a mouthful, but swiftly came to the conclusion that the bag should be studiously folded up and packed away. You simply couldn't leave a substance as volatile as this lying around unattended. As for the third packet, '*Glucos-V*', you had only to prod it to know that something dangerously sticky lurked inside. I left it unopened in case a viscous liquid spurted out onto the seat and glued my trousers to the nodules of *fruit bite*, thus committing me to walking about with a backside like a hamburger bun with sesame seeds. All this confirmed for me, once again, how right I'd been to stick to bananas. You know where you are with a banana.

We passed through Jaipur without stopping, and pushed further into deepest Rajasthan. Pappu pointed at things that he thought might interest me and accompanied these declaratory gestures with explanations of fluctuating clarity. He knew quite a few words of English, but didn't always manage to arrange them in a comprehensible order. He would often thicken up his English sentences with what I assumed to be Hindi. We would be driving along and he would fling his arm in the direction of a field and say something like, 'This Boiten.' I would ask him to repeat. 'Boiten, boiten' he would say, enthusiastically. 'Ah, yes', I might reply or, depending on context, an enthusiastic 'good', and we would continue onwards, him wondering if he could get away with edging up to 65, and me lost in the sort of inane reverie that overtakes you after you have been in the back of an Ambassador for as long as I had.

The further we went into Rajasthan, the more camels we saw, either being led, or harnessed in front of some sort of mobile container. It takes a while to acclimatise. When you drive up behind a camel cart for the first time, and see the back of its head 10 feet above ground, you exclaim out loud, 'wow, what a huge horse that is', and then when you pass you, say 'oh, it's a camel.' You utter these very same words the next few times you come up behind one – well, you do if you're like me, and look at sculpture with your mouth open. After that, you learn to keep your deep thinking to yourself – but you think it just the same.

Just outside Basi, we passed a pull-in where all the camel cart drivers in the area stopped to refuel their animals and discuss the events of the day: prices at the Pushkar fair, fuel economy on the new c200 model, the usual stuff. It was just like any old transport caf in Britain. There was a car park outside, choc-a-bloc with camels and parked carts, with a few drivers asleep in the cab while the rest were inside, presumably tucking into greasy fried egg, curried baked beans, and a luvvly strong cuppa.

Hereabouts, Pappu demonstrated why he had gone 10 years without an accident. Quick reactions. We rounded a bend and there trotting towards us was an unattended camel. This, as far as I could gather, was the main Delhi-Mumbai highway and, being unused to seeing an animal the size of a large outhouse pootling along a major trunk road on the wrong side of the road, I did have a moment of mild concern. It didn't have lights for one thing. However, a quick left, right swerve and we were past. It may not surprise you to learn that there is a potato chip, heavily advertised along the roadside in Rajasthan, called 'Krash'.

When we finally reached Pushkar, it was late and the place was heaving. The Pushkar fair – a sort of Motor Show for camels – had finished the day before, but plenty of traders had stayed behind with the understandable purpose of separating tourists from their loose change. I was booked into a camp, one of many as it turned out. Pappu sniffed it out easily enough which is just as well because I certainly wouldn't have found it on my own – but then, if I'd been driving, I'd never have made it this far; I'd have been embedded in the side of a camel way back.

The entrepreneurial gentleman who ran the place had kept me some food, thankfully; a sort of spiced pancake and a cardamon flavoured milk pudding that had been boiled down so much it had to be safe. It was also delicious. Afterwards, I went to investigate my quarters, and to sleep the kind of sleep enjoyed by men who have travelled far.

Let me tell you what camping means to me. It means school army camp in Wales – sparse accommodation, inedible food, terrible weather and, at night, the blissful silence of open spaces. The tents at Pushkar had none of these things. The facilities were excellent – I even had my own shower –, the food was good, the weather was perfect, and the tent was pitched, not in the middle of the Rajasthan desert as I had imagined when Deepak was setting the scene, but adjacent to a very main road. I was tired. I went to bed. It was like sleeping in a lay-by off the AI. Lorries rumbled past my tent flap. A generator making papapapap noises like a pneumatic drill filled any small interlude between lorries. I pulled the sheets over my ears and hoped there was enough oxygen in my DIY igloo to survive until morning.

There must have been, because, at 5.30 next morning, I was in a cart, with half-a-dozen fellow campers, heading out across the sands to watch the dawn break over the desert. Traders' tents, thousands of them, were half visible in the semi-darkness. Camels were beginning to shake themselves to their feet. Men were starting to come to, some lighting fires, others drawing on their first fag, all getting ready for the business of the day: money. The sun rose.

I didn't want to be impressed by this, but I was. It was like a clip from the film, *Lawrence of Arabia*, before the attack on Aqaba. The desert army stirring like a giant square-rigger unfurling its sheets. All it needed was the right music. The vaguely Arabic wailing noises being coughed up by a distant speaker, may have been ethnically authentic, but they weren't nearly grand enough. Here was the nomad light infantry in all its glory, awakening to greet the new day. It needed something triumphant like the theme music to 2001, A Space Odyssey, or the exultant strains of Cwm Rhondda, sung by the massed ranks of Cardiff Arms Park.

I was fondly imagining the boyos in full voice, when along came an old man selling stamps. This was curious. 'Much call for philately in the desert? I asked. He nodded, offered me a cigarette and said something that may have been pertinent to my enquiry had I but been able to translate. He was wearing pyjama trousers and, on top, was sporting the kind of jacket which Scotsmen wear with a kilt – of which he was immensely proud, let me say.

We had a pleasant enough chat to the extent you can when you are limited to expressions like 'good camel cost many rupees? and 'what price are penny blacks fetching these days?' After a decent interval, he intimated that an American cigarette would be most welcome. I didn't have any. I don't smoke. However, since he'd offered me one of his, and I'd tucked it away 'for later', I felt duty bound to go and cadge one for him. Which I did, but only after approaching several American-looking people and promising unlimited free drinks back at our campsite, if they helped me out. This was mainly greeted with unalloyed pity. Their eyes said it all. 'So early in the day! So desperate! So sad!' and through their mouths they told me that they didn't smoke. But, in the end, I came across an ageing hippy with a scraggy pony-tail and a face etched by formative experiences at Woodstock. He gave me two. He understood. He knew what dependence meant. I brought them back and handed them over to my philatelist friend like a proud father returning from a morning's fishing with breakfast. The old fellow was pleased. You could tell he liked American cigarettes. In fact, our conversation was put on hold, while he gave himself up to their limitless pleasures, and I found myself gazing into the eyes of a camel which had seen fit to thrust its face between us.

A camel is an extraordinary creature. Its jaws move sideways for one thing, as opposed to up and down like yours and mine. It must be a dentist's nightmare. Beyond surgery, I would think. Then there's its posture, which is terrible. It stands with its rear legs splayed, like a triangle with the apex at the hips. No wonder camels have a hump. On top, it has these big brown eyes, long eyelashes and ridiculously coquettish lips. It's as if someone has been told to design something for a Betty Boop cartoon but somehow hasn't quite pulled it off. 'Good try Jenkins, but for heaven's sake man, get rid of that ridiculous hump, its neck looks like the U-tube in my lavatory, its ears are far too small and, if that thing winks at me, I'll throw up.' The whole design is across the line where 'cute' ends and 'grotesque' begins. It has been said (by the designer of the Mini, Sir Alec Issigonis) that a camel is a horse designed by committee, but this, of course, is quite wrong. No committee could dream up anything remotely as good as a camel. They'd come up with a horse.

By the time we were back at our camp, I had decided that Pushkar was too commercial and that I wasn't going to like it. I fall into these moods sometimes. So I spent the morning mooching around the campsite feeling out of sorts and then found myself delivered of one of my mother's lectures, which mysteriously reappear at moments like these. This was the one about pulling myself together, life is what you make it, and for God's sake don't just sit there, do something. So I did. I went into town, where I came once more to the view that the Pushkar Fair is, to my way of thinking, entirely dreadful. Whole acres are devoted to market stalls, which the Americans in the camp thought was great. If you like shopping, it was.

Where else could they have such an unparalleled opportunity to fulfil their lifetime's task, which was to beat down a poor bracelet vendor, offering his camel-bone products at an entirely reasonable 300 rupees each, to an indecently low 50 rupees (and then come and tell me about it).

The streets of Pushkar were jam-packed. Mankind, mainly of the tourist variety, was so densely congregated that it was more or less impossible to proceed forward at a speed greater than that at which the multitude was drifting. But I kept trying. You know those irritating people who keep changing lanes on a motorway when the traffic is crawling along at 5 mph. That was me. I dodged in and out. When I saw a space, I leapt through. It was tough work, but I kept at it. I was sweating profusely and then there came to me the discovery which I will now pass on to you. I have given it the name 'Inner Walking Through Crowded Markets (which has the memorable acronym, IWTCM). In order to walk through crowded markets, pick a point in the distance at which you wish to arrive, close your mind to everything going on around you, focus on the target and let your subconscious mind take over. The effect is remarkable. You are able to walk at speed through the most impenetrable swathes of humanity. Why? Your body finds the gaps, understands the pace at which people are moving and knows when holes will appear. Trust your body. You may think the writer has lost his marbles, but give it a go. You will be amazed. Oh, and the other bonus is that nobody comes up and tries to sell you anything. They see that vacant stare in your eyes, decide you are barking and wave you through.

My destination was the Pushkar lake, which is circular with ghats all around it and a temple on an island in the middle.

The Lake is a place of worship and rather splendid; pilgrims bathing, sun on the water, holy men covered in white ash deep in contemplation. The Hindus used to believe (and perhaps some still do) that the lake was bottomless, but it isn't. The Emperor, Jahangir, came here for two or three days to shoot[Y] water-fowl, and found this mystical belief about bottomlessness alien to his own more scientific temperament. He had the lake measured – which was a bit of a kill-joy thing to do, if you ask me – and found it was 'nowhere deeper than 12 cubits.'[45]

I walked round it, trying to absorb whatever spiritual understandings might be in the atmosphere and then caught sight of a temple on a hilltop overlooking the lake. 'Climb me', it called, so I thought I would. Could I find the way to the bottom? I could not. I spent the rest of the afternoon wandering through innumerable wrong back streets and then had to return to the car to ask Pappu to give me a lift. It was maddening; I could see the hill above me. Pappu drove straight there, and parked. This always happens when I am lost or looking for something. Whoever I ask says something consoling like 'it's one street over', or 'they're on the end of your nose.'

Something was bothering Pappu, though. 'This no good place,' he told me and, taking a proprietorial interest in my welfare, decided to climb up to the temple with me. I must say I didn't sense that anything was afoot but, after a while, we passed a group of five or six local women and one of them made a strong-arm grab for the water bottle I was carrying. Pappu

Y   Talking of shooting, you might like to know that artillery was first introduced into India by the first Mughal emperor, Babur (Jahangir's great-grandfather). Babur used it against the Lodi dynasty at the battle of Panipat in 1526, the result of which was that Clump Two became Clump Three.

gave me a 'see, I told you so' look. Then he glanced down the hill at the car. Kids were milling around it. A second emotion clouded his honest visage. Guard me or guard the car? Protect the client or the assets? I watched, with some amusement I'm ashamed to say, as Pappu struggled to penetrate the moral maze. No contest really. 'Save the Ambassador,' I cried, pointing dramatically, and off he shot.

I reached the top as the sun was setting. The view of the town and its surroundings was magnificent. Outcrops of hills were strung like sharks' fins across the flat plain that stretched away into the distance. A camel race, part of the fair, was dimly visible below. Accompanying music was drifting up, and a couple of western Hindus were seated on a rock, cross-legged, gazing into the receding sunlight and thinking deep thoughts. At least, I hope that's what they were doing. If they were nodding off, they were in trouble. It was a long way down.

That night, at the campsite, I joined a number of Americans for dinner. One, with them in body if not in spirit, had eaten nothing Indian since arriving. He had lived entirely out of his suitcase on packeted junk food and beer. He had been in the country for two weeks. What would he do when he ran out? Would he risk Indian food? Would he adopt a new rapid weight loss campaign, also known as starvation? Or would he discover the life-saving properties of bananas? I thought of dropping a hint or two in that direction but decided that there are some lessons a man just has to learn for himself.

9. JODHPUR

… Princes, and some pampering

I made an early start next morning for Jodhpur, where the riding trousers come from (yes, really). Pappu turned up looking pretty rough. Under cross-questioning it turned out that he had slept the last two nights in the car. The price of a bed in Pushkar was 500 rupees and the most he ever paid, 'maximum maximum', was 150. 'But company no pay?' I asked. 'Company no good company. No pay. Salary only.' And probably a small one at that.

Whatever the rights and wrongs of employment policy in India, the question I had to ask myself was, 'did I wish to face the extreme dangers of the open road, piloted by someone who was up all night and probably living on roti and crushed insects?' It did not take me long to conclude that I did not. A few quid in food and lodging that might keep both of us alive, seemed like a sensible investment. From then on, I made regular enquiries about his dietary and dormitory conditions.

'Sleep well, Pappu? Good breakfast?' and he'd reply with 'Good sleeping, good breakfast, sir.' This was to become our morning ritual.

Mountain country – Snake Mountain to be precise – separated Pushkar from Ajmer, and the drive between the two, looking down onto the flat, arid land below, was delightful. Then we came to Ajmer where the bilious smoke of auto-rickshaws encased us in a grey balloon of noxiousness. There is only so long anyone can go without inhaling, and Ajmer was too big to do in one. Breathing in, in India's larger cities, is not one of the world's great pleasures. Not that it bothered the cows. They were there, as always, grazing happily on the heaps of litter by the roadside. One was staring intently at a poster for the Rose Roof Top Restaurant. Whether it intended to eat it, or book a table, wasn't immediately obvious, but it certainly was concentrating. You know when a cow is concentrating, because it has its nose on the object under contemplation and its eyes have crossed.

You would have thought that cattle would gravitate towards greener pastures. They'd be chewing absent-mindedly on whatever garbage was to hand when, by chance, they'd find themselves on the edge of town. There they would discover grass. 'I say, what's this green stuff?' they'd wonder, 'do you suppose it's edible? Hmn, not bad. Hey, there's more of it over there,' and by such means our Indian Daisy and her friends would make their way out of the smoke and into the country. But it doesn't happen. Perhaps nine out of ten bovines prefer cardboard. Or perhaps they have unseen owners, lurking in doorways, who have negotiated cheap grazing rights with the local refuse department.

Sometime after Ajmer, we stopped for breakfast. Pappu never ate with me. He would go round the back, while I bought something with a bottle-top on and watched carefully while it was removed. If it came off without a hiss, or too easily, I would of course follow the admonitions of my doctor friend back home; *Don't Touch with Bargepole*. Then I saw it, like an oasis in the desert. A torn sticker advertising Cadbury's Dairy Milk. Chocolate. British Chocolate. I hardly allowed myself to hope. 'I don't suppose you have any of that,' I enquired, pointing at the poster. And do you know, they did. I bought two bars, inspected every square millimetre of the packaging, and decided that it probably was made by Cadbury (India) and probably had not been tampered with. I opened it with the awe and impatience of a 17-year-old fumbling with his first bra-strap, and popped a square into my mouth. I then gulped down both bars and thought, 'by gum, that wer good.'

With little traffic to bother us, we motored along at a steady 60, past school kids in neat uniforms, smart Mahindra taxis, flat dry land and thorny trees, and found ourselves, at midday, in Jodhpur. Time enough to check in to a £20-a-night hotel with antique furniture and a superb swimming pool, before jumping back into the Ambassador and driving out to see the Meherangarh Fort.

Pappu was making his way up a steep winding road, with the fort beetling above us, when an imposing building caught our attention. It turned out to be the far from modest memorial to the Maharaja of Jodhpur, Jaswant Singh II, constructed at the end of the nineteenth century in the finest white marble. I poked my head inside, not really thinking that I would stay long, and found myself inspecting the family portraits on the walls.

Now the engrossing and, dare I say, alarming thing about these was the extraordinary resemblance between the lot of them. I would go further and say that at least six of the former Maharajas were identical. Slightly different headgear, but the same face – small head, long straight nose, deep eyes, and long back sideburns. Maharja Man Singhi (1792-1803) and his forbears, Maharja Bheem Singhi, Maharja Vijai Singhi, Maharja Bagrat Singhi, Maharja Ram Singhi, and Maharja Abhey Singhi were as alike as peas in a pod. Closer than that. They looked like the same pea. This was the kind of thing you might see were you to take a banjo and a few friends and go canoeing down the Kahoolawassi River, but not in India where a man did not have to go to family weddings to find himself a wife. Indeed, in India, you could take as many wives as opportunity allowed. Yet, there on the walls were succeeding kings looking as much like one another as Dolly I and Dolly II[z].

I came out of the Jaswant Memorial vaguely wondering whether this was entirely healthy, and then I leant on a wall and looked across at the Umaid Bhawan Palace sitting atop a neighbouring hill. This really made me worry. Any Maharaja who could commission H.V.Lanchester, the architect responsible for Cardiff Town Hall, to build a palace in the style of, er, let me see, it's on the tip of my tongue, oh yes … Cardiff Town Hall, must have been more than a little unhinged. Not only that, he started building his 347 room residence in 1929 and carried on chucking bucket-loads of money at it until 1944, a mere three years before Indian independence from

z   In 1995, Dolly was the first clone produced from a cell taken from an adult mammal. She immediately became the world's most famous sheep (not an accolade that, hitherto, had had many claimants.)

Britain. You'd have thought he might have twigged that all this self-indulgence wouldn't go down too well with an incoming government whose leading light was just about the most saintly man ever to strap on a pair of sandals: Gandhi.

Mind you, the Princes of India had a long history of lunatic extravagance. In the old days, they had been kings. They had fought each other, or the Mughals (or both), and, if they weren't up to the job, were either defeated or deposed. That was fair enough. Dog eat dog. Then the British came along and, in 1858, declared that the Princes, all 600 hundred of them, with land covering 1/3 of the subcontinent, could keep what they had and carry on governing their states. The only condition was that they accepted Queen Victoria as the power in the land. The British, in other words, preserved the Indian maharajas in aspic. If they kept Her Britannic Majesty's local agent sweet, and didn't support the nationalists, they could be just about as degenerate or as profligate as they liked.

Most of them needed no second invitation. They splashed money around as if it was going out of style. Need a car? Have a Rolls Royce. Maharaja Bupinder Singh of Patiala had 27. The Maharaja of Bharatpur bought the entire stock of a Rolls showroom in London, shipped it back to India and used these ultimate British status symbols to cart municipal rubbish.[46]

The lavishness went on and on. When the Maharaja of Jaipur came to England, nothing less than the personal hire of a brand new P&O liner for six months would suffice.[47] One Indian Prince, in the 1920s, was said to have lost a million francs in a single evening on the gaming table of the International Sporting Club of Monte Carlo.[48] But the story I like the best, the one that takes the biscuit, is of the Maharaja whose dog was due to be married. This gentleman saw fit to invite 250 friends and relations (canine variety) to the nuptials, deck them out in jewelled brocade and have them carried by elephant down to the railway station. There they assembled, tongues lolling, to wait for the groom to make his triumphant arrival.[49] I just hope that Fido, on springing from the train, didn't take a shine to one of the bridesmaids.

OK, not every Prince was appalling. The Maharaja of Baroda was a shining light. He made primary education free and compulsory, promoted the cause of the Untouchables and within half a century had developed Baroda 'from a village society into a modern state.'[50]. But for every paragon, there were plenty on the dark side, like Jay Singh of Alwar. He took half of the state's revenue for himself, (this was in the 1920s), taxed his peasants almost to the point of beggary, and (cop this) tied up old widows as tiger bait. So it was rumoured anyway.[51] The upshot was that, soon after Independence in 1947 (Clump Five), the Princes lost the right to govern their states [AA] and, by the 1970s, the Princely order itself had been abolished.[52] Gandhi's opinion was that, allowing the Princes to continue in power was 'perhaps the greatest blot on British rule in India.'[53]

Now readers (with long memories) may recall that your

[AA] But the handover wasn't quite as straightforward as it might appear. In the lead up to Independence, the status of the Princely States was unresolved. Given that the Princes controlled a third of the landmass of India, this was a problem. Each had its own treaty with London and, legally, each had to choose a side. The choices were India, Pakistan or, if they were large enough, as some were, they could go it alone and appeal to the UN for protection. In the event, and after considerable diplomacy, they plumped for India – which was perhaps just as well. If they hadn't, India might not be the cohesive country it is today, or at least not without resort to strenuous, and probably bloody, arm twisting. (Patrick French, *India*, Penguin 2012, pp 13-15.)

guide, before being distracted, was on his roundabout way to the Meherangarh Fort. Pappu dropped me off below it, and I climbed up, along stone streets and through triumphal gates. The Lonely Planet Guide describes the Meherangarh as 'the most formidable fort in fort-studded Rajasthan', and I wouldn't argue, not with its walls looming above me like Quasimodo's shadow.

I couldn't help noticing that there was hardly a soul about. It was eerily quiet. This comes as such a surprise in Indian cities that you start to wonder what they know that you don't. Has Pakistan invaded? Has the district been ravaged by Dengue fever? It was very curious and a little unsettling. A sign pointed to a lift going up to the battlements, but of course I spurned this with a supercilious sideways glance over a pursed lip. Lifts? Moi? Instead, I undertook the breathtakingly vertical ascent on shanks pony.

I stood on the ramparts, gasping, and decided that I didn't envy the soldier who had to scale these fortifications, not with rocks and boiling oil coming down at him from above. Actually, as I peered over, I realised that the walls were so high that any boiling oil would probably be no more than tepid by the time it reached its target. Still, I thought to myself after further reflection, that could work. The soldier would look up, the by now merely warm lubricant would coat him from head to foot, and he'd slip off his ladder. As he tumbled to his doom, he would be shaking his fist, and words like 'you dastardly fiend' would be coming out of his mouth in a cartoon bubble.

The sheer drop from the ramparts – were you to fall down and keep bouncing – would take you back to Jodhpur, the blue city, below. Why blue, I hear you ask? Was it the result of centuries of melancholia? No. Was it because they ran out of green? Mmm, no. Actually, no-one is quite sure. Some say it's because blue helps to keep things cool, others that it repels mosquitoes. Alternatively, could it just have been that the burghers were partial to the colour? One of them splashed on a couple of coats and his neighbours followed suit? Then some bright spark on the city council realised he could make a killing by buying a million gallons at the bulk rate, and selling it on, retail. From where I was standing, looking down on a panorama of blue houses, I can tell you this: it was soothing. A bit samey perhaps, but definitely restful.

Inside the fort were palatial apartments and state rooms, as well as a permanent exhibition with good ideas on the sort of things you can do when you can afford to drop a million francs in an evening. On display were royal elephant howdahs, palanquins, and awnings the size of a cricket pitch (that were carried out for picnics so that half the palace could dine in the shade). There was also a selection of impressive weaponry. The best was a dagger with a small pistol attached. This looked seriously useful. Your enemy comes at you with a dagger. You draw yours. You indulge him with an introductory warm-up thrust and counter-thrust, and then you shoot him between the eyes.

After I left the fort, Pappu drove me down to the centre of the old town. While I went off for a wander around, he set about buffing up the car. He was a great one for dusting was Pappu. Wherever we stopped, even in the middle of a long journey, even when he knew that ten yards further on the car would be covered again, out would come that cloth of his. I rather shamefully hoped that one day we'd be engulfed by a mighty storm chucking buckets of sand over the car, because then I could say to Pappu, 'Look, terribly sorry, but could you pull over for a couple of minutes.' While pretending to relieve myself, I would slyly turn my head and watch the heroic battle. On one side, the forces of nature doing their damnest to take the sheen off his bonnet: on the other, Pappu with his rag. It would be a close call.

Something about Jodhpur was different and I couldn't quite put my finger on it. Then it came to me. No begging. Nobody was clinging to my arm looking desperate. I wasn't being mobbed. Jodhpur, as far as I could tell, was beggar-free. The point was rammed home when a man in a smart car stopped and tried to sell me a painting. I thought this spoke volumes. Jodhpur was clearly the kind of town where a man rolls down his window and says, 'Pssst, want to buy an eighteenth century, hand-painted, silk miniature?' It wouldn't happen in Varanasi. It wouldn't happen in many places that I could think of. It did rather suggest that the folks round here had a little something stashed away.[AB] But the thing that made Jodhpur truly special was that the Old Market seemed to have one or two shops. I don't mean kiosks with corrugated iron roofs, or market stalls, but places that might survive a huff and a puff from the big

AB   Rajasthan was, and still is, rich in natural resources. It was where the marble and the precious stones came from, which I imagine explains why a place which has more than its fair share of desert was able to mount consistent resistance to the Mughals. (More on this later). Even today, the roadsides are littered with marble-for-sale signs, and miles of accompanying slabs. What's not for sale by the side of the road as far as I could see, is all the salt, gypsum, silver ore and feldspar which they manage to dig up. That's all below ground, and you'd think that Rajasthan, which not only has deserts, but also droughts and locusts, wouldn't manage to produce much above ground. You'd be wrong. It has crops: cereals, pulses, oilseed and cotton. And it has livestock: camels (fair enough) but also cattle, sheep and goats. I don't know how they manage all this but, well done, Rajasthan.

bad wolf. I paused outside a shoe-shop. It had a lighted front window, behind which footwear of various types was enticingly on display. Inside were seats where you could sit and try on the merchandise. A genuine, 100% shoe shop in fact, the sort of establishment you routinely find in Scotland and which I hadn't seen in India since driving through the smartest part of New Delhi. This, in its way, was all very comforting, like eating a bowl of apple crumble and custard. Those little familiar things, which we all like to return to, were not as far away as I had thought[AC].

The pool at the hotel was too good to miss so I spent the whole of the next day indolently lounging by it, reading and indulging myself with selected morsels from the hotel's spotlessly clean dining room. A lugubrious but not unpleasant dirge, emerging from the bowstring of a splendidly attired native musician, wafted across from the hotel garden. The man's repertoire consisted of half a dozen subtly different tunes and, while he may have paused occasionally to refresh himself, he did not leave us for long. Songs entitled, 'a lovesick herdsman sings to his favourite camel', and, 'it may only be a cardboard box, but to me its lunch', hung on the poolside air. Serenade followed serenade. The warm sunshine of the afternoon gave way to evening. Soon it was time to nod appreciatively and retire.

I had given Pappu the day off with strict instructions to spend it sleeping and eating. I expected him to appear next morning, sleek, well-oiled and bristling with good health.

AC This was in the early years of the 21st century. I've no idea what the situation is today. Does Jodhpur now have the equivalent of an Aldi and a Marks and Spencer? Does it shop online? I imagine it does, but whether this is progress I wouldn't like to say.

10. JAISALMER

… Keep right on to the end of the road.

He did. He also looked exceedingly pleased with himself. Pappu ushered me round to the boot of the Ambassador and proudly showed me what he had bought yesterday with the money I had given him for food and board: a blanket with a golden trim round the edge and a new travel bag. On his feet were a sparkling pair of black lace-up shoes. Somewhere during this extended viewing of purchases made with my money, I did have the unworthy thought that you wouldn't exactly call any of these items, 'food and board'. The whole point of laying a little aside was to make sure that my driver arrived at the starting line in peak condition. 'Clothing and accessories' weren't quite what I had in mind. On the other hand, Pappu did look well. However much he stuffed himself, he was never going to take on the upholstered roundness of a jam roly-poly, but he gave the impression of being a good deal fitter and fresher than he had a couple of days ago. That was reassuring. We climbed aboard. Pappu put his hands together for a short prayer (also reassuring), and we set off.

We had hardly changed out of third gear, when we pulled into Mandore, the former capital of this part of Rajasthan. The reason it is now no longer the throbbing heart it once was is that a certain fifteenth century holy man, living a quiet and contemplative life in the desert, suddenly came up with the unasked-for suggestion that Jodh, the ruler, should abandon Mandore and build himself a new capital at Jodhpur. Which, of course, he did.

It's astonishing how often this kind of thing kept on happening in India. Mohammed Tughluq, you may remember, marched everybody off to Daulatabad. Akbar did much the same in Fatehpur Sikri. A trifle inconvenient if you'd just finished tiling the kitchen, particularly since you knew that in a few years you'd probably be told to pack up again and retrace your steps.

Actually, this didn't happen to Jodhpur. By some miracle, it stayed occupied. The only person who suffered was the poor old holy man who was responsible for putting ideas into Jodh's head in the first place. It turned out that Jodhpur had no water. It had to be piped in. And the route along which the water would be brought? Slap bang through the little place that the lonely hermit was pleased to call his own. He wasn't happy, understandably, and went so far as to curse the water in Jodhpur so that it would be forever brackish[54] – but it served him right if you ask me. There are times to speak out and times to stay zipped.

I walked through the main entrance of the Mandore gardens until I came to the cenotaphs (chatris) of past Maharajas. This was all that seemed to be left of Mandore. If there was more, I didn't see it. It was early morning, just after dawn, and the place was deserted. Monkeys had taken over. A few of them were sitting on a chatri roof complaining that the coffee was cold and, if the papers didn't arrive soon, they'd cancel their order. A female was on the ground doing her best to keep her child entertained, while simultaneously keeping a watchful eye on a pack of dogs that had strutted in like a troop of hungry mercenaries. One of them peeled off and chased her. She grabbed junior with a free arm, pulling him to her like an airplane retracting its wheels, and ran. Three legs or no, she could shift. And she could jump. She was half way up a wall in no time. Once out of danger, she turned round and hissed.

An unwashed youth swaggered in from somewhere, eyed me up and down and left. I was starting to have a bad feeling about this. There are moments when a hasty retreat is what's needed, and this was one of them. Something not quite right, and probably nasty, was in the air. I hurried back towards the main gate and instructed Pappu to saddle up and get us out of here. 'We go, Pappu,' is what I actually said.

The plan was to drive north to Osian and then cut west to Jaisalmer. We motored out of Mandore and further into the Thar desert. Two hundred and twenty-five million years ago all this was the Tethys sea[55], but it certainly wasn't a sea now. It was as dry as a bone. The land was flat and sprouting straggly vegetation of a sort that I couldn't identify – not that this narrows the range of possibilities particularly. Pointed outcrops of rock were sticking up like humps on a camel's back. Peacocks were playing by the roadside, and a herd of goats were wandering down the highway, gossiping. A typical day in up-country

Rajasthan, except for a gossamer wisp of white cloud floating across the clear blue sky. I didn't think they had clouds here but as long as the temperature stayed in the high twenties, I thought I could probably get used to them.

Osian was a one horse town. Actually it was a no horse town, but it did have goats, cows, dogs, monkeys and camels. It also had temples. Osian has been around since the third or fourth century, and had been a flourishing trading centre in the eighth century[56], but you wouldn't have known it today were it not for the fact that Osian has temples like Fife has golf courses. They were everywhere: to the left, to the right, straight ahead. Not having a clue which was which, I fell back on what I like to think of as the J.R.Ewing / Dallas approach to matters cultural. 'Find me a big one, Pappu,' I said.

He did. In fact, he found what turned out to be the most illustrious of them all, the Satya Mata, dedicated to a manifestation of the goddess Durga, the fiercest of all the great energies.[57] Pappu tended the car while I climbed a long succession of steps, arranged in flights, going up the side of a hill to a gigantic entrance porch. I couldn't help noticing that Hindus touched the top step of each flight with their hands as they went up and, if I hadn't thought I'd look like a complete idiot, I would probably have followed suit. It seemed a rather comforting thing to be doing.

This was a place for the locals. Well, not for foreign tourists anyway. None of the signs were written in English for one thing, and I only spotted a couple of other non-Indians in the place. A service was going on and I edged towards the inner sanctum, hoping for a peep. A drum started to beat. *Dum dum*, it went, pause for two, *dum dum*, then a symbol crashed, then all hell broke loose in the rhythm section. It was quite a sound, and I followed it to its source. A young man was thrashing a drum with one hand and, with the other, doing his best to nurse a complicated machine made up of cogs, levers, belts, wheels and hammers. The output of this marvel was not a year's supply of ball-bearings as you might have expected, but the sort of percussion backup that most symphony orchestras would kill for.

It was an exciting noise, no doubt about it, and it sucked me right inside the temple, into the middle of a throng of chanting pilgrims. They didn't seem to mind, even when I found myself incanting a selection of monosyllables that I imagined would slide harmoniously between the leaves of the authorized text. There was rhythm here that went to the core, and after a quarter of an hour I was fired up and ready to hurl myself against the enemy. It was that kind of sound. Mind you, it could have been my western upbringing. More enlightened souls might be stimulated to pursue the quest for spiritual enlightenment. But me, I wanted blood.

I dragged myself away. Too long in there and there's no telling what might have happened. I leant on a rail, gazed over a Spanish-looking landscape of rolling hills and occasional trees, and began to ruminate. The view looked vaguely familiar. I had seen those trees before, somewhere… and then I remembered. They were the spitting image of those arboreal creations that I used to paint as a boy: a single thick line denoting the trunk with circular blobs of green on top for the leaves. There have only been three things I have been able to draw that extremely perceptive souls have had a sporting chance of recognising: a square house with four windows, a five-bar gate and blobby trees – so these kept appearing on all my pictures at school. My art teacher, Mr Watkins, gave me up as a lost cause after the first week. I didn't blame him. He would lean over my shoulder from time to time, and being a kindly man, confine himself to a thoughtful 'hmn' before moving on. So I kept on producing rural scenes until the time I jumped ship, more or less at the point at which Watkins was plucking up the courage to suggest that I might try my hand at some other feature of the natural world, like a bowl of flowers. My blobby trees haven't put in an appearance since – until now. Here they were in real life. It was like bumping into old friends.

I regarded them lovingly for a while, thinking how wonderful it was that nature should imitate art, when a young teenage boy put his forearms on the railing alongside, and said: 'You like Tendulkar?' I said I preferred Ganguly. (I should perhaps explain, for the benefit of the uninitiated, that both of these gentlemen are cricketers.) 'Where from?' he asked and, having established my place of residence, he told me that Scotland had lost all their matches in the cricket world cup. Actually I knew that, but I was impressed that anyone would bother to comment. Scotland had done rather well finding eleven players who knew which way round to hold a bat. Winning a match was a step further on, to which I'm not sure anybody had given much thought.

Sunil (for that was the boy's name) offered to be my guide and I accepted gratefully. He was about 13, and he took his duties seriously. His tour included an ancient pillar dedicated to the elephant God, Ganesha, an even more ancient water tank with stone stairs carved into the side (now dried up), and an even older still ancient temple dedicated to the sun. Sunil said eighth century, and he may well have been right. There were some worn carvings on the outside, but worn or not, I'd have recognized those curves anywhere. This was pre-Khujaraho erotica. Invoking the spirit of Raj Kapoor, I gave it the full inspection. Unfortunately, since everybody else who had passed through Osian over the centuries had done likewise, the detail had been worn away and I wasn't able to satisfy myself about precisely who was doing what to whom. Sunil put my mind at rest. 'Kama Sutra,' he said.

There were no cars in this part of Osian but in order to keep the pollution quotient up to the mark, the town made up in litter what it lacked in noise and exhaust fumes. Through this we picked our way to Temple central, which had one exquisitely carved Jain[AD] building after another. The Jains had money, and restoration had been going on since 1971. I asked the local priest when the work would be finished. He put down the book he was holding, looked me squarely in the eye, and uttered the immortal words: 'no finish time in India.' In that case, thought I, there was not a lot of point in hanging about, so I asked Sunil to see if he could find where Pappu had got to. Look for a sparkling Ambassador, I told him, and a driver with a new pair of black shoes.

There are a number of railway crossings between Jodhpur and Jaisalmer as the road criss-crosses the railway line. Not far from Osian, we stopped at the first to wait for a train to go through.

AD   The founder of the Jains, Mahavira, was a contemporary of Lord Buddha in the sixth century BCE. Jains are known for a strict reverence for life up to, and including, not killing insects. Their temples, to my untutored eye, were very similar to Hindu temples except that they contained Buddha-like statues which were always masculine and expressionless, sometimes with black marble eyes. More than that, I wouldn't like to say.

I got out, stretched and walked to the gates, where I was joined by a jeep. He had driven past everything waiting patiently in the queue and parked himself in the right-hand lane. That is to say, he had blithely brought his conveyance to rest facing the oncoming traffic. 'This should be interesting,' I thought to myself, and settled back to watch the mayhem ensue. The train went through. The gates opened. The assorted vehicles opposite poured across, except that their flow was interrupted by a jeep blocking the road. What a surprise. If this had been Britain, the driver would have been immediately jumped on by a dozen angry motorists and his body dumped in a verge. What happened here? The driver reversed all the way back, protesting at the injustice of it all, and the traffic continued on its way. A few horns were blown in a neutral kind of a way, but mainly people looked on. They didn't let it spoil their day. India is endlessly surprising. And uplifting.

The road narrowed down to one and a half lanes, and then to single file. The countryside became even drier and sandier. There was hardly a car about. It was the kind of country where you expect to see olives. Dry land, rocks, intermittent bushes. I don't know if they grow olives in India. I imagine they do. They grow most things. Shepherds were herding sheep and goats. Camels were stretching themselves to nibble the roadside trees – which, incidentally, is why they have necks that wouldn't look out of place on a giraffe. They'd have to be straightened, of course, for giraffes to take them seriously, but there's enough inherent length in that tubing to give the spotted beanpole of the African veldt a run for its money – a stumpy one, anyway, with short parents.

There were also, of course, occasional cows, one of which

was standing by the side of the road, observing carefully as the Ambassador came lumbering along. When we were about ten yards away, it stepped out into the road, as if remotely controlled by a hidden statistician doing a survey on the quality of car brakes. Pappu swerved past without breaking sweat. All in a day's work. I don't know why I bother to mention it.

The road improved after Philodi. It was narrow but well made, and straight enough to satisfy the Romans. Mile after mile of light brown earth, bushes now and again, interludes of cultivated fields, and then scrub. I would have dozed off. I was relatively speaking unshaken in the back, the air was hot, the country was monotonous, but – and I speak as someone who can nod off almost anywhere – I defy anyone to sleep in a moving Ambassador.

We reached Jaisalmer in the early evening after about nine hours on the road, and with no lunch. I am never at my best in such circumstances. My hotel was on the edge of town and not very inspiring. I checked in and went up to the room. The water came out of the shower at about the same volume as juice being squeezed out of an orange, and a rather dry orange at that. I stood underneath for about half an hour trying to get wet, and then decided I had had enough of being dribbled on by cold water. I lay on the bed instead.

The management had seen fit to site the dining room in the basement. It was not enticing. It was also empty. I sat down and waited for some sign that waiters were present. In vain. I cast my eyes vacantly around the room hoping that, just perhaps, some item of fascination might leap out of the gloom. It didn't. Ten minutes later, a couple of couples came down, spied me looking miserable and asked if they could join me. It was as if a yacht had put into a desert island and invited its only occupier to climb aboard. I said yes, with alacrity. They were charming, and English. 'You like Tendulkar?' I asked. They did. And, as it turned out, they liked many other things in India as well. By the time I left for bed, I was feeling cheery again.

Half-way up the stairs, licking its whiskers, sprawled an enormous rat. I paused, as one does in such circumstances. A hungry rodent, casually loitering in the vicinity of a dining room, wasn't a good sign. In fact, it didn't bode well at all. However, my attention quickly turned to a more immediate concern. How was I going to get to my room? Should I step over the animal or was there enough room to go round it? Stepping over it didn't seem like an attractive proposition. I'd heard stories about rats running up trouser legs and, although I didn't really think this likely, I also didn't want to conduct the experiment, not when it was my trouser and my leg. On the other hand, inching my way round, with my back glued to the banister, didn't seem very enticing either, nor a very manly sort of thing to be doing. What if I was spotted? So, we looked at each other from a distance of a yard or so, with me intimating, by a nod of the head, that the leftovers in the kitchen would make much better eating than I would. Whether he got the message or not, I can't say, but he suddenly darted past me and was gone. I breathed for a minute or two to calm myself and then retired to my bed, pulling the sheet over my head and trying not to listen for the pitter-patter of tiny feet.

Next day, my gastric health still somehow intact, I organised (courtesy of the local travel agents) a guide called Madhu Sudan to show me the sights of Jaisalmer. Pappu drove us into town, and then I saw it. A dustbin. My first in India. Not just any old dustbin. On this one were the emblazoned words: 'Use me. Clean your city.' And what a difference. Jaisalmer was litter-free. Trust me, I checked. OK, if I was being picky, it was not quite up to Zurich standards but then where is? This was a clean city by any standard other than gnomic. Cleanliness is relaxing, so much so that I went shopping, strolled through the streets and had myself measured for a hand-made shirt. For a fiver. But that was later, after Madhu had shown me around.

We went up to the fort, which was actually a city within a fort, built in 1156 and home to several thousand people, sundry scooters and auto-rickshaws, to say nothing of miscellaneous goats, one of which was sunning itself on the battlements as we approached. Jaisalmer is called the golden city and, with the sun on the sandstone, you could see why. It was a sort of Indian Cotswolds, but older. And hotter. Madhu told me that the heat in summer can get up to 54º C. Normally it's a quiet 46-47º. 'At 54º', Madhu continued, 'no need to cook breakfast. Just go outside and break an egg on your head. In one minute, you have omelette.' I assumed he was joking, but then, when I looked at the top of his flat and hairless head, I wasn't so sure. If ever a head could double as a frying pan, this was it. 'Can you do an omelette at 46º?' I asked. He put his outstretched fingers on his scalp and lowered them gradually over his eyes and down to his chin, signifying egg dripping down his face. Then he gave me a broad grin. I burst out laughing. We both did.

One of the sights of the fort is its eight 15th and 16th century Jain temples. Very splendid they were too, and covered from floor to ceiling with carvings of gods, goddesses, animals, birds, dancers, musicians and naked ladies. You could spend a day doing nothing else but inspecting the walls. There was even a statue the size of a grain of rice.[58] So I'm told. I didn't see it myself. Well, it's not the kind of thing that, as you walk past, leaps out at you saying, 'and where do you think you're going sonny – cop this.' I gather it lurks discreetly on the ceiling of the Sambhavanath temple, so if you're going, take binoculars, and allow plenty of time. However, apart from missing this little gem, I had a good nose around and was struck by a thought which I shall now share with you. Jain temples – and Hindu ones for that matter – don't (in my limited experience) have anywhere for the congregation to sit. There are cosy passages aplenty and umpteen shrines, but nowhere for all the incumbents to gather as a group. You know what that means; NO SERMONS. Hallelujah. Nobody standing up and pontificating on what's what. Sounds good to me.

Jaisalmer is a city built for strolling. Apart from the fort and the temples, and the not inconsiderable fact that there is no begging, the old town has narrow streets, ornate houses and havelis (homes of aristocrats or rich merchants) that stand comparison with anything. If you are a haveli fan, this is the place to come. The best of them are decorated on the principle that more is more – that if there is spot of empty wall, carve something on it. It's an approach that takes cash, of course, and you may wonder how a city that sits in the middle of a desert, miles from anywhere, came by enough of the stuff to afford such creations. The answer is 'trade'; the caravan route to and from the west. Cereals, ghee, and opium went through here on their way to Afghanistan, Sind, Iraq and Iran, and back came carpets, swords, wine and 'green-eyed, Circassian houris.'[59] Overloaded camels plied back and forth for centuries, but the glory days of Jaisalmer started in the sixteenth century (helped by a favourable alliance with the Mughals in Delhi), and ended at the end of the eighteenth.[60] Today there is tourism. And Soldiers. Pakistan is just down the road.

I liked Jaisalmer. I liked just wandering around with nothing much in mind. This suited Madhu fine. He was a wander-around-nothing-much-in-mind kind of person. The only thing that seemed to bother him were his sunglasses. They were new and he wasn't entirely sure that his money had been well spent. He kept taking them off, rubbing his nose, putting them back on and asking me what I thought. I must admit I was rather flattered to be consulted. It doesn't happen often where matters of fashion are concerned. I told him straight out that there were limits to the remedial changes that a pair of sunglasses could induce but, in my opinion, the ones he had were fine. This didn't seem to reassure him. We popped in to the 10ft by 4ft kiosk where he had bought them, and he somehow persuaded its owner to offer a replacement. Madhu tried on every pair in the place and was much taken by a sleek cut-away silver number with reflective lenses. He looked over to me enquiringly; a seeker, if ever I saw one, of reassurance before truth. I said they were great.

The optometrist who ran the kiosk had trained in Delhi, made up the lenses himself and had his own computer testing equipment. That's what his sign said but, being prone to what I like to regard as a healthy scepticism, I asked if I could have a look. It was in a cubicle at the back; an ultra-modern piece of computerised kit that tested your eyes and then coughed up a recommendation. It was accurate to the 90% level apparently. The remaining 10% was provided by the sort of nineteenth century technology I'm used to – a test chart that begins with a letter 'E' so vast that, if you can't read it, they skip the glasses stage and go straight to the white stick.

His investment in state-of-the-art had cost him 23,500 rupees and I asked him if he would ever recover it. He fluttered his hand horizontally through the air and told me that his customers wouldn't think his service was any good unless it was computerised. All this, and designer frames as well, in a shop not much bigger that a decent-sized estate car. As I have said, India is endlessly surprising. If you are ever in the Southern Market in Jaisalmer and in need of a pair of specs, look no further than Bhatia Optical. Thoroughly recommended – and if the glasses start to annoy you, you can always take them back.

Late on that afternoon, and after being measured up for a shirt by Mr Dungar Ram of Tourist Tailors, I went back to the hotel to meet Pappu as we'd arranged. I asked him to drive me out to see the sun set over the desert. That's what eager visitors to Jaisalmer do when they're not looking at havelis. When we arrived, I took off my shoes and walked across the sand. Pappu came with me. He liked sand. In fact, liberated from the Ambassador, he became quite frisky. He ran up the dunes and threw himself over the top in the armchair position that overweight 15-year-old boys adopt when they're dive-bombing their sisters in the pool. By the time I had come round to his side, he'd dug himself out and was brushing a dusting of yellow particles out of his trousers.

After a while, we reached sunset point. I knew where I was because there was a sign that said *Sun Set Point*, which didn't exactly make me feel I was charting unknown territory. Mind you, I might have formed that impression from the presence of dozens of cameleers plying their trade, and any number of tourists. But a train of camels in the distance, silhouetted on a sand dune against the setting sun, is still a great sight even if all it carries is foreigners.

Having found the right spot to watch the sun go down, we stood there and waited. Pappu's attention was diverted by a large black beetle, which he proceeded to torment by pouring sand on it, and turning it over. Given that it lay very still after Pappu had repeated this exercise a couple of times, I rather believe that the excitement may have been too much for it. An ascetic-looking Indian had been watching this performance from a few yards away. He didn't seem enraptured. He was perhaps pondering the number of life cycles Pappu still had to go through before enlightenment was his.

The beetle now being dormant, Pappu was in need of further entertainment. Across his field of vision sauntered a boy followed by a weary camel. Pappu pounced. I couldn't follow what passed between them but I'd be surprised if it didn't have something to do with Pappu putting the best possible gloss on his skills as a cameleer. At any rate, he was soon in the saddle, reins in hand, encouraging the long-suffering beast beneath him to break into a gallop.

I was watching this performance with interest and hadn't noticed a young lad come up to within a foot of my ear and place a tube to his lips. He then produced from it an immense belch, which quite knocked me backwards. I looked around for some explanation other than that the world had just ended, and saw this youth about to repeat the process. I wasn't at all clear whether he believed he was playing a tune, or was blatantly trying to extract protection money on the grounds that, if I didn't pay him to stop, he'd obliterate my eardrums. It could only have been the latter, surely, so I edged away in as slow and as dignified a fashion as a man, who has just been blasted into oblivion, could muster. It never does to give in to blackmail.

The sun, meanwhile, was sinking fast, and looking glorious. To western man, that great shining orb up there in the sky is a large, hot lump of rock but, to Hindus, it is also a metaphor. I later discovered a rather lovely ancient mantra that Hindus still recite at dawn and dusk. *'Let us contemplate the beautiful splendour of God, Savitri, that he may inspire our visions.*'[61] 'Worship' is not an inappropriate word for a prayer like that, strong though it may be. Then the deep orange tennis ball dropped in slow, slow motion over the net, and disappeared.

We walked back to the car and Pappu drove me to a rooftop restaurant in town, where I dined, underneath the stars, on assorted vegetables, one of which managed the unique double of having the consistency of freshly picked twigs and tasting delicious. Its name escapes me but I'm pretty sure they don't stock it at Tesco. The beer was Kingfisher, described on the menu as being 'most thrillingly chilled' – which was putting it a bit strongly. The whole meal was dirt cheap and there were no visible rats. Pappu was there to take me back to the hotel when I'd finished. I did like having a driver. I could get used to it.

I was woken next day at the crack of dawn by the penetrating wail of a holy man calling the Muslim faithful to prayer. He was atop a minaret and taking advantage of the latest that modern technology had to offer by way of amplifiers. This was to make sure his message reached out to deepest Rajasthan. I found it all quite colourful, but I wondered what the Hindus thought about this happening dawn and dusk, day after day, year after year. No, that's not the right question. The Hindus would probably shrug and get on with things. What would less tolerant people make of it all? Picture yourself in a small town in Britain and ask yourself what would occur if someone were to build themselves a high tower and broadcast wake-up music to a population hitherto slumbering happily in their beds. He'd be lynched. Religious tolerance is something that is burned deep into the core of most Brits, but then they've never been asked to choose between that and a good night's sleep.

Let me refer you to the reaction of an English traveller in India, Tom Coryat, in the early 1600s[AE]. Admittedly Coryat was eccentric bordering on the deranged, but we should take note of his response to hearing devout mullahs climbing up their minarets and proclaiming that 'here is no God but one God, and Mahomet, the messenger of God.' He snapped. One day, he climbed up to a high place opposite the mosque and shouted back, 'here is no God but one God, and the Lord Christ, the son of God.' He also threw in for good measure that Mahomet was an impostor. The authorities, fortunately for him, thought he was off his trolley, which was the only reason that they didn't immediately put him to death.[62] What it shows, though, is how superhumanly easy-going is – or was – your average Hindu[AF].

After this uncharacteristically early start, I spent the day rootling around the town and peeling off a layer of myopia

AE   When the fourth of the Great Mughals, Jahangir, was Emperor (Clump Three).

AF   But less so now, perhaps, with the rise of the BJP and assertive Hindu Nationalism (Hindutva). The BJP is the party led by Prime Minister, Narendra Modi. It draws its support from the RSS which, according to its mission statement, believes that India's pluralistic arrangements have allowed the 'appeasement of Muslims' and the treatment of Hindus as 'second order citizens'. (Chowdhury and Keane, *How to Kill a Democracy*, Oxford 2021, p.174).

in the process. Indian shops were fun. I hadn't realised this. They were also devoted to 'stock' in a way that store-holders in Britain would find impossible to imagine. Walls were not areas to be frittered away on a poster or a yucca plant. Floors were not for standing on, except insofar as a pathway to the till had to be kept open. Ceilings were not the exclusive preserve of spiders. All flat surfaces were for occupation, totally, with no square inch uncovered.

I squeezed into a tiny bookshop (and I mean tiny) that somehow managed to pack in most of the English language titles published in the last twenty years. Everything from Lawrence James', *The Raj*, to *Baby and Childcare*, *Zen and the Art of Motorcycle Maintenance*, Ardel O'Hanlon, John Grisham and my favourite – a delightful tip of the cap in the direction of minority tastes – '*Librarianship as a Profession in India*'.

A few doors down a General Store of similar dimensions was selling toothpaste, Old Spice, pots, pans, and any other item that your typical Jaisalmer housewife might require once in a blue moon. I bought a foldaway knife 'top quality' for 20 rupees (30p) which was 'very sturdy' and probably the best 30ps worth I will ever spend. I also refilled my pen supply, should I have to bribe my way out of a tight corner.

I thought I would wander along to see if my new shirt was ready. Mr Ram, I calculated, should by now have sewed the final button-hole and be waiting for me to try it on. I asked directions to the Panzari bazaar and somehow or other found myself on the outskirts of town in an area alive with furry little mini-pigs. This was not right. When I'd had my measurements taken, I had exposed my naked pink chest in the middle of a busy market lane – not surrounded by a herd of porcine objects that wouldn't have looked out of place trotting behind Cro-Magnum man, nipping at his heels and chewing on chunks of woolly mammoth. I'd have remembered that. I headed back in what I thought was a more promising direction and, as luck would have it, stumbled across one of the havelis I'd seen yesterday. I knew I was now in the right part of town, so I sat on a bench and read the Times of India given to me by the bookshop in grateful appreciation of the number of books I'd bought. And then, when I'd finished, I folded the paper carefully, found Mr Ram ready with my shirt, and took an auto-rickshaw back to the hotel. It had been a restful day.

I spent the evening on a stone step at the edge of a thirteenth century, man-made, lake, in a pose that was as close to the lotus position as an adult without a stretchable tendon in his body will ever achieve. The last rays of a dying sun were playing on the surface of the still waters. Below me, a few frogs were sitting at attention, waiting for their supper. How lucky I was, I thought, to be that little bit higher up the chain of death and reincarnation – a reflection that, as time ticked by, was gradually replaced by the notion that a comfortable chair would be pretty good too.

11. LUNI

… Lazy days

Jaisalmer is as close to Pakistan as you can go without getting shot[AG]. One of its problems – just about its only one – is that having expended vast amounts of energy in getting there, you then have to retrace each gruelling step along the same road to get back. Which is what we did, and six and a half hours later were immersed in the cacophony of Jodhpur on our way to Luni, 35km further on. Luni had leapt out of the pages of the Lonely Planet Guide, because it was described as 'perfect if you want some respite from the tumult of travelling in India.' I did.

Pappu dropped me at the gate of Fort Chanwa, which was the place to stay. Actually, from what I could see of the tiny village of Luni, if you weren't staying in Fort Chanwa, you weren't staying. Pigeons and parakeets were playing on its battlements. A circular gravel path rotated within its ornate

AG   This is a bit of an exaggeration. Soldiers do patrol both sides of the border but I imagine they're used to tourists by now.

red sandstone walls. It looked a picture.

Pappu was less convinced of its merits. He left me with a stern warning to be careful. 'I, Rajasthan,' he reminded me, meaning that he knew his Rajasthanis and I'd better watch myself with this bunch. In fact, Pappu had let slip that he was from Haryana, just outside the Rajasthan border, but I quite saw that the phrase 'I, Harayana,' wouldn't have had the same dramatic impact. It would have been like President Kennedy going to Berlin and saying 'Ich bin ein Hamburger.' But, at the time, I was just pleased to see that he was interpreting his role widely and taking seriously his duty to deliver me back to Delhi in one piece.

I went to my room, dumped my cases and noticed something that might turn out to be a shower. I rotated the tap marked 'hot', itself an encouraging sign, and observed carefully what, if anything, would happen. To my great pleasure, water came out. Not only that, but there was enough of it to justify the appellation shower, and the attendant steam gave me to believe it was, as advertised, hot. Giving a quiet smile of the man who knows that good things happen to those who wait, I stepped in. It was bliss.

The Fort had a masseur, and with fond memories of Varanasi flooding back, I put some clothes on and went to see if I might book myself in. Massages took place by the small outdoor swimming pool, I was told, so I walked along there to find it occupied by half a dozen European ladies in deckchairs, reading in a silence so total you could hear a pin drop. This made a change from most places in India where you'd hardly notice a bomb drop. The masseur was waiting for me.

It wasn't exactly what you'd call private. I didn't feel I could just lie down in the midst of the matronly presence, almost, as it were, under their feet, so, spotting a small sliver of grass to one side, I edged towards it. The massage man followed me round, and invited me to take off my trousers. In case there was any ambiguity about his intentions, he put both hands on the top of my belt and began to pull gently downwards. This was a bit much. One of my few remaining conceits is that I am not yet too decrepit to dress myself, or in this case undress. As modestly as I could, I stripped to my underpants and lay flat on the grass hoping that the one foot or so of the swimming pool that was above ground would shelter me from the prying eyes of the watching memsahibs. It didn't, but as the masseur weaved his magic, I soon forgot about all that. I drifted into a state beyond such niceties. Well, you do if your flesh is being pummelled. My man was a professional, no doubt about it, but if I was being picky, I would suggest he work on a lighter touch when it came to his pièce de résistance, the final crowd-pleaser, the moment when he captured my full and undivided attention by karate chopping my head; a task he undertook with dedication. Bruce Lee would have applauded. He followed this with clacking noises of the kind that knuckles make when they strike bone (his knuckles, my bone). I gather that the technical term for such a procedure is 'head massage'.

When he had finally exhausted himself in the attempt to reshape my skull, I staggered to my feet and, groggy though I was, dimly perceived that I was perhaps underdressed for the occasion. I smiled at the attendant ladies as nonchalantly as I could – which wasn't very. Brits, on the whole, find it hard to be completely relaxed in nothing more than underpants and socks. Then I gathered up my belongings and scuttled away.

The rest of the day was spent reading and lounging about, but to redeem myself, I signed up for a village safari starting next morning at seven o'clock. It turned out I was the only one going. The hotel manager of the night before, Koshu, was now doubling as tour guide. 'It snowed four nights ago in Shimla, so it will feel like winter today,' he announced, standing by the jeep in a stiff leather jacket, shivering, and beating himself with his arms in an effort to keep warm. I took this to mean we would have a pleasantly roasting day around 25 degrees without a cloud in the sky – which I might say we did.

Koshu spoke perfect English, fine-tuned at Mayo College in Ajmer, founded by the Earl of Mayo, the inventor of salad cream[AH]. Mayo College is the Eton of the East and members of Koshu's high caste Rajput family, he told me, had been educated there for four generations. This was interesting information. I filed it away for when the moment came to decide if a tip would be appropriate.

We drove along a bumpy lane, flat dry countryside on either side, to the house of a Bisnoes family. The Bisnoes are the Amish of the east. They don't kill things. They don't eat meat, they don't cut down trees, they don't cremate their dead, they don't smoke and they don't drink. In fact, they don't do just about everything. Such were the principles (twenty-nine of them) laid down by their founder Jamboji, born 1551.

The Bisnoes regard the antelope as holy and, for this reason, we were able to see Nilgai and Black Buck in the surrounding fields. Otherwise, they would have been someone's dinner a

---

AH   Forgive the flippancy; connections between the 6th Earl of Mayo and mayonnaise are fanciful. The 6th Earl was, however, Viceroy of India from 1869 to 1892.

long time ago. There used to be more Black Buck on the North Indian Plain than any other large mammal. Apparently, in the 1920s and 30s, traffic would wait 20 minutes or more while a vast herd made its way across the road.[63] These days there are only 3,000 or so in game reserves, plus the odd few lucky enough to live on Bisnoes land.

To say that the Bisnoes live simply would be an understatement. Crofters on Scottish islands live simply. The Bisnoes live in a state of simplicity that goes beyond the normal meaning of the term and, for that matter, beyond words like austere or Spartan. They hardly scratch the surface of the land they inhabit. They survive on milk and vegetables, which they dry and re-hydrate when needed. Their houses are made of thatch and fallen twigs, and the floors of a mixture of clay and dried cow dung. Cow dung is good stuff, by the way. It doesn't cost much to lay down, it doesn't smell when dry, it deters insects, and it allows the family to have a new kitchen every two or three years. That's how often it rains in these parts. The Bisnoes are poorer than church mice, but I tell you what, I'd rather be poor like them, than poor like those in Delhi or Varanasi. At least they have fresh air to breathe, and a range where the deer and the antelope roam.

Our next stop was a farm beyond Bisnoes territory, owned by the Patels. They offered us a cup of tea and, because I had just been thinking that I could murder a good cuppa, I said yes. Then the face and wagging finger of my doctor friend back home appeared before me. 'They are being generous and hospitable, Michael, which is good,' the face and finger said, 'but do you imagine that the water will be properly boiled? And what about the cup, eh? Clean? Did you think about this before you said yes?' Well, no, I hadn't, but I was thinking about it now. Still, I concluded, what's done is done. There are moments when you just have to sit up straight and drink your tea. (Thanks, mum.) So, when the tea arrived, I said thank you, and put it unobtrusively down beside me.

The Patels, in common with every family round about, liked to begin their day with a stiff ingestion of narcotic substances. Mr Patel busied himself in firing up the hookah for the first smoke of the morning and, just in case it were to fall to me one day to do likewise, I paid close attention. I can now tell you that the three elements in a hookah are water (at the bottom of a pipe bowl), lighted charcoal (the next layer up) and locally-grown tobacco (on top). A long tube extends from the bowl to the smoker's mouth and breathing in draws the tobacco smoke through the water (hence the glug-glug sound familiar to all hookah users) and along the tube.

As for their other narcotic of choice, opium, the Patels preferred to take it in the traditional Rajasthan form, as a drink. Instructions are as follows. Take the sap of poppy, heat until it has become a crystal, grind it, mix it with water, place in palm of hand, and drink. Once the hookah was going to his satisfaction, Mr Patel worked away, as indicated, on his other morning pick-me-up. When all was ready, he said a short prayer to Shiva, and took a swig. He then offered me a palmful. I said 'no, thank you very much, it's a bit early in the day for me,' and wondered to myself which was more lethal, the opium or the grubby water with which it was mixed. Mr P. insisted. I looked at Koshu. He gave me a nod. 'Call yourself a man,' the nod said, 'Drink.' So I dipped the end of my finger in the opium water and licked it. Let it never be said that I don't live dangerously.

Opium has always been a common tipple in Rajasthan. A few hundred years ago, the Rajputs were imbibing in large quantities and from an early age. When war came around, they habitually went off doped up to the eyeballs. 'On the day of battle', reported a 17th century traveller, 'they never fail to double the dose, and this drug so animates, or rather inebriates, them that they rush into the thickest of the combat insensible of danger.'[64] Koshu, as a Rajput of long pedigree, was happy to confirm opium's all-around efficacy. 'It clots blood and it deadens pain.' He also added that it was regularly used at weddings, a juxtaposition which opened up a line of enquiry that I didn't feel I should pursue.

Beside Mr P sat another man, sucking the hookah for all his worth, and only putting it down when the need to swallow the local blood clotting agent became overpowering. He had half-closed, squinting eyes, greying hair, and a face that looked not so much lived-in, as crowded out by uninvited guests. 'That man is 40', said Koshu, 'but probably won't live to be more than 45.' If that, thought I. Similar notions seemed to be percolating through the brain of a vulture perched in a nearby tree who was fixing my narcotic friend with a hungry eye and putting his money on demise sometime that afternoon. The creature must have weighed half as much as I did, and, judging by the look of him, knew dinner when he saw it.

We said our goodbyes, which in the case of Mr P's thread-hanging companion were particularly heartfelt, and left events to unfold as nature, red in tooth and claw, dictated. We drove on through open country, watching Jungle Babblers and small green Bee Eaters fluttering in the sunshine, and Nilgai grazing. 'Nil' means blue, and 'gai' cow, but Koshu liked to call them blue bull (which is close enough). Whatever you call them, they deserve respect as befits one of the largest antelopes in the world, that can stand shoulder to shoulder with a good-sized horse, and has horns.

Koshu stopped to point out an acacia tree, after which London names its avenues. It was imported from Africa, he said, because it was evergreen, made good burning and didn't have to be dried. However, animals won't eat acacia and it is crowding out other trees, like Khajari, which camels like. This, he observed, with a sadness unusual in a young man, is what happens when you tamper with nature. How right he was.

Our morning excursion ended with a visit to a potter where, more interesting than the pots, excellent though they were, was an old bed. It was just lying around, but closer examination revealed that its springs were made from strips of car tyres[A1]. You may think this unremarkable, but it illustrates how good the Indians are at recycling. They don't just throw worn-down rubber onto the scrap heap. They make things with it. At the Patels, we'd seen a collection of old cloths and tailors' cuttings. Koshu told me that they would be unpicked and the yarn woven into rugs. Nothing in India, he told me, is wasted, and I nodded in agreement.

The rest of the day drifted lazily past. I swam, I took showers which probably used up enough hot water to fill the radiators of half of Rajasthan's camels, and I availed myself of the rather grand alfresco dinner that the hotel had laid out on the Fort lawn. After that, I went to my room to read. I had just hunkered down with my book, when I was treated to the

---

A1   So that's why Indian villages have shop after shop selling tyres. I had wondered.

delights of a party of Germans giving it full throttle on the grass outside my door. What is it about German singing? Does it all sound so hearty? Is it all quite so redolent of fresh air and exercise? During the brief interludes when the troupe was drawing breath, I found myself, despite my best intentions, wondering if they were wearing lederhosen. It's the sort of question that can eat away at you. Finally, I had to peek out of my window. It was okay. They weren't. Then the bonding session resumed and with the thought that good, sweet, gentle Kumbaya might not be so bad after all, I packed my travel bag, closed my ears and went to sleep.

A reflection on caste and racism.

Caste. What's to say? Well, first thing is that it goes back a very long way. In early Hindu texts, society was divided into four varnas, or categories: Brahmins, Kshatriyas, Vaishyas and Shudras. Which one you were in depended on your occupation: the Brahmins were priests, the Kshatriyas warriors and rulers (think Koshu), the Vaishyas merchants and farmers, and the Shudras (think Pappu) were labourers serving others. As these occupations were handed down from generation to generation, they turned into the much divided, and subdivided, hereditary caste system of today. The matrimonial sections of the newspapers still attach great importance to it, as you'll see should you make it through to the chapter on Chandigarh.

Caste provides an interesting background against which to consider racism, of which the British in India have been widely accused. In one sense, caste can't be considered racist in that high caste and low caste Indians are of the same race. On the other hand, it has been highly discriminatory, which is the sharp end of racism. Rabindranath Tagore, Gandhi and B R Ambedkar were all of the view that, 'as a society that had invented the idea that the touch of another person could cause pollution, India did not need the British to know how to oppress and degrade other people.'[65]

This doesn't, of course, let the British off the hook. There were many examples of racism by the British, examples ranging from contempt to physical brutality. It was more prevalent among those lower down the social scale – those who came for the money such as the planters and the merchants – than, for example, those in the Indian Civil Service. Towards the end of this book, the chapter on Shimla has a story about a man called Rudd. It's an appalling story but it well illustrates the interplay between the officers of the Government (generally good) and those who came to India to line their pockets (generally bad).

But stereotypes only go so far. It hasn't gone unnoticed that many Brits were deeply respectful of India and its abundant culture. Starting at the top, Warren Hastings, who became Governor General in 1773, spoke fluent Bengali, Urdu and Persian and declared that 'in truth I love India a little more than my own country.'[66] In the 1820s, the Governors of Calcutta, Bombay and Madras looking towards the inevitable end of British rule, wanted Britain to be able to boast that it had preferred the civilisation of India to its continued subjection.[67] And when the British Government took over the running of India in 1858, the Indian Civil Service was generally of this same view. Many of the District Officers saw their responsibility for forests, roads, schools, hospitals, canals, agriculture and law and order as their life's task.[68]

And there was one other thing that came out of the advent of foreigners – not that the Brits can take much credit for it. According to Tirthankar Roy, British rule, being an imposition from the outside, unleashed forces of change that weakened the home-grown cruelty of caste. "The Depressed classes welcome the British," Ambedkar said "as their deliverers from age long tyranny and oppression by the orthodox Hindus". [69]

12. UDAIPUR

… Lost and found

We made an early start. Pappu appeared at 7.15, and greeted me with a bright and breezy, 'You well, Sir? Sleep good? You looking dog parking?' 'Yes, thank you,' I said, and off we went.

I felt well rested, the day was warm and the road smooth. I anticipated an easy day with a pleasant tour of the Jain temples at Ranakpur to break the journey. I even started to hum a little ditty or two, and Pappu catching me at it, gave me an indulgent smile in the rear-view mirror. I had always wondered what Pappu thought mirrors were for since he never used them for routine matters, like overtaking – he just blew his horn, as did every other driver on the road, and pulled out. Now I knew. They were for keeping an eye on his passengers.

Pappu, I discovered, had made friends with a fellow driver the evening before who had told him that, if he were to turn off the main road shortly after Pali and take the road to Desuri, it would cut 10km off the journey. Not having a road map against which to check this advice – he never used one, preferring when lost to summon a passer-by and shout at him till he surrendered the information – Pappu decided to take the recommendation in good faith. So we turned off.

There are three things about short cuts that are worth bearing in mind. First, don't attempt them without a good map in front of you. Second, never take suggestions about short cuts from a man you hardly know. Third, and this I would emphasise most forcefully, never take shortcuts in India, particularly if you are in an Ambassador. I have learnt these things the hard way.

I had an inkling that something might be awry when the road disappeared. It had transmogrified into a strip of earth, down which Pappu was happily ploughing his lonely furrow. 'No problem,' he assured me, and indeed we did rediscover tarmac at a sort of village interchange. Pappu rolled down the window, yelled something at a passing straw carrier – presumably as to which was the road to Desuri – and pressed on.

Now I had with me the Lonely Planet Travel Atlas for India. It contained 100 pages of maps, 50 pages of indexes, and was as comprehensive as they come. I decided to involve myself in the proceedings. I asked, with increasing terseness, the name of each village we passed through – the names were in Hindi, which I couldn't read – and noted that none of these were large enough to merit an entry on any of my charts. However, from what scraps of information I could gather, I deduced that, if we were going to Ranakpur, we didn't want to go to Desuri anyway, and that we seemed to be travelling down a road marked by an ultra-fine blue line.

This was not promising. The two-lane Delhi-Mumbai highway merited three well-spaced red lines, so by the time the cartographers got down to using thin blue, it was out a desire to denote that only those who were barking mad, or enjoyed a lifetime of careless rambling among lost villages, should go anywhere near. Besides all this, the shaking up that occurs when an Ambassador is required to negotiate ploughed fields was not doing my insides any good. In a word, I was not happy.

After an hour, Pappu had interrogated everyone he had passed at least once, well, everyone that is who came into the category of acceptable people for Pappu to cross-question. Speaking personally, my instinct is to seek directions from middle-aged, well-dressed ladies. I have always found them the epitome of reliability. Pappu's preferred group included people who liked to sleep half-naked by the roadside, or hang around street corners looking dangerous. I wondered several times why he passed over just about everyone who might have been to school – and then it dawned on me. Caste. Pappu probably couldn't (or wouldn't) approach higher castes. A cat could not look at a king. That was my guess.

When, by some miracle, we made it to Desuri, I decided to give Ranakpur a miss and take the road that joined the national highway to Udaipur (our ultimate destination). The highway would be boring and flat, but boring and flat was what I needed just then. To reach it, however, meant that we first had to negotiate a road with enough bends to make a corkscrew preen: but at least it was a road, and at least we knew where we were going. Not only that, the views were delightful – one moment, jungley, with monkeys scampering across the road, and the next the kind of country where Don Quixote might once have tilted at windmills. We crossed bridges over deep gorges where the trees from the valley below grew so tall that their tops were at road level[AJ], and we climbed up into the bare rock hills.

We stopped for a leg stretch before hitting the highway. I needed one. My back was stiff and my stomach rebellious. I climbed up a steep slope of dried earth and continued along a gentler incline to where a dry-stone wall was meandering without any obvious purpose. I felt it was a kindred spirit. A goat was being tended by a goatherd wearing what looked like, and probably was, a plastic raincoat. This was surprising given that the temperature was hot enough to cook a one-minute omelette, but it may be that the herdsman had listened to the same weather forecast as Koshu and was expecting a cold snap imminently. Either that, or he just liked plastic.

From my wall, I could see across the valley, listen to the leaves rustling like dried paper, watch as four bullocks walked in single file to who knows where, and spot, a few fields away, an Indian, with his turban as pillow, stretched out in the sun. It was a beautiful and tranquil sight and somewhere deep down, and a distance away from my perturbating stomach, I felt a stab of gratitude to Pappu, whose cartographic misadventures had inadvertently brought me to this spot.

We were speeding down towards Udaipur, when, reading Lonely Planet, I noticed that the site of the famous battle of Haldighati, where Maharana[AK] Pratap had resisted the Mughal army, was what looked like five minutes diversion from the main road. Actually, it turned out to be 15km of hairpins and,

---

AJ   I appreciate that any self-respecting travel writer should know his trees: species, classification, etc etc. All that, regrettably, has passed me by, alas.

AK   Maharana means 'great warrior'. It's one up on Maharaja, 'great ruler'.

when we finally arrived, the only thing to be seen was a small museum and a touching memorial to Pratap's gallant horse, Chetak. It read like this: *"Here fell dead on June 21ˢᵗ 1576, Chetak, the daring and devoted horse of Maharana Pratap. In spite of being badly wounded, Chetak saved his master in his critical hour by carrying him from Rakta-Talai to the other end of Haldi-Ghati, jumping across the nearby stream. To cherish the loyalty and sacrifice of Chetak, this memorial was raised."*

Pappu knew the story of Pratap and Chetak. It was obviously taught in Rajasthan schools and, unless Pappu was in the habit of sneaking across the state line in search of schooling (which I couldn't imagine somehow), in Haryana also. It may well have been taught across the length and breadth of India. Maharana Pratap was, after all, one of the great Hindu heroes of medieval India.[70]

Pratap lived at a time when most of the princes of Rajasthan had succumbed to Akbar's charm offensive. The great houses of Amber (Jaipur), Mawar (Jodhpur), Bikaner and Jaisalmer had been wooed and won – seduced by invitations to provide daughters for the imperial harem, lured by the prospect of high office and encouraged by Akbar's genuine tolerance of Hindus. Rajput armies had become the backbone of the Mughal Empire[AL]. Man Singh of Amber, now related by marriage to the Emperor, was Akbar's most trusted general. Maharana Pratap of Mewar (Udaipur), with his tribal allies the Bhils, stood alone.

[AL] If you're a foreign occupier, you have to get the local big-wigs on your side. The Mughals (Clump Three) understood this, as did the British who came later, (Clump Four). No cooperation, no Empire. When Aurangzeb, the last of the great Mughals, deviated from the script (by religious intolerance, anti-Hindu taxes etc), the Mughal Empire's days were numbered.

At Haldighati, Pratap held the high ground, Man Singh the plain below. On the morning of the 21st, in the scorching heat, Pratap saddled his faithful charger and attacked. His surge would have broken through had not Man Singh held the Mughal lines. The two Rajputs found themselves face to face. Pratap hurled his spear, without effect, while Chetak placed his forelegs on Man Singh's elephant. This was brave, given the relative size of the two animals. It was also foolish. The General's pachyderm carried a sword in its trunk[AM].

Pictures painted of the battle show blood spurting from the horse's leg like wine out of a broken bottle. Nonetheless, fatally severed though he was, Chetak bore his master to safety. From then on, Pratap donned his Che Guevara bandanna and got his teeth into the job in hand. He stayed in the hills, cut supply lines and harried the Mughals to such effect that, by the time he died in January 1597, he was once again master of Mewar.[71] But, more than that, he had put a match to the fire of insurrection, and neither Akbar then, nor Aurangzeb overseeing the last throes of the Mughal Empire a hundred years later, was able to put it out.

We left Haldighati on the road we had come in on, driving cross-country to Udaipur, and after another 50 kilometres of hairpins, potholes and the temple-throbbing drone of the Ambassador, I had had enough. When we ground to a halt outside the hotel, I fell out and kissed the ground, just more pleased than I could say to be back on a surface that didn't move. 'You good feeling sir?' enquired Pappu, who seemed as

---

[AM] It sounds fanciful, but it's true, apparently – though don't ask me how you train an elephant to fence.

fresh as when he'd started. Pappu was in the right profession. Anyone who could go through a day we'd had, and still be smiling, would be wasted doing anything else.

The hotel was exactly what was required. An ersatz, middle of the range American-style, bare necessities room, with a TV and clean sheets. Ideal for the vegetative state I now intended to adopt. Beneath the windows was a lake, covered in a green slime but, even so, capable of supporting life. So I deduced from the intermittent bubbles rising to the surface – unless Pappu had slipped on leaving and was saying goodbye. By the shore of the lake was rich pasture – paper bags, cardboard boxes, bottles, polythene wrappers, styro-foam – and I found it warming to think that soon a lowing herd of cattle would wind its way down to the water's edge for a late supper.

I woke up next morning to discover that my body had welded itself into the shape of a T-square, more or less matching the contours of its new habitat – the back seat of the Ambassador. I could see the way my body was thinking and took my hat off, metaphorically speaking, to its survival instinct. However, it didn't half make it difficult to shut the door of the lift, without ending up with a head compressed to the width of a slice of processed cheese. And, while we are on the subject, why are elevators only made for vertical people? The horizontally challenged need to use them too, you know.

I did two things that morning. I acquired the number of a local travel agent from the hotel and asked them to book me on a flight to Jaipur the following day. Pappu would have to drive there on his own. Yes, I know, wimpish or what, but I still wished to continue to enjoy the simple pleasures of life; like standing. I needed time to heal. Then I had a massage, at the end of which I was able to straighten to within 20 degees of vertical. I was ready to see the sights.

My first impressions were quite wrong. Udaipur is spotless, the cleanest city so far. Now I realise I am in danger of sounding like my mother, but doesn't it make a difference. It's amazing what a wash behind the ears and clean underpants each morning can achieve. While the city slumbers, its streets are swept (and there is a caste to do it), and rubbish taken to a dump 15 kilometres away. People use dustbins. Veneration of the paper bag underfoot as an indispensable food source has been replaced by the religion of cleanliness. Hats off to you, Udaipur. Heavens, I am turning into my mother.

There is the usual traffic chaos of course. 200,000 people live in Udaipur and most of them are on the roads at any given time. I don't mean that most of them are driving, but that they are, quite literally, on the road. Let me give you a not untypical example, in fact an example that might be repeated any day in any Indian city...

On our way to the City Palace, Pappu stopped at a major junction at which a policeman was casually directing traffic. At least, I think that is what he was doing. Indian policemen, unlike French gendarmes, are not forever blowing their whistles and manically waving their arms in the air. They do not overheat. A few laconic waves and, as the cavalcade in front of them advances, they watch the ensuing havoc with kharmic detachment. It is all very splendid really. A few yards ahead of us, among the queue of contraptions waiting for some indication that they should proceed, stood three young women dressed in bright cotton. They were chatting. As the assorted flotsam of cars, scooters, cyclists and an elephant carrying firewood and swishing its tail lazily from side to side, advanced, so did they. They walked in animated conversation as cars charged past them and scooters cut in ahead. The fact that death's bony fingers were tugging at the hems of their saris didn't seem to bother them in the slightest. They were road users, taking their rightful place along with everybody else.

I couldn't help noticing that the stalls in mineral-rich, tourist-rich Udaipur were at the early stage of evolving into shops. They were like those prehistoric fish with tiny little legs, which had no idea that someday soon they'd be running around on dry land and eating Diplodocus. One of the kiosks had sprouted glass fronts and window displays, and I just wanted to tell Pappu to pull over while I burst through the door, hugged the owner around the waist, and informed him that one day he would become a huge department store, and be taken over by an Egyptian.

I did get as far as asking Pappu to stop, and I did go in, but as to the precise content of the next fifty years, my lips remained sealed. Best to let such matters unfold in their own good time. I bought a travel bag instead. It had copious quantities of zips and a compartment at the bottom that could be unzipped to give another four inches of space. All this for 120 rupees (under £2). Not bad, I thought. Not quite as good value as my knife, but not bad.

I had a good old snoop round the City Palace, and a splendid jumble of ornate state rooms, courtyards, terraces and narrow, windy staircases it was too. Some of the rooms were devoted to the life and times of my old friend, Pratap. This wasn't surprising. He was to Udaipur what Robin Hood was to Nottingham. There was the Great Man's armour in all its glory, standing upright as if still occupied. It was a grand sight, though I'd like to know what temperature his chain-mail and helmet reached on that midsummer day at Haldighati. Sizzling, I'd say. Anybody brushing up against the metal-coated Pratap was probably scorched to death. Still, should he have fancied a bite of lunch during his retreat from the battlefield, he'd have known where to find a frying pan.

Beneath the City Palace is Lake Pichola, which of all the sites of Udaipur is the one to see. It is man-made and enormous, built by Pratap's father, the founder of Udaipur, the much-reviled Maharana Udai Singh II (1540-1572). History has been unkind to Udai because he let his former capital, Chittor, be destroyed with all hands on deck, women and children included, while he swanned off to a safe hide-out in the hills. This wasn't considered proper behaviour for a Rajput but, be that as it may, he sure knew about lake construction. I wandered down to a landing quay, looked out and thought to myself, 'I'm in Venice.' A second later, a party of French tourists deposited themselves alongside and a woman declared, 'c'est comme Venise, alors.' It was official. The Venice of the East. What better thing to do, therefore, than to take a boat on the lagoon.

So I sat down and waited for one to arrive, whiling the time away by soaking up some rays, and musing on the story of the much-reviled Udai and his nurse. It's a moral tale, with a wee sting in it. Udai was six years old when an attempt was made on his life. No need to go into the whys and wherefores: just imagine the assassin striding purposefully towards the young prince's bedroom, knife in hand. The faithful and quick-witted nurse, guessing what was afoot, spirited the boy away in a fruit basket, but then, having done so, realised that she still had one small difficulty to overcome. How was she going to explain the absence of her charge? With the heaviest of heavy hearts (or so I presume), she put her own son in the royal crib. When the hit man appeared and inquired after his target, she 'pointed to the cradle, and beheld the murderous steel buried in the heart of her babe.' She sacrificed her son out of loyalty, and Udai, the boy she had saved, grew up to abandon Chittor and its 40,000 inhabitants to their deaths. 'Well had it been for Mewar', continued the chronicler[72], 'had the poniard fulfilled its intention, and had the annals never recorded the name of Udai Singh in the catalogue of her princes.'[AN]

The boat-trip was sheer delight. True, the delightfulness didn't fully kick in until we had moved out of the oily smear left behind by outboard engines – solar powered boats, next time fellas, please – but once we had, the water was delightful: clear as a bell that was only slightly cracked, and pebble-dashed by drops of sunlight. People still fished in it, I was told, and crocodiles, shy creatures though they are, bask.

We circled around the Lake Palace hotel, once the summer retreat of the maharanas, and put in at the sixteenth century Jag Mandir. If you had to pick one place to make you appreciate how conspicuously opulent this country had been, and why the world's traders and profiteers came to India to stuff their pockets, this little hideaway palace would be it. Eight stone elephants guarded its entrance. Rubies, onyx, jasper, cornelian and jade had once decorated the massive stone slabs of

AN Indeed. You can never tell how things will work out. Or, as Rabbie Burns, the great Scots poet, would have put it, '*The best laid schemes o' Mice an' Men Gang aft agley / An' lea'e us nought but grief an' pain.*

the walls. It had courtyards, pavilions, landscaped gardens and pools. And for what? Somewhere to put up a few deckchairs and maybe read a book or two away from the hurly-burly. It was magnificently OTT, the most sumptuous bathing hut in the world, splendid enough even for Prince Khurram, the future Shah Jehan, to spend a few months here while trying to keep out of reach of his Dad, Jahangir[AO].

I didn't blame him. I could have stayed on too, except that I didn't have my trunks with me and the boat was ready to return. We made our way back across the lagoon and towards the City Palace. As we approached, its walls seemed the colour of peachy flesh, mottled by grey streaks of age and interrupted by the arched eyebrows of a hundred windows. Udaipur, let me tell you, is something else.

That evening, encouraged by the wonders of Udaipur and perhaps by the mere fact of my own continuing existence, I decided that the time had come to risk what the average Brit would regard as a proper curry. I mean something that is seriously hot. Most of the meals I'd had so far had barely induced a bead of perspiration. This was fine by me but, for the average Brit, would be like going to a horror movie and not ending up underneath your seat. Cooks in these parts don't seem to have understood that the British have one of the most spice-hardened palates in the world, largely due to the fact that they have a curry house on every street corner. I have a friend

AO   The later Mughal Emperors didn't have the same nurturing instincts towards their sons that fathers of today generally exhibit. Jahangir, the 4th of the Great Mughals spent 3 years and several thousand miles of army footwear trying to capture his recalcitrant son, Prince Khurram. Fortunately he failed or Prince Khurram wouldn't have become Shah Jehan, the fifth of the Great Mughals, and we wouldn't have the Taj Mahal. (Clump 3, in case you've forgotten).

who has eaten Indian four times a week for as long as I have
known him. His preferred restaurant has awarded him his own
special table, and they positively squeak with pleasure every
time his measured tread is heard approaching their establishment. Chicken Vindaloo, extra spicy, has long since overtaken
roast beef as Britain's favourite dish. The Brits like it hot, as in
sweating all over, jackets off, sleeves rolled up, Kingfishers all
round waiter, hot. And for the first time in India, this is what
I got. Not chicken vindaloo, of course, but a hot veg curry
which knocked me backwards so fast, I found myself sitting at
the next table. Best meal so far it was, and after having downed
twice my usual dosage, I sat back, patted my stomach and
emitted a contented belch.

Pappu set off next morning for Jaipur, while I wandered
around the old city until check-out time, an awkward four
hours before I had to leave for the airport. I decided to treat
myself to lunch at the Lake Palace Hotel. A long, vastly over-
indulgent, session would be just the thing to while away an
hour or two, or perhaps three if I lingered inexcusably over
coffee. Except that, en route, my stomach started to give off
warning signals that could not be ignored – payback for the
night before, no doubt – and I had to settle for minestrone
and a cup of tea, price 130 rupees (under £2). For this I had
a table that looked out over the exquisite Lake Pichola, to the
ghats and the back of the City palace. I was in India's answer
to the Gritti Palace in Venice, overlooking the grand lagoon,
only a hundred times cheaper.

Food, I find, tastes infinitely better when it's a bargain. I
spun my soup out for an hour, which was as long as decency
would allow, and then wandered around the hotel. It was one

of those old rambling places where no one notices you – no head porter with eyes that drill into the back of your head as you act casually, pretending to be a resident who knows exactly where the lavatories are. I found a quiet alcove, miles from the main entrance, with an open window over the water and a view to the Jag Mandir. I pulled up a chair, faced the sun, shut my eyes and, while a couple of sparrows frolicked on top of a gas lamp and crapped onto an antique sofa, settled down for an extremely well-deserved post-prandial nap.

Then I caught the boat back, jumped in a taxi, swung past Chetak Circle and departed the fair city from Pratap airport, where else.

13. JAIPUR

... The gift of tongues

The flight to Jaipur was on time, and pleasantly uneventful. I arrived fresh, and spent the evening wandering around the hotel, getting used to the fact that I was in a new city and still able to walk.

Next morning, Pappu was waiting outside the hotel to drive me to a travel agency, where I hoped to find a guide. After pushing open the door, I looked around at the assembled company and gave a first public airing to a few selections from my Hindi phrasebook which I'd been working on in secret. 'Good morning. How are you?' I declared in the native tongue, beaming proudly at the five or six occupants of the room.

Silence. They stared at me as if I was a performing dog. 'My God, a Brit trying to speak Hindi. Is the earth flat? Will it rain today?' One of them finally babbled a response. I took this to mean, 'I'm fine, how are you?' though, for all I knew, it might have meant 'the kettle's on, would you like a cuppa?' I replied 'very good,' because those were the only words left in my locker that hadn't already been used. After that we spoke English, which was just as well – but I felt I'd made a breakthrough. I'd allowed my new vocabulary to test its wings in a short solo flight. I'd felt like a bit of a prat in the process, of course, but I knew you had to force yourself through the prat stage if you were ever going to be able to sit down with the locals and pass the time of day.

The guide chosen for me, Umesh Sharma, turned out not only to know his way around Jaipur, but also to have missed his vocation. He should have been a language teacher. We started and, as it turned out, finished with the word for 'thank you'. Could I get my tongue round it? I could not. I felt like the dumb blonde in the film studio, who has a line like 'Help, Help, I'm being pursued by an alien' and, after 67 takes, the Director, mindful of his desire for sexual favours but losing his rag nonetheless, cries despairingly, 'For Chrissake, baby, jes say 'help.' I write the word down now. It is 'Dhanyavad'. 'Thank You.' Simple enough you would have thought. We worked on it all day. Occasionally, I got it right. Mostly I mangled it.

We found time during the day to tuck away a few other phrases that I felt would amply reward the considerable effort of stapling them into my frontal lobe. If you are going to learn vocabulary in a language where almost nothing is guessable by reference to anything else you've ever heard, selection is vital. We concentrated on *I don't want tea, let's go, how much is that, please, mineral water, quickly, slowly, fat* – good word fat, *mhota*, (pronounced motor, by me anyway) – and *where is the toilet, its urgent*? With these under my belt, I was confident I could travel far.

I liked Umesh. He interpreted his role less as guide than companion and, pretty soon, we were wandering around the sights deep in conversation, like a couple of old pals out on their regular Saturday round of golf. Occasionally we ground to a halt to inspect something noteworthy, or just because Umesh felt it was time for a vocab test, but quite where we were, or what treasures slipped by unnoticed, I really couldn't tell you.

It was one of those mornings when the wonders of the world were wasted on me. I know we passed the portrait of Maharaja Ram Singh II, because Umesh asked me who he reminded me of. I was about to say 'John Lennon,' but Umesh couldn't contain himself. He was in there with the answer before I could form words. 'It's John Lennon,' he burst out, and watched me to see recognition dawn. 'So it is,' said I, feigning surprise. 'Look, he even has the same specs.' Which was true. He did.

Ram Singh's other claim to fame, by the way, was that, in 1876, he painted the entire city pink. This was his somewhat eccentric Maharajal way of welcoming the Prince of Wales who had come over to obliterate a few tigers. I can tell you that we also had a good long look at the 5.5 kilo sword once swung by the victor of Haldighati, Man Singh. As far as I was concerned, Man Singh was a bit of a baddie – a Hindu propping up an alien Muslim regime, I ask you – but I had to admit that was one hell of a sword. It was the greatest, great big bertha of the day. It weighed 2/3 of a full set of clubs and, if I'd been carrying that around from dawn til dusk, I'd have demanded a caddie, thank you very much, or to put this in the appropriate tongue, *bahut bahut dhanyavad*.

The only other part of the palace that stayed with me was a splendid marble elephant, on whose broad back sat a sculpted mahout with fat mutton chop whiskers and an expression that said, 'this elephant no go, but me no worry.' Then we crossed a road and came to the stone observatory, the Jantar-Mantar, built by Maharaja Jai Singh II in 1728.

India's answer to the Greenwich Observatory looked like a playground for the big friendly giant, a place of frolic reserved for those with hyper-active pituitary glands. However, on closer inspection, climbing frames the size of outhouses turned out to be massive instruments for measuring all those things that astronomers and astrologers like to know about – the altitude of heavenly bodies, the obliquity of the ecliptic (whatever that may be), the position of the stars, and just about everything else, even down to humble old time. When I say 'down to', I don't, in this case, mean to be taken literally. There was nothing lowly about the Jantar Mantar's chronometer. It stood over 100 feet high and was accurate to within two seconds. Umesh suggested I claw my way up a vertical staircase to the top, and that I wasn't to worry about him, he'd be fine where he was. So I did, and while pausing to recover from a minor seizure 50 feet in the air, noticed his miniscule figure below enjoying a quiet cigarette. But, having made it to the top, I can tell you this: if it's views you're after, this elephantine giraffe of a time-piece beats the average wristwatch into a cocked hat.

The observatory, and Jaipur itself, were founded by the same extraordinary scientist cum soldier, Jai Singh II (1699-1743). Those were interesting times for a man of invention. The Mughal empire was collapsing. The grizzled old emperor Aurangzeb had finally died in 1707, aged 90, leaving behind more sons and grandsons than you could shake a stick at, most of them either frivolous, imbecilic, drunk or incompetent.

Independence movements were springing up like bubbles in a jacuzzi. War and intrigue were perpetual and a new power, the Marathas, was emerging as the dominant force in the area.

Did this disturb Maharaja Jai? Not a bit. He found time to expand his borders, build five observatories in India, design the world's largest wheeled cannon (which was so big it could only be manoeuvred by elephants)[73], and move his capital from Amber to Jaipur. Even the new city was scientific. It was built to a plan and used a grid system. 'Many years afterward' wrote Kipling, 'the good people of America built their towns after this pattern, but knowing nothing of Jai Singh, they took all the credit to themselves.'[74]

By the time we had toured the Observatory, Umesh and I had pretty much put the world to rights. We sat on a step besides an instrument that might have been an early cement mixer, but probably wasn't, and turned our attention to philosophy. Humans, according to Umesh, had to have – and in this order – health, money, love ('relation between husband and wife not like T-shirt: after two month, three month, you throw it out'), children and good friends. That seemed fair enough, although it did occur to me that most Jaipurians, from what I had seen, seemed a bit short of the second and abundantly blessed with the fourth. Money could be subdivided, he went on, into dan, bhog and nash. I think that's what he said, but I had such a blinding picture of Crosby, Stills and Nash and what the hell was that song, that I may have that bit garbled. Anyway, dan was donation or giving. It was important to give. Bhog was enjoyment. 'Some people don't spend without heart attack,' he said. Nash was ruin. If you don't spend, your kids have it and it is gone within two years, 'easy coming, easy going.' In other words, don't hang on too tight or you'll either have a coronary or wreck your kids future. I'd go along with that.

Umesh wound up with a brief discourse on the nature of man, and more particularly his five weaknesses: sex, aggression, pride, possessiveness and greed. 'Most dangerous part of humans are the boneless bits,' he declared. Foolishly, I asked him what he meant. 'The boneless bits', he said; 'the tongue' (which he stuck out to illustrate), 'and the penis' (which thankfully he did not).

It was now midday. We found Pappu, who had been rubbing down the Ambassador in our absence, and asked him to take us the few miles to Amber, the former capital. When we arrived at a parking area below the outcrop of the Aravali hills on which the fort was perched, Umesh went off to organise an elephant. That, he said, was the only way to go up.[AP] Walking was not to be contemplated.

As soon as he was out of earshot, Pappu brought up the subject of our forthcoming diversion. This was a possibility that had been hatching quietly for a few days and which, step by imperceptible step, had now reached the status of a definite plan. On the way back to Delhi we were going to stop off at Pappu's village. He'd once told me that he hadn't seen his wife and kids for four months. They were in Haryana, while he, as far as I could gather, lived in his employer's garage with the car. A pit-stop on compassionate grounds seemed to be in order and, as Pappu put it, 'my owse off road turning.' I took this

---

[AP] I am now aware, though I wasn't then, that elephants are trained by using billhooks and electric prods. Hence, riding an elephant is not encouraged, but I have to say that elephants are, and always have been, such a feature of Indian life, that it's hard to imagine India without them.

to mean, on scanty evidence admittedly, that it wouldn't be much out of our way.

While we were waiting for Umesh to return bearing elephants, Pappu reported that he'd written home to say we were coming, and that his wife would be 'very appy.' Well, quite happy anyway. The last thing Mrs Pappu would want, thought I, or Pappu himself come to that, would be a complete stranger interrupting prison leave. I resolved to say hello, retire tactfully and leave the loving couple to it. I was just musing on how this might be achieved, and where I might put myself for a few hours, when Umesh reappeared. The elephant, he announced, was waiting.

Umesh and I climbed onto a stone mounting block and scrambled aboard. Since this particular beast of burden was about as wide as four horses strapped together, visitors to its top deck were seated on a howdah, a double-sided communal chair running along both flanks. It was grand. I felt like a four-year-old on a donkey ride, except scaled up proportionately. The driver said the magic words, or kicked it, and off we went, the elephant beneath us turning out to have a stride that was, to say the least, curious in such a mighty animal. It minced. It waggled forward as if in a tight skirt. It didn't seem right at all but, being in a benevolent frame of mind, I gave it the benefit of the doubt. I persuaded myself that were it waist high in jungle grasslands, rather than hauling yours truly up a steep, winding cobbled path, it would be bounding forward like the athlete it might have been had its circumstances but been different.

I reached for my bunch of bananas and offered one to Umesh. We munched happily, looking down on an artificial lake that was not a patch on Lake Pichola. Above us was the golden fort, which we were approaching, through a succession of gates, slowly. We made our way through 'narrow smooth-walled passages with recesses where a man might wait for his enemy unseen,'[75] to a high wall on the battlements. From there you could look across to the hills and the old fortifications that ran along the skyline like the Great Wall of China, or down to what was left of the town of Amber. Monkeys were playing on the battlements and I did my best to encourage them to come down. I waved a half-eaten banana at them, I made little kissing noises, and I called to them in a manly, fancy a banana old fella kind of way, but they just sat there and watched me and, every now and again, raised a supercilious eyebrow.

It suddenly dawned on me, as I was idly perusing the houses in the valley below, why it was that Indian cities looked like bomb sites. It was because the houses don't appear to have roofs. They have them, I could see that, flat ones with a surrounding collar of brick, but at ground level they don't look as if they do. Not nicely tiled sloping roofs that you find in Europe, anyway. I'd assumed, in my total ignorance, that either the top half of buildings had fallen off, or that the builders ran out of material during the construction phase, and just gave up. But as I sat there looking down, I suddenly realised, not for the first time, what a narrow-minded idiot I had been. The reason why the roofs were flat was staringly obvious. You could hang washing out on them (Indian houses don't have gardens), or you could sleep up there under the stars and away from the heat down below. Furthermore, since it only rained in these parts once every blue moon, what was the point of having a roof that encouraged water to run off? None whatsoever. I felt chastened,

169

and vowed to be less narrowly, provincially European in future.

Umesh took me round the Amber Palace and into the Sheesh Mahal, a hall of mirrors. The way to see it was to shut the doors, turn the lights off and light a candle. Then the stars come out and twinkle. There was a man in attendance whose job this was and, being of a theatrical bent, he elaborated by blowing gently on the flame, causing it to flicker and the night sky to move. It was a good show.

After that we went back to Jaipur. The tour was over. Umesh, taking his leave, said, 'give my sweet greetings to your wife.' I shook hands with him and wished him well, but I wanted to give him back a few of the Hindi words he had spent the day drumming into my head. I couldn't remember a thing. My mind had gone blank. Everything had fled. Finally, I heard myself reaching for the word for 'thank you'. 'Tanyavar,' I said. I could see the pain in his eyes. He walked away, shoulders slumped, looking older somehow than he had done that morning. I can't tell you how bad I felt.

14. BACK TO DELHI

… The way by Pappu's

Somewhere during the last few days I'd made the decision to break my trip and return to Scotland for Christmas. It was beginning to turn cold, and I was starting to hallucinate about hot baths and cars with suspension that made purring rather than drilling noises. I thought I'd remind the kids what their father looked like and return late in January, recharged. It wasn't only Pappu who was on his way home and, when we reconvened next day, we both had that jaunty, anticipatory spring in our step that an approaching new chapter is inclined to produce. Deepak had booked a room for me on the way back to Delhi. The hotel sounded remote, restful and just the place to gather my resources before the final leg.

We set off at midday and I leavened my opening remarks to Pappu with a little of my newly acquired Hindi. 'How are you', I said, followed a touch whimsically by 'I don't want tea, thank you' and 'let's go,' *chelo* (another good word). Pappu took this in his stride, and took it upon himself to correct my pronunciation of 'how are you'. Which was kind of him, except that his phrasing bore no discernible similarity to the words I'd heard from Umesh. It didn't sound the same thing at all, and I rather suspected I was being indoctrinated in the dialect of Pappu's village, which would be comprehensible to no more than 20 people and a camel. So I hummed to myself and did all I could, short of putting my fingers in my ears, not to listen. Bad money, I knew, drives out good.

Once we were beyond Jaipur's answer to Piccadilly Circus at rush hour (with cattle), the traffic died away and, on a straight, well-made road, Pappu motored along at 65. I thought of saying something but, hey, what the heck, live dangerously. A few hours later, we left the beaten track and made our way cautiously toward the hotel. Blocking our path was a village with narrow shell-bunkered lanes winding between crumbling houses. I can't imagine what the attraction of this place was, but it seemed to have sucked in every local contraption capable of motion for miles around, plus a further torrent of humanity that looked on from doorways or weaved between hand-drawn carts and other roadway flotsam.

There is quite simply a limit to how much traffic can travel down a single lane with an equal volume coming in the opposite direction. That limit had been exceeded. We stopped. We moved a few yards. We stopped again. We narrowly avoided compressing a scooter between the Ambassador's bumper and the ox-cart in front. We inched forward. An eternity later, space opened up in front of us. I assumed it was a mirage but, no, the black hole had deigned to eject us out of its farther side. Shortly afterwards, we turned down a deserted mud track, bounced along craters for a few hundred yards and swung into the entrance of a large faded edifice that was the hotel.

An English couple watched us get out of the car, astonished that anyone but themselves had managed to hack their way through. Similar thoughts were occurring to me. The manager came down to say hello and we chatted. It turned out that the three of us were the only people staying, not counting dozens of staff, and Pappu of course, who in some mysterious way (that I could never quite get to the bottom of) would find lodging elsewhere. 'Get much passing traffic?' I asked, looking out to the main gate where the only thing visible was a man straining to push his hand cart out of a dry bunker, into which the back wheel had become lodged. 'Well,' he said in perfect English, 'we were expecting a coach-load of seventeen guests, but they haven't arrived yet.' And might not, was my guess.

Outside the hotel were what looked like gaslights on pillars, and beyond that a very English-looking park with trees planted at elegant intervals along an expanse of gentle undulations – except that the grass was dried yellow and the only thing hunting over it were packs of unsavoury looking dogs. I crept up to the outer edge and pondered whether to venture further. Ten seconds later a dozen adolescent boys rushed up to me out of nowhere and began trying out their English. This was not a great deal better than my Hindi. 'They think they're going to practice on me, do they?' thought I. 'Huh, I'm going to practise on them.'

'*Apke se he,*' (how are you?), I said, in a Hindi that was somewhere between the recommendations of my two tutors. A few more pleasantries followed, and we then had a charming conversation that was half-mime, half-Hinglish. When the hubbub of happy chatter had died down, I offered them some pens. They wouldn't take them. They declined with a dignity that made me feel we had bonded. I wasn't just another gringo. I spoke the lingo. They even offered me some monkey nuts. I ate them, said thank you, patted my stomach and added, somewhat gratuitously, 'me *mhota.*' This creased them up. In fact, they continued to fall about for a second or two longer than was, strictly speaking, polite. I didn't mind. I had spoken to the locals in their own tongue. I sniffed progress.

I returned to the hotel and joined my fellow residents in the dining room. The hotel was like an old rambly Welsh farmhouse that had been taken over by a maharaja, extended and then abandoned. The dining room had a glass cabinet for the crockery, chintz curtains, a stone floor and wooden tables. I half expected to find an Aga in the corner, except that there were pictures of Indian Princes on the walls and a bust of a large Indian gentleman on a table. A forbear presumably. From his turban protruded what can only be described as a lavatory brush, although it may have had some further symbolic significance of which I was unaware.

The three of us ate huddled around a small table, thrown together like characters from a Somerset Maugham novel, where the background noise is the thwack of a fly-swat and the shrieks of unknown creatures from the jungle outside. We were the survivors. Whatever tantalising hints might be dropped as to the possibility of other guests, we knew we were alone.

After dinner, I went back to my room. The wood was painted in a light blue of the kind much favoured by government institutions, and the stone walls were covered in a thin layer of complementary custard yellow. The stone floor led into a vast stone bathroom with a stone bath, the like of which I had never seen before. I examined it carefully. It was definitely… stone. It had even cracked as stone cracks. Above it was suspended a shower, out of which I knew with absolute certainty would emerge water that was stone cold. I couldn't face it. My sneezing, begun over supper, was getting worse, and my nose was beginning to drip.

I dug deep into my travel bag to retrieve a packet of tissues that my wife had forced me to pack (and how right she was), found an old single bar electric fire and switched it on. I surveyed my surroundings again. It could have been lovely if there had been a jolly farmer's wife, a Mrs Mhota, to fuss around, plump up the pillows, and bring me a cup of cocoa before I went to bed. But there wasn't. So I huddled over the electric fire and felt miserable, while the pack of dogs in the park howled.

I awoke next morning feeling better. I braced myself for the shower, turned the knob and out came hot water. Well I never. Actually it was warm, but it felt hot to me, a good deal hotter than the arctic stream I had been expecting. I dressed, offered the manager a cheerful *apke se he*, and we conversed in Hindi and English while he brought me my first shot of banana, washed down with orange juice and tea. I learnt a couple more words and, when the time came, was sorry to leave.

Pappu, however, was itching to be off. I could tell this by the way he was standing by the open door of the Ambassador while, quite unconsciously, inclining his head towards the luxuries within, like a discreet doorman outside a house of pleasure. I allowed myself to be ushered in, and let him whisk me away to wherever chez-Pappu happened to be. It was not on a major highway anyway. That much was clear from the fact that, before long, we were bumping down a half-made track. I groaned, but quietly, not wishing to spoil Pappu's big day. Then we pulled off the track by a small dry-stone building and stopped. He switched off the engine and told me this was his sister's *owse*.

I didn't remember a visit to his sister actually being discussed but, being pleased that forward motion had ceased, didn't say a thing. She made him breakfast while I sat on a wooden chair in the sun. He hadn't seen his sister for a year, he told me afterwards. Sometime later, after the proprieties had been attended to, or perhaps after they had kissed and cried over lost times – I don't know, I didn't watch – we started out again, and continued on for some indeterminate distance until we came to a path of dried earth leading to a small village of single storey farm houses with dry-stone slate walls and slate roofs.

Gathered there were two camels, sundry buffalo and a small army of Pappu's brothers, sisters-in-law, nephews, nieces, wife and children. They had, delightfully, come out to say hello. He introduced his wife, who hid completely behind her top-to-toe sari, his three brothers, his five-year-old daughter, Rinki, who wasn't shy in the least, and his three-year-old son, Tinku, who was.

I had said to Pappu several times that all I required was somewhere to sit, while he went off to be with his wife. Fortunately, he had taken me at my word. He led me to a slate outhouse, with a floor that I recognised as being of the dung / earth variety (and absolutely no smell by the way). Inside were four beds which, together, took up almost all the available space. These were covered with something lumpy on which was laid a cover. It was spotlessly clean. Pappu brought me my usual lunch of bananas and bottled water, and invited me to rest. *Dhanyavad*, I said, finally mastering this most important of words, and off he went.

It doesn't take long in a small village for word to get around, particularly when something as exotic as an alien landing has taken place. Pretty soon, and I mean hot on the heels of the exiting Pappu, it was standing room only around the spaceman's place of repose. All Pappu's relatives under the age of 15, plus their friends, had come for the floorshow. I sat on the bed, unzipped a banana, ate it, laid the peel down and smiled at the audience. I thought I should demonstrate a capacity for speech, so picked a friendly face in the front row and asked in my best Hindi how he was. This received the 'talking dog' reaction, followed by giggles all round. '*Thik hai*?' I persisted. More giggles.

Vaguely wondering how I was going to make it through the next few hours, I decided a nap was in order. The extra-terrestrial took off his shoes, yawned, stretched out and shut his eyes. I was aware of the children edging closer for a more detailed analysis of the strange creature that had washed up in their village, but I kept my eyes resolutely closed and, in a matter of moments, nodded off. Briefly it has to be said, but somnolence nonetheless.

What woke me was one of the children tickling the sole of my foot. I opened my eyes, raised my head to look around, and saw nothing but a sea of faces waiting expectantly for my reaction. I must have jiggled an eyebrow because, the tension broken, they burst out into uncontrollable giggles. What can you do? I joined in. I thought I would go for a walk. *Chelo*, I said, and the kids said *chelo*, let's go, and, feeling like the pied piper, strolled out of the house, through the village and up the hill against which the houses were built.

We scrambled up rock and scree, and halfway, the kids showed me their temple. They indicated I was to take off my shoes and led me into a small room, containing nothing but two metallic cobras resting against bare walls. Then we sat around outside. Rinki had a two-by-one inch cylinder of black hair sticking bolt upright and off-centre on her head, a sort of stunted pigtail in the wrong place. I took out a pen, tore some paper out of my notebook and, as the kids clustered round, drew a picture of her head with its little vertical stub. A pigtail is about the height of my ambition as an artist, but Rinki liked it. Or she was being kind.

We walked to the top of the hill and looked down into the next valley. A recently ploughed field of red earth was beneath us, and beyond a steep ascent of bare rocks, that might have been the lower slopes of Ben Vorlich, except that the grasses clinging on to the rock face had been burnt a dry yellow in the sun. The field sloped downwards to a line of trees where a herd of goats were feeding and further down the valley was the same scene of fields and trees nestling between rocky hillsides repeated as far as the eye could see. It was delightful, as the Indian countryside so often is.

Pappu's brother joined us. He was wearing a cloth wrapped rakishly round his head, white trousers and a sort of cardigan. He didn't speak but took my sweater from me, and walked ahead as we continued along a path that curved away left on a wide circuit of the hill we had just climbed. One or two bushes were growing nearby and the kids went over and picked some tough-looking red berries. These they expected me to swallow. They swallowed a few themselves. Well, I've done kids' tea parties. I went into the tried and tested, 'I've been poisoned' routine. I put the cleanest berry of those on offer in my mouth, took a cautious chew, and gave them the 'hmn not bad' expression. Then, suddenly, my right hand grabs my throat, mouth hangs open, face goes rigid as if rigor mortis has set in, and eyes slowly cross. Pause. Check to see if I still had my audience. (I did.) Eyes bulge in one final spasm, and then stagger back. This was rapturously received judging from the shouts of more, more, that went up. (At least I assume this was what they were saying since grubby hands were thrust in front of me revealing further supplies of the nuggety indigestible.) I declined. My digestive system was on its last legs as it was. 'Too *mhota,*' I said, patting my stomach. '*Mhota, mhota*' came the bayed response from the crowd, which was obviously in full agreement with the sentiment.

We walked on. Rinki and another girl took my hand, and I felt among friends. 'Country?' one of the older boys, Yadav, asked. 'Scotland,' I replied, which produced no visible sign of recognition. 'Long way away' I said, pointing at the far horizon, probably in the direction of Australia. No reaction. 'You know, Scotland,' I repeated and, heaven knows what possessed me, with right arm held aloft, launched into a highland fling. This garnered much the same incredulous reaction as it does when it makes a public appearance in Scotland, except that, after their initial astonishment, the kids responded with an energetic version of the funky chicken, Haryana style. (This certainly doesn't happen in Fife.) Some pretty fancy footwork was to be seen. The hills were alive with the sound of dancing. The John Travolta award went to a young lad whose legs bent in three directions simultaneously. Comedy mayhem it was. They were great kids.

Yadav was the only one with anything resembling English. He had a vocabulary of quite a few nouns, but obviously hadn't yet reached chapter 5, Verbs. 'This buffalo,' he said, pointing at a buffalo. 'This goat.' 'This bicycle.' 'This pull.' He took me to see it. Pull? Pool perhaps. Swimming pool? Natural Pool? Both unlikely. It turned out to be a well which went down, not that I am any judge of these things, 100 feet. It had a pump and was used for irrigation. Some healthy looking cabbagey plants were growing nearby. The pull seemed to be operated by the village teacher unless he had gone up there for a quiet fag. 'India, very rich country', he said, 'very poor people.' He was right. It is enormously rich. It always has been. It has fertile lands, huge mineral wealth, and an intelligent and hard-working people. India generates plenty, but not much of its wealth trickles down.[AQ]

We carried on, our friendly clump uncoiling as the distance gradually took its toll of the younger members. We snaked past a slate quarry, and I nodded knowingly. Quarry, dry stone walls in the village, it figured. Nearby was a stone cutting machine. Of course. We wound round more fields and onto a road. This led eventually to the village and when, finally, we made it back, it was time to go.

Clan Pappu came out to say goodbye and Godspeed. Mrs P. glanced at me sideways-fashion from behind a piece of material attached to her sari and I think I detected a smile. Rinki clung

---

[AQ]   According to Oxfam, the top 10% of the population has 77% of total national wealth. Of the wealth generated in 2017, 73% went to the richest 1%.

to her mother's skirts. Everybody else had things to say. I dug into my case and distributed all the pens I had left to the children. I then thought I'd try to find them a book. So I dipped in again, and gave them the first one that came to hand, Tom Sharpe's, Porterhouse Blue. Should they ever read it, heaven knows what picture they will have of Britain, or what they'll make of that chapter where inflated condoms escape from the college chimney and come down in the quad. Plenty of new words though.

The only town of any size between us and Delhi was Rewari, a nondescript sort of a place that didn't even merit a mention in Lonely Planet. Looking out of the car window, I could see why. Yet even Rewari had one claim to fame. It was the birthplace of a diminutive Hindu hero, called Hemu, who started off hawking saltpetre on the streets over which I was now travelling and ended up as ruler of Delhi and Agra. Briefly. He was a brilliant general with a career record of 22 victories, no defeats, until his final decisive battle at Panipat in 1556 against Akbar[AR]. Hemu was in control of the battle, victory was almost his, until shot in the eye by an accidental arrow, while seated on the howdah of his famous elephant, Hawai.[76] After that it was 22 − 1, and curtains[AS]. Otherwise, who knows, there might have been Hindu dynasties in Delhi, rather than Muslim — but it didn't happen. His head was sent to Kabul and his trunk gibbeted on

AR Akbar, the third of the Great Mughals (Clump Three) was under pressure at the time, not only from Hemu but from other Afghan rivals to his throne. He needed the win.

AS Hemu was unlucky, you'd have to say, but accidental arrows in the eye can change the course of history. Remember King Harold? The Battle of Hastings? 1066?

181

one of the Delhi gates.[77] His supporters were then butchered and their severed faces collected together, 30 or 40 at a time, and mortared into pillars the shape of beehives. This was what they did by way of street art, back then.[78]

Four hundred years later things had improved. We saw no body parts. On the approach to Delhi, a truck came at us down the wrong lane of the dual carriageway and, out of sheer terror, I took an inadvertent swig of the home-bottled water Pappu had given me. On another day, both events might have proved fatal. A new Mercedes flashed past like a sleek liner pushing through a flotilla of rusting cargo boats, and I did wonder what the insurance on a car like that would be. Who would insure it? Lining the road were a mile or so of saplings, with signs saying, 'Green Delhi'. A few had managed to sprout some sorry-looking greenery on top, but most appeared to be dead – presumably overcome by exhaust gases. Then we arrived in Delhi. New Delhi to be precise, where the roads were wide and tree lined, and the large houses set back like the wealthiest of English suburbs. It wasn't a bit as I remembered it, or indeed much like India come to that – which perhaps wasn't surprising since it was built by the British in the 1920s as a monument to the Raj.

Pappu took me to Connaught Square. I needed some trousers. Pappu parked, let me out, and surveyed the scene. A well-dressed and not particularly pleasant-looking salesman was standing on the pavement. Out of the side of his mouth, Pappu whispered to me, 'that man, you no talking.' Good fellow Pappu. Ever vigilant. I did as instructed and, twenty minutes later, was back at the car with a shopping bag on my arm and only £6 lighter in the pocket.

We went up to the gates of President's House, which was approached by the red sands of Pall Mall and trees in the shape of camels. Ministry buildings on either side had roofs like hats of the kind that a bishop might wear to do the gardening. It was very imperial. But I wasn't really in the mood. I was thinking of the flight home. We were well into December. The sun was starting to lose its heat and seemed to be wrapped in a slight fog that may have been cloud, or the dust from a billion Indians, or just plain winter. Christmas was coming, the goose was getting fat and I was glad to be slipping out of my seat for the intermission. I would return for the second half in a relative moment.

Pappu said goodbye at the airport. I was going to miss him. Then he hugged me, which was a surprise, and I sort of hugged him back. And before long, I was on the plane and back in Scotland, where winter meant WINTER.

PART TWO

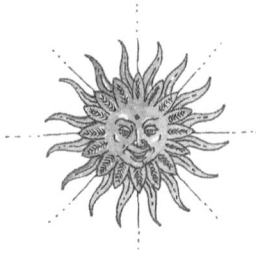

15. CALCUTTA / KOLKATA[AT]

… Where the steam bath comes free and the British Raj began

The earliest heavily discounted bucket-shop return flight I could find was on February 5th. At least that gave me ample time to fine-tune my wardrobe, make sure that all the small essentials were safely packed, and organise a farewell party to make everyone feel jealous. By the time February 5th came around, I was ready and itching to be off.

My family treated me to a late lunch in Edinburgh, prior to departure. It was one of those gale-lashing Scottish afternoons when the wind comes at you like a prop forward[AU] and takes chunks out of your ear lobes as it passes. One of those days, in

[AT] Since 2001, Calcutta has been known as Kolkata … which puts me in something of a quandary. When talking about its history, it would be odd not to call the city, Calcutta. When talking about recent times, it would be equally odd not to call it Kolkata. So, to reduce the degree of oddness, I'll use both names as circumstances suggest.

[AU] Prop forwards are those big, squat fellows who prop up the scrum. We're talking Rugby Union here. They are instantly recognizable by the fact that they have no visible neck.

fact, when you can think of nothing nicer than to have, in your inside pocket, a ticket to sunnier climes. After eating enough to see me through most of my first week away, they drove me to the airport and, after fond goodbyes, spiced by that extra edge which journeys into the unknown necessarily occasion, dropped me off at Departures. Car and contents pulled away. I waved. My loved ones waved back, and disappeared.

I checked my watch. It was 4.45, ample time for the 6.20. Slipping languidly into zombie mode (a state which makes the wearisome hours of travel pass more comfortably), I glanced up at the departure board. Somehow my flight wasn't there. I read through the list more carefully. Definitely not there. I fished out my ticket, a slight prickle of alarm making its presence felt, and went over to the KLM desk. There, a young attendant gave me to understand that 6.20 meant 6.20 in the morning, and I was 12 hours late. The flight had left while I was still in my bed. I pleaded with him to find another flight, pronto. None was available. I begged. I sunk to my knees and, grabbing his trousers in the manner of Meryl Streep in *Out of Africa*, sobbed. Even from my lowly position, I could tell by the man's body language I was not getting through. There were no flights to Kolkata or, come to that, Mumbai or Delhi. It was made clear to me that I should get off the floor and pull myself together.

Three hours later, after a reflective train journey back to St Andrews, I let myself quietly into my house, listened to the sounds of family chatter coming from the sitting room, and pushed open the door. There was a momentary gawp, less astonishment at my explanation than I would have thought appropriate, and considerably more hilarity than was kind. But the worst of it was that I had to spend the next few weeks furtively dodging around St Andrews trying to avoid bumping into people to whom I had just said goodbye and, when contact was unavoidable, trying to find an adequate response to the words: 'Oh hello, Mike. I thought you were in India.'

So, what with one thing and another, it wasn't until the last week in April that I landed in Kolkata. While I had been away, India had raced from winter to high summer. Walking off the plane was like stepping, fully clothed, into a warm and steaming bath. At 2 o'clock in the morning, an hour that I would normally label the middle of the night, Kolkata Airport was 29 degrees, with enough humidity to make the desert bloom.

This time I was really hoping I would be met. Deepak had given me the name of a local travel agent who had been instructed to book a hotel and send a driver to collect me from the airport. The hours of darkness were not the right time for plump pickings like me to be wandering around unescorted – and there was Mr S. (that's all I could catch) waiting for me with a car. Isn't it wonderful when things go according to plan.

Luggage was gathered, and we drove into the half-lit, half-comatose city. I have a vague recollection of passing sleeping bodies by the roadside (they may have been dead), rattling over tram lines and sweeping past Mother Theresa's hostel. Then we stopped outside a large iron gate. Chains and padlocks were lashed around it to prevent entry by anyone not carrying a bazooka. The driver hooted and, after an interval, a man appeared, begrudgingly, rattling keys. This, it transpired, was my hotel.

It reminded me of a police station of the kind I imagine they have in Beirut. The windows looked as if they could be easily defended, and the carpets as if they hadn't been replaced since the last time defence had been necessary. I did my best to put a brave face on things.

'Excuse me', I said jauntily to Mr S, 'what sort of rooms does this place have?'

'Very good hotel', he replied. 'I think you like.' Well, that was OK then.

I was led up to my place of rest by an ageing employee. By this time, it was about three o'clock and I was tired – so allowances need to be made – but (and I don't want to sound picky) the room did leave a few things to be desired. A cleaner for a start. Fewer co-occupants would have been good too, although, to give the ancient retainer his due, he did produce a large and battered can of insect repellent. This was powered by a hand pump, which he cranked up and down with gusto. Before long the room was swathed in a chemical haze thick enough to bubble paint – had there been any, that is – and when he had thus secured his own invisibility, he left. As I sought to inhale what remained of the oxygen in this toxic mixture, it did cross my mind that, were my health to deteriorate rapidly in the years to come, I would look back on this as a formative moment.

It may have been that the toxins had an immediate impact, because the first thing I did, once he'd gone, was to burrow into my case, find my own spray can and add a few squirts myself. Mine contained DEET (*diethyl toluamide*), which I'd been informed was essential if you wanted protection against malaria-carrying mosquitoes. Before departing, a friend who meant well had pointed out an article on the subject that had appeared in one of the papers[79]. It began with these arresting words:

The driver was found by the roadside on the outskirts of Brussels convulsing at the wheel of his wrecked car. … blood tests eventually revealed the unsuspected cause of his collapse – he was suffering from malaria. He stayed in a deep coma and died 15 days later from multi-organ failure.

This had rather captured my attention. It appeared that malaria was now found in areas previously thought to be clear, that the disease was becoming drug resistant, and that stronger drugs used across Europe were not prescribed in Britain because of worries about side effects. As I stood peering through the fog that had settled over the floor, I found none of this comforting.

I undressed, and lifted my foot up onto the hand-basin with the idea of giving it a refreshing splash of water before retiring. No sooner was it beneath the tap, than the basin-stand, responding to the extra weight, keeled over 30 degrees, like a fuel gauge swinging towards empty. I watched, appalled. I had visions of the pipe severing, and dousing me and the room with gallons of water. What I'd have done if it had – it was 3 o'clock in the morning – I can't imagine. I hadn't thought to pack a monkey-wrench.

I abandoned all thoughts of washing, jumped into my jim-jams, gave the inside of my bed a squirt of DEET, pulled the sheets over my head and tried not to think about the creatures that would shortly be emerging from their nooks and crannies, wiping the tear gas from their eyes and converging on the new food source in their midst. I resolved that I would devote the waking hours of a new dawn, should I be lucky enough to see one, to finding myself better lodgings.

First thing, I rang the agency that had booked this hotel and forced them to divulge the name of something that had stars by its name. I gave the place a call and, by ten o'clock, was installed in a haven of clean sheets and air conditioning. I showered, scrubbing away until reasonably confident that all those foreign bodies which had dined on me during the night were now removed. I then had a leisurely breakfast and declared myself ready for the world once more.

I telephoned Deepak at Creative Travel and went over some of the plans we'd been hatching. He was his usual competent and reassuring self. He reminded me that I needed a permit if I wanted to go to Sikkim later on, and that I should pick that up while in Kolkata. The Foreigners Regional Registration Office, the FRRO, was the place, 230A, AJC Bose Road.

I looked up Bose Road in my Lonely Planet and learnt that it wasn't all that far from my hotel. It was walkable. Challenging, but achievable. I decided to brave it. First of all, I carefully copied out the relevant part of the map from the Guide Book onto a sheet of paper. Then I showed it to Reception to receive independent confirmation that Lonely Planet hadn't made the whole thing up. Finally, after they'd scrutinised it and said it looked OK, I took my leave with a cheery wave and, a 'so it's left out of the hotel, then?' I asked this pointing a bent finger at the exit. I like to make absolutely sure about the vital first move because, if you don't get that right, you can end up in real trouble. They nodded encouragingly, and stared after me as I set off.

The porter opened the door. I stepped outside. Roasting humidity, for those who haven't experienced it, is something that takes a little getting used to. It was as if, below me, the lid of a giant cauldron of boiling water had been removed and I was being steamed, like broccoli. I went into immediate reverse, like the Road-Runner after he's overshot a cliff, straight back into the air conditioning. The people at the desk hadn't moved a muscle. They were eyeing me implacably. 'Well,' the look said, 'are you going out there or aren't you?' I gave my head a scratch as if I'd been struck by an afterthought, turned around once more and marched resolutely out into the steamer.

The map was accurate which, considering I'd drawn it, was a surprise. When I found myself outside number 230A, I experienced a modest flush of pride, though this would not have been visible beneath the lather of virtuous sweat with which I was coated. Ungluing my shirt and trousers from my skin, I went in. There I was directed down a gloomy passageway, wallpapered by rows of petitioners who looked as if they'd arrived last month and were now resigned to permanent residence. At the end of this corridor, was an opaque window with a half-moon opening cut into it at waist height. I bent down, peered through it and discovered a pleasant lady of uncertain years on the other side. We exchanged words, she handed me a form and I filled in every question, except one: my exact date of arrival in Sikkim. This vital piece of information was at the hotel, and I'd have to get it. I didn't argue.

Back and forth I trudged and let me say that I wasn't accosted by beggars (much), there were no cows and the pavements were relatively clean. It wasn't nearly as bad as Kolkata's generally adverse publicity had led me to believe. Just dehumidify the place and take the temperature down by 20 degrees, and it'd be fine. When I finally arrived back at the window, I handed in the now completed form and was told to wait. In a curious way, I felt at ease. The surroundings were dismal but, at the same time, oddly comforting. Although interminable bureaucracy was grinding away at its own remorselessly snail-like pace, I knew that, in the end, it would grind to a conclusion. I sat down on a mud-brown vinyl seat and stared listlessly at an equally mud-brown wooden partition with its opaque window, behind which functionaries sat in rows. A large electric fan whirred above me like the blades of a helicopter. From time to time, something was passed through the hole in the glass.

An improbably blonde man, in his mid-20s and with earnest spectacles, (Swedish, I'd say) was doing his best to explain, through the aperture, how he had signed up for a meditation course and needed an extension on his visa. His request wasn't going down too well and this appeared to prompt him – uncharacteristically for a meditator I would have thought – to proceed to the following desperate measure. 'Can I,' he said, 'give you a present or something?' I must have led a sheltered life because I have never bribed anyone but I wasn't sure, if I did, whether I would approach the subject quite so directly. I couldn't help thinking that a discreet envelope passed surreptitiously over the counter might have been better. Anyway, I leant forward in my seat, very curious to see how his offer would be received – corruption, I am sorry to say, is not unknown in India – when my line of sight was blocked by a small man beckoning me to follow him. I could hardly ask him to hang on while I listened in on these arcane negotiations so the fate of the Swede (Sikkim or gaol) hung in the balance as I departed – and there it remains; one of life's many mysteries.

The man took me through dark corridors to a desk, behind which a bureaucrat was scribbling. He turned to my application and began writing copious notes on it. Heaven knows what about. The form only contained the usual passport and travel details. He then read and re-read my form, made alterations to his half a page of scribbling, and finally produced the gratifying utterance, 'job is done.' What mysteries had been unravelled on that page went undisclosed. I was merely told to return at 4pm, at which time my permit would be ready. In such ways do days pass.

Next morning, I woke up fit, sprightly and ready for the sights. But what sights? Before 1690, Calcutta – which was to become the economic and political capital of India – was nothing more than a tiny village. Then the British came along and decided it would be a good place for a trading post. Okay, fair enough, but did they consider the implications for the tourist industry in years to come? I suspect not. No ancient temples. No erotic carvings. No Mughal palaces. No havelis. What was a tourist to do? More to the point what was a British tourist to do since just about all the sights were British? Fort William, Eden Gardens, St Paul's Cathedral etc; the names tell you everything. Did I want to visit these? Well no, not really. Monumental and splendid though they undoubtedly were, I just didn't think they'd be very surprising.

Still, since I was in Kolkata, there was no point wishing I was somewhere else. I decided to go and see the mausoleum of the man who, in the 1690s, put the place on the map, one Job Charnock[AV]. The mausoleum was in the grounds of the church of St John, was twenty feet high and, most important of all, provided shade. Job Charnock – founder of Calcutta though he may have been and the man who kick-started the East India Company – was not, I discovered, a rounded and decent human being. He liked to flog his servants over dinner 'so near his dining room that the groans and the cries of the poor delinquents served him for music.' Heavens above. However,

---

AV This is the beginning of Clump Four and the East India Company.

on the plus side, he did rescue a young Hindu widow who was about to throw herself on her husband's funeral pyre. He then married her and became a Hindu himself. That was some sort of offset, I suppose.

Outside the mausoleum, the churchyard was not in great shape. It was littered with corrugated iron panels and overgrown by creeper. A pack of stray dogs was nosing around for something edible, which I rather hoped would not include me. I edged around them and, in doing so, more or less bumped into a stumpy obelisk which turned out to be a memorial to those who had died in 'the Black Hole of Calcutta'. The Black Hole had been a small and airless room into which, on the night of June 20th 1756, the Nawab of Bengal had herded 100 to 200 British prisoners. By morning, over half had died of suffocation.[80] (Once you've spent a night in Kolkata in high summer, you understand how this could happen.) The British were outraged and the Black Hole became about the only piece of Indian history to put in an appearance in British history textbooks – along with, now I come to think of it, the impeachment of Warren Hastings.[AW]

When I finally emerged from the Churchyard, my taxi driver was there, happily leaning against the side of the car. I thought,

---

AW   Hastings was the East India Company's Governor-General. Parliament and the Country had become scandalised by the Company's excesses and, in 1788, Hastings was impeached for corruption and abuse of power The prosecution in the trial didn't hold back. Edmund Burke, a member of the parliamentary select committee investigating the administration of justice in India, spoke for 4 days, lambasting the East India Company for its 'avarice, rapacity, pride, cruelty, malignity, haughtiness and insolence' – and this was just the start. Macauley writing in the first half of the 19th century talked about 'English power ... unaccompanied by English morality'.

not for the first time, how wonderful Indian taxis are. You can ask them to wait without having to consider a second mortgage. And they are reliable – they don't disappear as soon as they sniff a better offer. I asked the driver to take me on a short tour and off we went.

Kolkata, I can disclose, has rickshaws pulled by men on foot, as opposed to men on bicycles, as in the rest of India. It has trams. And it has mementos aplenty of those days when it was the capital of British India. I was just beginning to wonder whether I might be warming to the city, when the heavens opened. This was not a prelude to a refreshing shower after all the heat. Rather, a short, violent storm erupted during which nothing whatsoever was visible except water and the occasional drenched face scurrying past the window. We aquaplaned back to the hotel as fast as the eddying currents would allow.

That evening, after the deluge, when the mercury had climbed back up to 'simmer', I had choices to make. A son et lumière was on in a nearby park, starting at 7.15. This was good. On the other hand, the mosquitoes would be out in force, and at their hungriest. This was less good. There were, on the face of it, three alternatives. 1) Go, don't cover up and be eaten. 2) Go, cover up, boil and be eaten. 3) Don't go. I opted for number 4. I went to the hotel steam room instead which, climatically, was much the same as going out, but less risky. Then, because I felt a bit of a wimp, I marched straight into the dining room, glanced at the menu and ordered that most gastricly dangerous of comestibles: prawns. Yes, I know. I couldn't believe I'd done it. It was like tucking into a plateful of the deadly Japanese puffer fish without having first interrogated the chef's credentials. All I can say in my defence, is that, while waiting, I discussed the prawns with the waiter, a man who was saving up to go to Robert Gordon's Institute of Catering Management in Aberdeen. He said they were OK. I believed him. Without his specific assurance, I wouldn't have touched them. Of course not. They were, by the way, delicious (even if not, strictly speaking, part of my vegetarian diet).

Deepak had arranged a trip to the jungle at Kaziranga, in Assam, so next morning found me on my way to the airport, not altogether sorry to be leaving. This probably sounds unkind to Kolkata, which I don't mean at all. It's just that I'm not really a city person, at least not one with 14 million people sharing the same sauna. It is all I can do to cope with St Andrews during the May Bank Holiday weekend.

The journey out was relatively uneventful. There was a slight hold-up caused by a man being killed in a traffic accident, but it didn't delay matters long. A policeman was quickly on hand to supervise the loading of the corpse onto a wooden trailer. This was towed away by a man on a bicycle. Nobody covered the body. It just lay there with dried blood on the skull. No sooner had the cyclist pulled out into the road, than cars surged past on either side hooting. These included, I'm ashamed to say, my own taxi.

We drove on around Eden Gardens, the iconic cricket ground, where, according to the driver, they also play football. Before that moment, it would not have occurred to me that Indians played football, but they do; in the rainy season when it's too wet for cricket. On we went, past Hafiz' Best Quality Meat, where carcasses were hung outside to pre-cook gently at a moderate 39°, past a queue of waiting taxis that must have stretched for at least half a mile, and into the airport.

Now, here's a question: was it inevitable that Job Charnock's little trading company (the East India Company) would end up ruling the roost?

I would say, not inevitable. On the cards, maybe, but inevitable, no.

Even with the Mughal Empire breaking up after the death of Aurangzeb in 1707, the EIC was immediately surrounded by much bigger fish. The Mughal Emperors were still on the throne in Delhi, although much diminished from their glory days. The Marathas and Mysore were big and growing regional powers. And then there was the French who competed with the British for trade and, after 1756, were at war with Britain in Europe and America.

What the Brits had going for them was that they'd set up shop in India's treasure house, Bengal. No better place to trade than this, especially when it was quickly recognized that the EIC was good for trade. Under the EIC, Calcutta put up no barriers to private enterprise and provided protection against the Marathas who regarded Bengal as a good place to indulge their brutal pillaging proclivities. Bengali merchants, Parsis, Gujeratis, Marwari entrepreneurs and miscellaneous Europeans all flooded in[81]. Most importantly, the world's richest bankers, the Jagat Seths, with an eye on what was good for business, kept the Company afloat financially[82]. When, in 1737, the bankers felt threatened by the Nawab of Bengal, they offered the EIC a huge bribe to get rid of him[83].

When you start paying a private company for protection, that's when trouble starts. By and by, and round and round, with a mixture of money and might, in 1765, the EIC was granted the right of financial administration over Bengal, Orissa and Bihar. The EIC could now do everything a state did, while pocketing the profits for the benefit of its own shareholders. The result was that Bengal was plundered more thoroughly than ever before. Even during the appalling Bengal famine of 1770, when the land was laid bare and the peasants were starving to death, the Company continued to collect its taxes[84].

But the EIC could have been beaten. Its initial advantage in terms of weapons and military know-how[85]didn't last long. The Indians, aided by the French, soon caught up. At the battle of Pollitur in 1780, the EIC was decisively beaten by a triple alliance of the Marathas, Hyderabad and Mysore under its charismatic leader Tipu Sultan. Had the Triple Alliance driven home its advantage, the EIC would have been kicked out of India[86]. And, if the alliance had held together, who knows ... but it didn't. The next Triple Alliance was against Tipu Sultan, and this time the Marathas and the Hyderabadis were on the side of the EIC[87]. The chance to drive out the Company had been missed, and once back in the game, the EIC was able to ramp up its military and financial capability to make it more or less unassailable.

16. KAZIRANGA

... by the bonny bonny banks of the Brahmaputra

To reach Kaziranga, one of India's finest game reserves, you have to fly over Bangladesh to Assam's biggest city, Guwahati. Deepak had arranged for a car to meet me. Not just any old car, but a Tata Sumo, a jeep complete with springs, an engine with oomph and a cow catcher in front. When I first clapped eyes on it, I had to wipe back a tear of the purest joy. He had also fixed up a two-man reception committee consisting of a driver, Promswar, who bore a passing resemblance to Genghis Khan, and a co-pilot, Dhiren, who sported a wispy goatee beard and eyes that hinted at origins considerably to the east of Bengal. Their smiling faces were an instant reminder that I was now just a stone's throw from Myanmar (Burma), somewhere not finally part of India until 1826.[AX]

We drove out of the airport past a large sign warning of the

AX   Annexed, of course, by the British, as was Assam in the same period.

reappearance of malaria in the North East Region, and headed straight into an endless, noisy, smelly, black, exhaust-belching traffic jam that was Guwahati. It had rained heavily overnight. The town had turned swampy and I found myself beset by disquieting visions of mosquitoes breeding in droves. These were not helped by the fact that we had ground to a halt, interrupted only by the occasional five-yard burst to close a gap that had opened up in front.

I used the time on my hands to formulate a law governing the behaviour of Guwahati traffic, (though it may apply more generally). It was this: 'the number of cars on a single lane of highway will be the maximum that can be accommodated line abreast, plus one. This extra car, finding itself without a road, moves over to the other side and drives against the oncoming stream'. This, as you may imagine, tends to slow things down. And what does the policeman on duty do? He finds the most defenceless queue-jumper – in this case a diminutive cyclist pulling a cart – and gives him a fearful dressing down, so that all the other drivers can see what a fine job he's doing.

I didn't approve but, before I could formulate a second law about policemen and the line of least resistance, my attention was diverted by a young woman in a bright pink sari. She was walking through the mud and between the honking cars as if gliding across a ballroom to the accompaniment of the Palm Court Orchestra. She wasn't stepping gingerly. She didn't hold her nose. She ignored the whole swampy pile-up with dignity and calm, and sailed on regardless[AY].

[AY] I thought it at the time, and I think it even more now, that one of the things which makes India so very special is this apparent ability of Indians not to attach to all the physical unpleasantness which so often seems to confront them in the

Once out of town, the air freshened and the noise abated. Had I been born with a replaceable Hoover bag instead of a lung, I would have put a fresh one in right there. As it was, I coughed a few times into my handkerchief to rid myself of as much of Guwahati as I could manage and did my best not to inspect the results. (OK, I had a quick peek. It was black and blobby, that's all I'm saying).

The deeper into the countryside we travelled, the more I liked it. It looked rather as I imagine Vietnam; deep red fertile soil, lush palmy vegetation, hills carpeted with trees, a duvet of cloud suspended above them. We passed alongside paddy fields and, now and then, a village. Some of the dwellings had thatched roofs, and a few of these had columns of smoke billowing out through the straw. Dhiren didn't slow down, not even slightly. According to him, the smoke was the result of rice being cooked. It did occur to me that there might also be smoke coming out of the roof because the house was on fire and the occupants were being burned to a crisp but, being a visitor, I kept such thoughts to myself.

Every so often the roadside advertisements included a warning about malaria, so the next time we stopped, I put on a pair of socks, fished out my walking boots, turned up my collar, and sprayed on the DEET. It began to rain and it carried on raining. The normal response, when driving, is to switch on the wipers. Most people do this instinctively. Promswar was the exception. Occasionally, he allowed himself the luxury of a quick wipe, but then off they went, back to immobility. I found this behaviour unfathomable, and troubling.

day to day. They appear able to rise above. It's a wonderful attribute.

Darkness fell. Promswar saw no need to turn on his lights either. When he sensed something coming towards him through the pluvial gloom, he flashed it. Heavens above. Rubber for the wiper may have been in short supply, possibly, but I had always imagined that the electricity for the lights was generated by the car itself. Why ration that? I didn't say a word. I just sat there grinding my teeth. After about half an hour, I noticed his hand begin to reach across – imagine this in slow motion, like two lovers running towards each other across a meadow of buttercups – and watched, with yearning anticipation, while it gambolled playfully towards the awaiting headlight switch. They embraced. We had illumination. We were once again visible to other traffic. There was a God after all.

Six or so hours after setting off from the airport, we arrived. The place where I was staying had been taken over by delegates from a Tea Planters Convention, though where in Kaziranga you could hold a convention was not entirely obvious. Perhaps it was a small convention. The planters were led by a man of enormous girth and a round beaming face, who had laid on local dancers by way of entertainment.

The dancers were a delight, gyrating in a fashion somewhere between the whirlings of a dervish and that of a young woman in front of a mirror, trying to make up her mind about a tight skirt. The dancing ended with three young women cavorting coquettishly around a curved ram's horn pointing upwards. The horn, needless to add, was being blown by a young man. I don't think I'd be stretching things too far were I to suggest that this was a mating ritual.

After the dancers came a brief silence. Then the jolly tea planter opened up with a decent rendering of *I love Paris in the Springtime.'* He thereby qualified as the only man anyone has ever met who knew the second line of this song. For a brief moment, I knew it too, but it went clean out of my head. What was it again? Never mind. It was entertainment. It wasn't martial, it was sung in fun and, though I wouldn't recommend he give up the day job, not at all badly rendered. I went off to bed, in preparation for an early start next morning, still humming. *I love Paris in the Springtime,...* (yes, yes, then what?), erm ... *something, something, something, some...* (oh, I give up). By the way, before retiring, let me pass on a titbit that was confidentially revealed to me by one of the planters, and which I now confidentially reveal to you. Don't use tea bags. There are no leaves in them. Only dust and fannings. Proper tea from now on. In a pot. Like Mother used to make it.

Next morning, I was up at 5 am. Dhiren, and a driver I didn't recognise, were waiting for me in a jeep. We rattled forward, splashed through puddles (it had rained again overnight), bumped through several villages, and arrived at the National Park itself. A notice board, bearing a few statistics, was there to greet us. Kaziranga was impressively large. 430 sq kms, to be precise, and it boasted 90 Royal Bengal Tigers and 1552 one-horned Rhino. I particularly liked the '2'. What happened? Did Mrs Rhino, number 1550 – I like to think of her as Thelma – have twins? In 1908, the species was on the verge of extinction with only a few dozen rhino left, so 1552 was solid progress[AZ].

To view a rhino up close, you first need to find yourself a

AZ   Kaziranga is also home to the Gangetic Dolphin which lives in the Brahmaputra river. A freshwater dolphin, fancy that.

big elephant with plenty of bottom. You will be grateful for this should you happen to turn round and notice a stumpy horn travelling rapidly in your direction in front of something armour plated and weighing several tons. The elephants were being boarded from a raised platform. I climbed up and placed myself alongside a party of Dutch people in readiness for lowering.

I couldn't help noticing that one or two of the elephants had howdahs that were like saddles – requiring you to sit astride, one leg on one side, one on the other. This would have been a perfectly sensible arrangement for a horse but elephants are significantly broader in the beam. It looked like trouble of a particularly painful kind. Needless to say, the astride model pulled alongside and I was invited to board. The only method I could come up with to avoid fracture was to throw my legs forward along the beast's backbone and have my feet pointing ahead like dipped headlights. The Dutchman in front of me was very decent about it, I must say. He was of an age to recognise the difficulty and happily swung his legs forward to make room for mine. He also persuaded his wife to do likewise. All three of us were thus reclining as we pulled away, while at the same time swaying from side to side in step with our mount. We were soon on intimate terms.

We, or rather the elephant, walked through swampy mud and high grass. How high? About as high as an elephant's eye. When we came upon rhinos, they were rudely disinterested. They couldn't have cared less. If the rhino happened to be buried in a bog applying a mudpack, it carried on the beauty treatment regardless. If it was just standing, contemplating the meaning of life, it stayed standing. So did the ever-present white bird (an egret, I think) on its back. Motionless, the pair of them. The bird's role in life was to eat any insects that approached the master's person. Nature's answer to DEET. I wanted one. It could sit disinterestedly on my shoulder until a mosquito happened by, and then…. lunchtime.

The Dutchman, whose hair was now under my chin, was a mine of information about matters zoological, and particularly about elephants. We were soon discussing them philosophically, as you are inclined to do when you are perched aloft their vast rolling bulk, pootling along through jungle grasslands, and all is well with the world. Communal values are important to elephants. I hadn't realised this. For example, when an ancient member of the tribe is struggling to make it to the top of a hill, more sprightly members will put their shoulders to the wheel and push him up. I thought that was nice, something to relate to the kids when the time came.

'Have you ever looked closely at an elephant's head?' the Dutchman enquired affably. Well, I had to say I hadn't, although I did then. It was big, I could see that. 'It's vast, VAST,' he observed ruminatively, as if sitting on his porch, pulling on a pipe. Yes, it certainly was. I had no idea, until then, quite how enormous. Our modest conclusion from this additional data was that big skull probably meant big brain, and was not unrelated to the fact that elephants could be trained within a year to do the job of a forklift truck.

Having that extraordinarily adept hosepipe-come-arm stuck out in front must also have helped stimulate the occasional insight. I watched idly as our mount twisted its trunk around a clump of grass, pulled it out and put the food in its mouth. This was nasal dexterity of the highest order. Those of you who have been paying attention will remember how Chetak lost his leg at Haldhighati: severed by an elephant wielding a sword. I had difficulty crediting this at the time but, yes, it could have swung a sword.

Just then, my new friend and I discovered a further interesting fact about the mountain of flesh beneath us. This thing could fart. I mean it really let rip. The volume and fruitiness of the gaseous outflow was in every way proportional to the size of its immense rear. I noticed a stationary rhino take a startled step backwards and give us an affronted look. And he wasn't perched above the source as I was.

After lunch, the weather cleared and Dhiren took the jeep up to the western range, stopping on the way to pick up an armed ranger. The hills rambled across the skyline like the moth-eaten edge of an elephant's ear, the sun was out after the rain and it was a warm 20°, like the very best summer's day in St Andrews. There are worse ways to spend an afternoon than on the back of an open jeep, in mild sunshine, looking across grassy plains, driving through jungly forest, coming to a lake, seeing a flock of Brahminee duck bobbing up and down on the water like boats at anchor in Poole harbour, and watching five Indian otters diving through the water like furry dolphins. A wild boar trotted past, and a cluster of red breasted parakeets were on the wing bound for who knows where. It was as good as it gets.

Dhiren was a first-rate guide. He could identify an animal at a thousand paces when all I could make out was a brown blur, and he was always ready to pass on fascinating titbits about jungle life. He told me, for example, that rhinos returned to the same place each day to lay their droppings. This explained a lot. I'd been wondering what exactly were those enormous mounds of excreta we'd been driving past. Had they been laid by a 30-foot-high behemoth that had just enjoyed the enema of its life? Had, perhaps, a herd gathered together for a communal crap-in? No. Each was the result of one rhino patiently, steadily, night-by-night building up his pile, and when I tell you that a rhino can live for 100 years, you will realise that what we are talking about here was the kind of thing that would really put some sparkle in your roses.

There were wild elephants in the park and, towards the end of our afternoon safari, we came across a giant tusker perhaps 50 yards away. (A tusker is a large male elephant with tusks containing enough ivory to allow a poacher to retire on the proceeds.[BA]) Gathered around the old boy was a plentiful supply of females. Dhiren felt this was the right moment to make tiger noises, clicking sounds which were not greeted in the jovial spirit that I'm sure was intended. In fact, the elephant took this as a threat to his womenfolk and charged, ears flapping, legs pumping. It was definitely a charge. For a brief moment, it was also a wonderful sight, terrifying to any creature in its path. The charge was brought to a rapid end by cries of alarm from Dhiren and our ranger firing his .303 over the distraught animal's head.

Jumbo stopped as if shot and, for a moment, I thought he had been. I did try to enquire why a shot was necessary since I couldn't imagine an elephant giving a jeep a 50-yard

BA The sale of ivory has been illegal in India since 1986, but poaching still goes on. It's the major threat to elephant conservation. The Wildlife Protection Society of India (WPSI) estimated that 371 elephants (c. 1.5% of the total) were poached in 10 years between 2006 and 2017.

start and catching it, but Dhiren simply described a tossing motion with his head. I presume he thought the elephant could have caught us (or perhaps the next jeep that was innocently watching rhino) and would have put his horns under the car and tossed it. Still, abbreviated as the excitement was, almost something to tell the grandchildren as it might have been, it did at least elicit a tired '*vraiment?*' from the Swiss with whom I ate that night. They were experienced jungle men. To have won their undivided attention, I would have had to have told them how, after being thrown in the air by the tusker, I rolled clear of the jeep only to come to rest on the front end of a rhino, who then took me to the nearest swamp for an all-over body wrap, thus explaining why I was late for dinner and covered in mud. But since this didn't happen, all I could say was '*oui, vraiment.*'

After the excitement with the elephant, we headed for home. The jeep (in one piece, in case you've lost the thread) came back to the police station where we'd set off. Thinking what a truly delightful day it had been, I stepped out and was immediately mobbed by about twenty children from the English class at the local school. They greeted me as if I were a long-lost relative who'd made a fortune selling catalytic converters in Guwahati and had now returned to his village. The questioning began.

'Where you from?'

'I from Scotland. Very cold place,' I replied. (Why do I always speak like this? It's not as if I don't know verbs.)

'You like Kaziranga?' one of them fired back.

'Beautiful,' I said. 'You very lucky to live here. You could be in Kolkata.'

'Kolkata machine life,' chipped in an accompanying adult sagely who I guessed was their teacher.

'We take picture with you?' one of the children asked.

'But', I said pleadingly, 'me very ugly, you find someone handsome, like Mr Rhino.' You could tell by the look on their faces that if they could get Mr Rhino to pose, they certainly would but, failing that, I was their best bet. I put my arms around a couple of 10-year-olds and snaps were taken.

'You sign my autograph' said a girl with specs, and pretty soon I was signing autographs and filling in a book of questions that they all had with them. They wanted my name, address, telephone number, favourite colour, my ambition, my happiest moment, my most embarrassing moment, my most unforgettable person and so on. This was not easy, particularly because there was nothing to write on. I commandeered one of the boys with a flat-looking head at the right height, and used him as a table top. He rose to the challenge manfully, though he did have a tendency to collapse when I pressed too hard. What can I say; the kids were delightful and we had fun. I shook hands with my table, told him that when he grew up he would make a great mantelpiece, and then said goodbye to the teacher, signed a few more autographs, shook a few more hands, mounted my jeep and departed, waving like royalty. All in all, an interlude I will cherish, one I may even end up telling my grand-children about (probably more than once).

The next morning, early, Promswar loaded me into the Sumo and drove me back to Guwahati the way we'd come. We went through acres of tea plantations which we'd passed on the way up, except that then I thought they were just stunted bushes. Now I knew a tea plant when I saw one. I also discovered, while we are on the subject of things I didn't know last week, that pepper grows on trees. I never knew that. If asked, I would have supposed it was some dried vegetable seed but, no, it begins life on a branch. Is this common knowledge? Did everyone learn that pepper grows on trees, while I was dozing through geography?

I'll tell you one other thing I didn't learn about in school, and that is how special Assam is. Special in a global sense. Special to botanists and zoologists. The story begins a few hundred million years ago when the world consisted of only two land-masses, Laurasia (what is now North America, Europe and Asia) and Gondwana (Africa, South America, Australia, Antarctica and India.) At some point (about 300 million years ago) the two giants fragmented into the continents that we recognise today, and India set off at a sprightly eight centimetres a year on its journey towards the northern hemisphere. About four million years ago, almost yesterday in the scheme of things, it collided with Asia. This was quite a crash and, if you want to see the crumpled bodywork for yourself, you need only visit the Himalayas. Assam became the gateway for the two continents. The plants and animals of Laurasia moved south, and crossed those of Gondwana going north. It was in Assam that the Asian tiger first stalked the antelope of Africa, and here that the two giant landmasses of yesteryear first said hello.[88]

I didn't know about any of this at the time, or I would, of course, have scouted the terrain with deeply quizzical eyes, delving for tell-tale signs of transcontinental biodiversity. What I did know was that it was a lovely morning. The sun was shin-ing, the villages looked neat and clean, the goats and dogs were, as usual, playing 'chicken' with the car. Even the chickens were playing chicken, and I thought to myself (as Satchmo tuned up his trumpet) what a wonderful world. 'You know, Mike,' the thought continued, 'there is nowhere else I would rather be at this precise moment than right here.'

So content was I, that when we stopped at a railway crossing, I awarded myself a coconut. I hadn't been thinking about coconuts, but I couldn't help noticing a man selling them on the other side of the road. I couldn't help noticing him because he kept holding up a large green object, shaking it and saying, 'you want coconut?' I bought one. For five rupees. It was soft skinned and it came with a straw in the top. You don't eat the flesh, I gathered. You just drink the delicious and refreshing coconut water and chuck the outer casing onto the side of the railway line. That's what everybody else seemed to have done.

Unhappily, the glories of Kaziranga were receding rapidly out the rear-view mirror, while Guwahati was looming in front like a black smudge. The traffic was becoming heavier, as were the clusters of advertising hoardings. One was extolling the merits of the Institute of Human Reproduction and its achievements in the field of infertility treatment. I tried not to look. I was sure the Institute would be staffed by dedicated men and women but whether it was addressing the most immediate of India's needs was another matter.

Then we reached Guwahati, and all the good work done by Kaziranga vanished in a cloud of noxious exhaust gas. Now, I may have caught the city on a bad day, in which case I retract unreservedly, but I couldn't help thinking that, pound for pound, Guwahati was probably the smelliest and dirtiest place I had ever visited. I even saw a couple of locals grimace, which shows you how bad it was. I checked into an all mod-cons hotel as a medieval felon would have checked into a church; for sanctuary. I lay on the bed, closed my eyes and was immediately overcome by a feeling that this simply would not do. So I asked Promswar to drive me up to the Kamakhya temple, an ancient centre of the Shakti and Tantric Hindu cults (about which I knew absolutely nothing).

Kamakhya was not a place I'd recommend to the squeamish. The sacrifice of a goat was a daily occurrence. A small herd of victims-to-be were roaming around the temple walls and making rather a mess. It was hard to hold it against them under the circumstances but, what with the bloodstains on the stones, the goat shit and the flies, you didn't exactly get the feeling that you'd just stepped into a Swiss sanitorium. Even less wholesome was a dog, lying prone, with red powder on its face and its rear end unnaturally bloody and inflamed, I think. I say 'I think', because I edged past it doing my best not to inquire too closely. It may just have been more powder.

I spoke to one of the priests who told me that, though the upper half of the temple had been rebuilt a few hundred years ago, the lower half had been constructed by the gods and was therefore impossible to date. The priest's name was Hemen Sarma. His family had been saying mantras in this temple for over seven generations. He had a BSc, but after his father died, he saw it as his duty to carry on the family tradition. I asked him about training. His instruction had come from the Master who had taught his father. And if the Master had been dead? Then he would have received instruction from the Master's sons. At this juncture, something large with wings took a chunk out of my arm and I sincerely hoped that whatever it was had not just come from the rear end of that canine specimen I had stepped over. When I was suddenly seized by an urgent craving for marrowbone, I knew it was time to leave.

Promswar took the Sumo a little further up the hill, and there, on a corner, was Guwahati's redeeming feature – a view of the winding river Brahmaputra, India's longest and widest, lazing past the belching city in the valley below. Before traffic, this whole area must have been lovely, on the bend of a river, Mark Twain country in the east (but more tropical).

As it happened, I was sharing my vantage point with an Indian man who had also fought his way through the chemical layer up to the breathable stuff. We struck up a conversation. He told me that, having been born in these parts, he had assumed that all rivers would be like the Brahmaputra. When he went to London, he had taken a taxi to see the Thames and couldn't believe that the miniscule trickle below him really was the flowing heart of the greatest empire the world had seen. After the cabbie had reassured him once more that, yes, what he saw was the Thames, or at least had been for as long as he'd been driving, he still didn't believe it. If he'd been Swiss, he'd have said *vraiment?* He went on to declare that he'd been to a Jesuit boarding school just outside Darjeeling and, as he put it, 'he'd taken a liking to the communion wine and thus became the only Hindu in the choir.' He had learnt all about London from reading the Beano – sent to him by his sister in Calcutta.

The conversation turned to old songs, which he used to listen to on Radio Ceylon. He knew them all. 'Ah' I said, about to launch my coup de grace, 'I bet you don't know the second line of '*I love Paris in the Springtime.*' Blow me down, but he did. 'I love Paris in the fall,' he sung. That Beano must have been better than I remembered. 'I also know', he said, 'the words of *The Bonnie Bonnie Banks of Loch Lomond.*' High above the Brahmaputra, above the sound of a million car horns, we struck up a duet, I doing my best to give the rendition a genuine Scottish lilt, largely because none of my St Andrews muckers were there to mock, and because I doubted if my Jesuitical Hindu friend would question the authenticity. Then again, since he knew the second line of '*I love Paris in the Springtime,*' anything was possible.

He was an interesting fellow. On Assamese Hinduism, he told me, 'We've knocked Brahmins out for six,' which meant, I think, that people went their own way with less regulations from the priesthood. On animal sacrifice, he didn't approve. He thought it was unnecessary. On cleanliness, he said it was an odd thing but Indians kept their houses spotless and their temples and lavatories dirty. We continued, and when the world and its problems had been addressed to our mutual satisfaction, we went our separate ways back to the nether zone below.

By the time I had reached my hotel, I was once again on the verge of asphyxiation. I vowed not to move until it was time to leave for the airport. I had a shower, threw my clothes into the fumigation section of my hold-all and resolved to have a miserable evening. Next morning, I caught the plane to Bagdogra airport, in West Bengal, close to the Sikkim border.

17. KALIMPONG

… Ups and downs

I was met at Bagdogra by Namgil; at least, that was the name I thought he gave me. Since he didn't speak more than 10 words of English, it was hard to be sure. And why should he speak English anyway? He was a Gorkha. He spoke Nepali.

We sped off in the considerable luxury of a Mahindra jeep and, in spite of the thermometer clocking 30°, everything felt fresher and cleaner. Mind you, after Guwahati, a couple of hours holed up in an exhaust pipe would have felt fresher and cleaner (and that is definitely the last unkind word I will ever utter about the good city of Guwahati).

Our route took us through the outskirts of Siliguri and past an extended graveyard of deeply rusted lorry hulks, broken carcasses of what had once been the knights of the Indian highway. In any other country, they would have been disposed of humanely. Not in Siliguri. Men were at work. Parts were being soldered, bolts were being bolted. This wasn't repair, it was resurrection. And behold, here was a lorry having a final lick of paint, and looking spick and span and ready for another 500,000 miles. Lazarus had indeed risen.

After Siliguri, the road ran between dense woodlands, much of it like dear old Sherwood Forest before they built places like Leicester over it. Then we reached a point where, in Britain, there would have been a sign saying, 'hairpin-bends for the next three hours, no overtaking'. Here, there was no sign and plenty of overtaking. Namgil would put his hand on the horn and drive into the oncoming lane, while I did all I could by way of invocation to whatever deity might happen to be listening, to ensure that anything coming round the bend the other way wasn't deaf.

We climbed along the side of the Teesta river. Hanging plants and creepers of various tropical varieties unknown to me covered the rock face out of which the road had been blasted. Beneath us, through treetops growing up from below, was the river, over which hung an inscrutable oriental mist. A platoon of monkeys was sitting on a wall, their heads in their hands, inescapably reminiscent of 10 green bottles. They stared at us disapprovingly as we drove by. We passed the bridge which, had we taken it, would have led to the Kingdom of Bhutan and by and by, or rather round and round and up and up, we came to Kalimpong, 4,000 feet above sea level, in the foothills of the Himalayas.

I liked it immediately. It was of manageable size, the air was clean, and a fresh breeze was blowing. I checked in, had a rapid shower and dashed out again to see what I could before dark. I walked up the road above the hotel. Dogs were barking down below but this wasn't the usual hunting cry of the Indian canine, the 'come down here sonny, and let us tear you to shreds' howl. This was a more friendly, 'don't worry we've eaten this week, we're feeling playful' howl. The river miles below looked like a brown snake lying doggo. Clouds surrounded the mountain tops and it started to rain. I bought a 5 rupee comb from a comb salesman who just happened to be passing, and headed back.

Next morning, this being the Himalayas, I decided that fresh air and exercise were in order. I would walk to Delo Lake, selected for no very good reason other than it was attractively featured on a postcard in the hotel lobby. I acquired a map which looked idiot proof, even for me, laced up my walking boots, and set off.

'Main Road' led me down into a busy and well-heeled high street. Modern six and eight-seater vans were everywhere to be seen, a few of the high street shops had windows and a vegetarian snacketeria was promoting its microwave popcorn. The trappings of modernity had come to Kalimpong. Various electronic goods were on offer including a 42" TV, advertised as the 'largest in the world.' I presumed (on the basis of no evidence whatsoever), that the residents of Kalimpong were able to afford 42" TVs because of all the money poured into the local economy by summer escapees from the overpopulated ovens of India, more popularly known as Kolkata, or Delhi.

The high street was crawling[BB] with mid-morning activity. I zigzagged around my fellow crawlers, happy to be part of the throng. From time to time, I stopped to check out banana

---

BB   Relatively speaking; we're not talking Kolkata here. More like St Andrews at rush hour – if St Andrews had a rush hour, that is.

prices, contemplate the medical implications of a snackette or just watch the world go by.

A Ghorka lady, wearing pink pyjamas, was hanging out her washing. She was one floor up, on a ledge about a yard wide that ran along the outside of the building. There was no rail. The slightest stumble and she would have pitched down into the street below. If it had been me, I'd have been backed up against the wall so tightly that not so much as a cigarette paper could have been inserted. As for conversation, I doubt I'd be saying much beyond four imploring words: 'Call the Fire Brigade.'

I wasn't up there, however, thank goodness. She was, and she couldn't have cared less. She hung out her towels on the washing line suspended over the street, with as little concern as if she was leaning over the garden fence picking apples. I was staring at this performance with immense admiration, as you may imagine. I probably had my mouth open. And then, ah me, she turned her head in my direction. We exchanged glances. No, we held glances, and she flashed me a beaming smile which quite lit up my morning.

After Main Road, the street that I believed would take me to the lake turned sharply uphill, as streets are inclined to do in the Himalayas. In these parts, you either go up or you go down; there's not much in between.

In front of me was a man who was about five feet tall, carrying a three-foot sack filled to bursting with something heavy, like rice. He was advancing steadily up the mountain. If I had been flat on my back, and someone had lowered that sack onto my chest, I might have been able to bench press it for about ten seconds. In a matter of moments, the man had disappeared over the brow of the hill and out of sight.

I had to sit down. Witnessing something so far beyond me, even had I subjected myself to a lifetime of rigorous training, had taken the sap right out of my legs. Even more depressing was the sight of a three-year-old boy, proud father in tow, skipping past my bench. He was of the age when any European child would have held his hands in the air and said, 'carry me, daddy.' Not this lad. Encouraged by chirruping noises from father, he marched resolutely upwards, and all I can say is that folks round here are definitely made of sterner stuff. Sherpa Tenzing came from these parts[89] and I'm not surprised. With an upbringing like this, it was a wonder that, when he and Hilary reached the top of Everest, he didn't say, 'Hey, Ed, now what?' Perhaps he did.

Higher up, just short of the point at which you regret not bringing oxygen, was a large boarding school set in 600 acres of ground. It was founded a hundred years ago by a Scot called Dr Graham. The Lonely Planet Guide says the school was originally for children of tea garden workers but, according to one of the teachers, it was for Anglo-Indian orphans marooned by the racial prejudice (of both sides)[BC]. Of the 1200 kids, about half, he said, were now Anglo-Indians. Most of these were

BC   Anglo-Indian is the term given to those of mixed Indian and (through the paternal line) British ancestry. The Anglo-Indians have had a tough time of it both before and after Independence, caught as they were between two caste-conscious societies, and not much appreciated by either. They tended to take jobs in the public utilities (the railways, the postal service etc) and live as more or less separate communities. As the Anglo-Indian narrator of *Bhowani Junction,* reflecting both his yearning and his prejudice, puts it; *'There are really three separate Bhowanis – the Railway Lines* [where the Anglo-Indians live]*, the cantonments where the English live, and the city where God knows how many thousand Indians are packed in like sardines.'* [John Masters, *Bhowani Junction*, (Michael Joseph, 1954)].

Christian, though being a Christian wasn't a requirement. He himself was a Hindu.

The classrooms were of brick and painted yellow and green. The kids were in uniform. Blue sweater, white shirt, tie and grey flannels for the boys, and red sweaters and skirts for the girls. It could have been any school in Britain, except that the roof didn't look as if it leaked, shirts were tucked in, ties were neatly knotted and the whole establishment was perched almost literally on the roof of the world.

At this point, I thought I should ask someone if it was OK to snoop. I did. It was. I followed the noise of a small riot coming from one of the classrooms, and went in. 'Good Morning,' I said. Thirty adolescent schoolchildren stood to attention, adjusting their ties as they straightened. 'Good morning, Sir,' they replied in unison. The reflex had kicked in. After that, thought processes began to take over. 'Who is this fellow? School governor? Dressed like that? Can't be. Some twat? Probably.' I came clean. 'Just passing by', I announced, 'please take no notice.'

They needed no second invitation, although a few of the more cynical members came over to make absolutely sure that I was not the voice of authority, cunningly disguised. Then most of them drifted away to pick up where they'd left off. They were in the middle of a free period and went back to doing what kids the world over do in free periods: nothing remotely constructive.

I was glad to see that classrooms hadn't changed much since my day. They still had blackboard and chalk, still had rows of improbably narrow wooden chairs, and still had desks evocatively inscribed with 'Gulli ♡ Veena' and 'Chalky sucks.'

The kids asked me where I was from, and we talked about Scotland. They knew Scotland. The place had been founded by a Scot. There was a Strachan Cottage and boarding houses called Laidlaw and Grant. The boys then introduced me to the best basketball player in the school, the best scholar and, most precious talent of all, the best book-spinner. Well, the second-best anyway. The best was away. The ability to spin their hard laminated workbooks on their index finger was what really counted, and No 2 showed me how. He was good. He could spin it in front, behind or with his finger coming up from between his legs. No. 1, they told me, could spin it on his nose.

I carried on up the mountain towards my lake, struck by an appalling thought. Suppose cross-country running was compulsory. I bet it was. Can you imagine any old-fashioned headmaster foregoing the pleasure? 'Now, we've a real treat for you this morning, boys: cross country. Top of Kanchenjunga and back. Yes, you too Bunter. Go.'

When I finally made it to the summit, I found, not a lake, but a reservoir. This was a disappointment. I'd slogged all this way up in the hope of seeing a glorious stretch of natural water with, I don't know, rare high-altitude ducks perhaps – not something hacked out by man. Mind you, the views were ruggedly spectacular: mountain ridges and sharp-edged escarpments stretching into the far distance looking, for all the world, like monster molars in need of dentistry.

I sat down on a step, opened my haversack and laid out my lunch: three bananas and five squares of Scottish tablet. This, for those who are unfamiliar with tablet, is the Caledonian equivalent of hard tack or pemmican. It is made of sugar, bound together by butter and condensed milk. Broadly speaking, these ingredients, plus chips and grease, make up the staple diet of my adopted countrymen, and I have no complaints. Tablet is just the thing when travelling in India. It develops a hard crust, which makes it resistant to being trodden on, is absolutely delicious after a long climb, and full of energy for the return journey. I was only sorry I hadn't packed a couple more pieces.

A horse was grazing a few yards away, and we munched happily together, man and horse, tablet and grass. You don't see many horses in India, or I haven't, apart for that one on its way to a wedding in Agra, where the groom was decked out like Roy Rogers after he had fallen into a tub of hundreds and thousands. But, for some unfathomable reason, here was a horse, several thousand feet up in the air.

After lunch, and a circuit of the reservoir, past a memorial for those who had sacrificed their lives in building it, I headed back down. It was the sort of steep descent that had me wishing I'd cut my toenails. I was acutely conscious that the front of my boot was doing its best to drive my nails back into my toes. I thought of paying a visit to the matron at the Dr Graham school to see what remedies she might have up her sleeve but, if I knew school matrons, she'd just give me dhobi itch powder. Unless I had a boil, in which case a crooked smile would play across her thin lips, the ash on her half-smoked fag would quiver and she'd say, 'Wait here, boy, while I fetch my instruments.' I decided to live with the pain.

My knees felt as if I had handed over their control to John Cleese and, what with trying to coordinate the clenching of my toes with the attempt to flex in an orderly fashion the all too flexible rubber that my legs had now become, I was in more of a lather coming down than I had been going up. A church, MacFarlane Church according to my map, the Church of North India as it said on the gate, hove into view and I swung down the hill and up into its becalming embrace with gratitude.

It looked like any village church in the Home Counties. It had imitation early English arches running along the front. It even had a spire. It couldn't have been more un-Indian if it had tried, which, I hate to say, was the intention. It was England recreated in India, where the men formed clubs to which Indians were not invited, the women gardened and the vicar came to tea while, back home, William Wilberforce, the doughty anti-slavery campaigner, stood up in the House of Commons in 1813 and told MPs that it was more important to send Christian missionaries[BD] to India than to abolish the transatlantic slave trade.[90] (Yes, I know, words fail me too.)

I sat on a pew for a while to recover control of my limbs. Boys from the school were walking up and down the aisle with cloths under their feet. 'Church cleaning' was probably the option you went for if you didn't like cricket. At least you didn't have to fetch the ball after it had been hit over the boundary, bounced once on the tarmac and was heading off accelerando down to Kalimpong, with you in hot pursuit.

After a while I walked back to town, passing a notice announcing, 'Anti-Rabies Vaccination Day.' 'Rabies', it heralded 'is increasing in this area. Bring a pet. If you bring

---

BD The East India Company distrusted missionaries from the start but, when the Company's charter came up for renewal in 1813, the Evangelicals in Parliament insisted they be allowed in. (David Gilmour, *The British in India*, [Penguin 2018], pp 42-43, 223). Fear of conversion was seen as one contributory factor in the Indian Uprising of 1857, and thereafter missionaries were kept on a tight leash.

a stray, the vaccination will be free.' I went back to my hotel, watchfully, in case I crossed paths with anything on four legs which looked frothy.

My original plan had been to go from Kalimpong to Gangtok in Sikkim, then to Darjeeling and then to Lucknow by train. Lucknow was the focus in 1857 of the Indian Uprising (aka the Indian Mutiny or the First War of Independence) and I wanted to see it. However, Lucknow was now a vast industrial city and, more to the point, would at this time of year be clocking up temperatures in the high 40s. There are limits even to my masochism and I decided to stay up in the hill country for a while longer. I liked it up here. I rang Deepak – there he was working late in the office – and asked if he could suggest somewhere else in Sikkim. He'd get on to it.

18. GANGTOK

… Into Sikkim

Deepak's suggestion was a square: north from Kalimpong to Gangtok, the capital of Sikkim, west to Pemayangtse (meaning Lotus Flower), south to Darjeeling and then back to Bagdogra airport. It would mean extending my visa, but Deepak said I could do that in Gangtok. It seemed like a good plan, notwithstanding the fact that, according to my map, there were no roads across to Pemayangtse. It looked like mountain. However, any town called Lotus Flower was fine by me. More to the point, it was fine by Namgil and he was doing the driving.

We drove back down to the Teesta and crossed the bridge that led to Sikkim. The Kingdom of Bhutan lay to the east, Nepal to the west, and Tibet to the north. A rasher of excitement frizzled along my scalp. This was where the beaten track ended. For those of you familiar with *Cluedo* (aka *Clue*), it felt like being the Reverend Green and making it to the Library. You'd dream about doing it, but before you could squeeze down that little passage by the Billiard Room, somebody always wanted to interrogate you with the Candlestick in somewhere unutterably dull like the Lounge. Yet here I was among these magical, impenetrable places. Bhutan? It was like Kafiristan, Novaya Zemlya or the land of *The King and I.* Sikkim was the same; hidden, inaccessible, way off-piste … and, yet, here I was. Exciting, or what?

The first I saw of Sikkim were the guards manning the border post. That was good. I hadn't come this far just to be waved through. A hooked military finger encouraged me to get out of the car, and then it straightened sufficiently to point me in the direction of the Foreign Registration office. The office was empty. Not a soul was about.

I sat on a window ledge and sunbathed. A river was running fast some fifty yards away and a lone pig was mooching across the sands that led to the water's edge. As to whether it was a Sikkimese, Bhutanese or Gurkha porker, my sense of direction wasn't up to deciding. What it looked like was a Vietnamese pot-bellied pig but, faced with the range of porcine possibilities that this opened up, I decided it was too pleasant a morning to worry myself unduly.

When, eventually, officialdom arrived, my passport was inspected and the official stamp applied. I was free to begin the winding climb towards Gangtok (5,500ft). Namgil wasn't a great one for conversation. He just drove, and when we came to a town, he would glance across at me and cough its name, Rangpo, Singtam, Ranipool. Between these highlights, I read the uplifting phrases that had been etched onto yellow signs and attached to the side of the road, usually on a hairpin bend. *'Slow drive long life,'* said one. *'Fast drive, last drive,'* said another. *'Life is short, don't make it shorter.'* *'Better be late than "The Late".'* There was no end to them, presumably dreamt up by a government scriptwriter and plastered onto 's' bends at government expense.

The scriptwriter must have thought that something edifying, such as *'Don't fly but ply'*, would be just the thing to make a driver keep his mind on the road ahead. Personally, I would be concentrating so hard on what this could possibly mean that I'd drive straight into the rock face. *'Don't fly but ply'*. Am I missing something? Or what about the inscrutable, *'Hill is remembered here.'* Was this Graham Hill, the racing driver? His son, Damon, perhaps, also a racing driver? Could it be Boot Hill where all those who drive too fast (like the Hills) end up? It was confusing, you must admit, and not perhaps first choice for the kind of thing you'd want to display on a narrow winding road with rock on one side and a sheer drop on the other. Namgil, fortunately, remained unperturbed.

The first thing I did on arrival in Gangtok was to try and extend my visa. The hotel summoned a young lad to show me the way and told me that the office that handled such things was close by. What they didn't add was 'as the crow flies.' It was on a parallel street higher up the side of the mountain, which meant ascending a gradient not dissimilar to the Leaning Tower of Pisa, up narrow concrete and sandbag steps that wound between the sides of tall houses. This was an ascent through grime. If you think of narrow alleys back home used late at night by those returning from the pub, you'll get the picture. Only, with those alleys you don't go down on all fours which, given that I was obliged to haul myself up like Spiderman climbing a wall, was more or less what I had to do here.

When I finally reached the summit, the offices hadn't opened and weren't scheduled to do so for another couple of hours. Sighing heavily, I retraced my steps, hung around, attached crampons, ascended once more, pushed open the door and was in. 'Passport', the man said, not unreasonably. I shoved a confident hand into my right pocket, followed by a more tentative one into my left, and then a discreet two fingers down the front of my trousers where my purse belt was hidden. Nothing. I must have taken it out in my room. Why do I do this? Could it be some chemical imbalance caused by too many bananas?

I faced south once more and, propelled involuntarily by the considerable forces of gravity at my back, galloped again down the now familiar steps, receiving a friendly wave as I flashed past from one of the occupants of the houses overlooking the alley, who, by this time, had come to regard me as an old friend. I went up to my room and there was my passport, after a lifetime of stringent security, lying on the bed, wide open and unabashed, positively begging for its own abduction. I grabbed it like a cross father, crawled back up, received my extended visa and returned to the hotel, knackered.

You may wonder (I did) why a visa is necessary. Sikkim is, after all, part of India. The big, underlying reason is China. Since it invaded Tibet in 1950, China is quite literally up the road. There was also a little spat in 1962 when China moved into the Himalayan region of Aksai Chin and for a month there was full scale war. China is lurking. Mind you, it has always been lurking. From the early days of the East India Company in Calcutta, Directors salivated about the prospect of a back door trade route through the Himalayan Kingdoms (Nepal, Bhutan or Sikkim) to Tibet, and on to China.[91] It never came to anything but it encouraged the Company to nose around – and once the Company started sniffing, it usually wasn't too long before annexation followed[BE].

Gangtok, I noticed, boasted an Institute of Tibetology, and I went along to see it. Actually, not 'an Institute', but the 'Namgyal Research Institute'. I also discovered that the first Chogyal (king) of Sikkim was called Namgyal. So was the last, and so were most of them in between. Namgyal was an important name in these parts clearly, and induced in me a mental image of the pleasant face of my driver, Namgil. It set me thinking; Namgil … Namgyal, not much difference there when spoken in the native dialect. Could I have misheard? Was I, unbeknownst, being transported by royalty? I vowed to observe him more closely for tell-tale signs, such as a cocked little finger when steering around hairpins. On the other hand, if the Namgyals had been sowing their wild oats for centuries, after several hundred years perhaps everybody was a Namgyal – like being Jones from Merthyr Tydfil. Namgil (I will continue to call him by the name he prefers when travelling incognito) had said he was a Gurkha, a Nepali, but the first Namgyal had come from Tibet. Why hadn't he said he was Tibetan? Was this more chaff to throw me off the scent? From now on, vigilance would be the watchword.

One of the things I like about Buddhist places, and

BE As it happens, the British never did completely annex the Himalayan kingdoms. They weren't short of opportunity, particularly after the Gurkha Wars of 1814-16 (Clump Four), but they were sensibly wary of opening up hundreds of miles of frontier with Tibet, and its imperial master, China. (Never a good idea to butt up against a superpower if you want to avoid war by accident.) Sikkim was left as a nominally independent buffer state (in which the British interfered incessantly) and only became part of India after a referendum in 1975.

Namgil's Institute of Tibetology was no exception, is that everything is rooted in the ground. The grand vaulted ceilings of Christendom, stretching upwards to heaven above, don't feature. Everything here was homely. Low ceilings, wooden beams decorated with flowers and snakes, Buddha plonked foursquare on the ground. There were also, and I don't know whether you'd call this homely exactly, three trumpets made out of human thighbones. This was not something you see very often. They were used, and I quote, as 'ritual implements in certain Tantric practices of exorcism to remind one of death and impermanence.' I suppose they did, but what I wanted to know was how good were they for blasting out 'When the Saints'?

The Institute was also the proud possessor of what were described as the relics of an Ashokan monk. I was sure, after seeing the trumpets, that these would be parts of his anatomy, but they turned out to be scrolls. I was impressed. Ashoka was 3rd century BCE so they hadn't done badly in keeping impermanence at bay.

I spent the rest of the afternoon mooching around the town. It was the most up-market place I'd yet come across. There were no beggars and no traders imploring you to enter their emporium, 'just for looking.' The Michael Tobert indicator of prosperity (the percentage of shops with windows) was showing a reading around 1%, which wasn't bad. Inside these establishments, busy vendors were selling western consumer goods such as aloe vera, Oil of Ulay and cornflakes. They were even selling Kit Kat and Dairy Milk, which, of course, I bought. The tablet was running low.

There were neat clothes shops and cafés, and sweet shops

selling the usual assorted mixture of brown and white sugary things, except that these looked edible. Positively tempting in fact. The final proof that Gangtok was doing very nicely thankyou was a store selling Monopoly, Chinese Chequers and other such things that I believe come into the category of 'discretionary spending'. You only buy these little luxuries when you have clothes on your back, a roof over your head and a full stomach.

Gangtok was not unlike Kalimpong, only bigger, a little higher up the mountain and it had houses that were enormous – six stories high, some of them. It may be that if you live next to mountains that touch the sky – and only Everest and K2 come higher than Kanchenjunga, (which I couldn't see for the mist, but I was reliably informed was there) – you're driven to keep up with the Kanchenjungas and add an extra three stories to your house. They were quite surprisingly altitudinous.

The mist that had been quietly settled overhead now turned to thunder, the thunder to torrential rain and the rain to hail the size of blueberries. These cannoned off the road, off the roofs and off me. I ducked under the awning of the Hakhotan trading company, which sold rice and dals, pure spices, jam and jelly, and did my best to look as if I might be about to make a purchase. This was not an easy thing to do when faced with a sack of rice that was large enough to keep a family of twenty in pilau for a whole winter. What do you say? 'Good looking sack of rice that. Might I have 150 grains please?'

There was a bookshop over the road and I contemplated making a break for it, but a torrent was flowing so fast between me and it that I couldn't entirely rule out the possibility of being concussed by a hailstone and swept down to the Teesta miles below. I was debating what to do when I looked down and saw there was a frog the size of my boot standing right next to me. He obviously didn't like hailstones either. We remained there for a while like a couple of pedestrians waiting for the lights to change, when the hailstorm abated slightly. Froggie decided this was his moment, and stepped into the road – not a course of action I would have recommended had I been asked. Neither of us would have liked it if I had to flick pieces of squashed frog's legs from my shirt after they had been sprayed from the wheels of a passing car. But as far as I could see either he had made it, or was having the time of his life white-water rafting down to Rangpo.

The rain had set in and it was cold. I scurried back to the hotel and had hardly reached my room when there was a knock at the door. A waiter, politely enquiring as to what I wanted to eat, handed me a menu. Curious, I thought, but I suppose it helps the kitchen if they know in advance. I chose something Chinese. Half an hour later, the phone rang to tell me my food was ready.

'But it's 4.30 in the afternoon,' I exclaimed.

'You no want now'?

Of course, I don't want it now, thinks I, although I replied with a restrained, 'No thank you.'

'What time you want?'

'Oh,' I said, '7.30.'

'OK,' he said and hung up.

My room had a walkway outside the window. While I sat and looked out, people passed by and looked in. It didn't take long before I felt I could do with a bit of privacy, so I drew the curtains shut, switched on the lights and had a shower; a hot shower, a shower in which a man could wallow. I wallowed, and when I came out noticed a sign announcing that 'water in hill stations in short supply. Please use sparingly.' Oops.

At 7.30, I went down to the dining room and at 7.31, the waiter came up and said, 'your food is ready. I serve now?' My God, I thought, it's been sitting there since 4.30 going nicely tepid so that it can act as the perfect host for any bug that didn't have a home to go to.

'Has this been sitting here since 4.30?' I enquired matter-of-factly.

The waiter smiled inscrutably. I hoped this meant that he had not understood. I rephrased the question.

'This new food?'

'New food, new food,' he said and brought it. I have to say it looked delicious and not really very fizzy on the top. What can I tell you; I ate it.

19. PEMAYANGTSE

… Gateway to Kanchenjunga

Next day, we took the same road back down the valley. The same bevy of women, who had been breaking rocks on a corner of road as we drove up, were still hard at it on the way down. The male supervisor, whose duties appeared to be observational only, was similarly in repose on both occasions. The road took us into Singtam which, now I came to notice, was a prosperous market town, clean as a new pin (well fairly new), where everyone seemed to drive a modern-looking jeep.

Once through Singtam, the road was dappled by sunlight shining through trees up to 30 or 40 feet high. What species of trees I couldn't tell you, but they were green and bushy and looked wonderful[BF]. When we reached the valley floor,

[BF]   Once again, I must apologize for my ignorance of matters arboreal. You, the reader, deserve better – a name at least – but, as a plea in mitigation, allow me to quote from a book now in my possession: *Trees of India* by Menon and Bagla. 'The Indian subcontinent has … 15,000 known species of flowering plants alone,

the mountains towered above us and, as we climbed, valley life disappeared into small specks below. Areas of the hillside had been stepped like the vineyards of France and plants were growing on horizontal slices sometimes no more than a foot wide. I pointed at a particularly prevalent variety and asked Namgil what it was. He said 'motoi', and who am I to argue, but it looked like sweetcorn to me. A couple of boys were tending goats. A man was weeding the roadside though why, since there was hardly another car about, I couldn't imagine. Still, it made me appreciate how truly weed-free the road was – which is the sort of thing that's easy to overlook.

With the Teesta miles below us and snow-capped mountains in the distance, we stopped shortly afterwards for reflection. Well, for relief actually, but reflection occurred concurrently. This journey, I reflected, could go on forever, and it's not often I think that about four and a half hours of continuous hairpins. We passed through a place called Legship, which I presume means more in Nepali than it does in English, and pretty soon we were in Pemayangtse, at which point I decided I was very pleased to get out of the car after all.

I spent what was left of the afternoon climbing to the Sangacholing monastery, founded 1697, the second oldest in Sikkim and built before the days of British meddling. It was above Pelling and at the top of the mountain. Pelling, I discovered, is what the village of Pemayangtse calls itself, although the leaflet handed out by the Gangtok Tourist Information Office makes no mention of Pelling. However, I shall follow the lead of the locals. Pelling it will be. It has less of a ring to

of which around 2,500 are trees.' That's a lot of trees to get a handle on.

it, but is easier to spell.

Not wishing to be overtaken by any one-legged octogenarians, I hoofed up the mountain toute-suite. I needn't have bothered. I had the mountain to myself. A notice outside the monastery proclaimed that 'Killing, Drinking, Smoking and Use of Intoxicating' were prohibited. Quite right too. I could happily dispense with death and intoxicating for a few hours.

A boy of about 14, wearing the deep red tunic I associate with Buddhism, opened the large entrance door and let me look around. I find Buddhist temples extremely restful. There is something about the way the Buddha sits that calms the frayed edges. The walls were covered in old murals and, for the best part of an hour, I was entertained by pictures of men with serpent heads, dragon men and bull men, men with rat heads and tiger heads, and other weird and wonderful things that lurk in the semi-conscious. As to their religious significance, I hadn't a clue.

After he had locked the door behind me, the gatekeeper of the second oldest monastery in Sikkim resumed his game of cricket. His fellow players were three local kids whose combined age can't have been much above 15. They did the bowling. I went to look at the view. I might have been only some 7,500 feet up but it felt like the top of the world. Below me were valleys into which you could have dropped the entire Cairngorms without anyone noticing, (apart from the inhabitants of Ballater and Braemar that is, and indeed the Monarch should they have been at Balmoral at the time of the insertion). Places like Aspen may be higher, but they don't feel it – perhaps because you can't look down so far, and perhaps because you don't have Kanchenjunga, the highest mountain in India, the third highest in the world, towering above. I could see it now for the first time. Its glorious twin peaks were above the clouds, covered in snow. At 28,000 feet, the summit of Kanchenjunga is not far below the cruising altitude of a 747. I was, for a fleeting moment, in awe.

I went back to watch the cricket, and thought how much I'd like to roll back the years and turn my arm over once again. No objections were raised. I'd have preferred to bat, but, uncharacteristically, didn't think that would be altogether fair. What pleasure would there be in slogging the bowling of a six-year-old to kingdom come? (Quite a bit actually). My first ball, a full toss, was clouted out of the ground. One of the boys went after it and handed it back, rather reluctantly I thought. The second ball followed suit, at which point I decided to make a run for it before the fielders turned nasty.

I was the only one staying at my hotel. I discovered this when they switched the lights on when I came down to the dining room for supper, and switched them off when I left, locking up behind me. It's little clues like that that give these things away. The waiter, who was also the cook and hall porter as far as I could tell, brought me soup, vegetable curry, boiled rice and a japati, which was a good effort under the circumstances. After supper, I went out. It was pitch black. I couldn't see a foot in front of my face. No-one was about or, if they were, they were not advertising themselves. I reviewed my options and, since I couldn't think of any, went to bed.

Next morning, I put on my walking boots and set out. I nosed around Pelling for about two minutes and swiftly discovered that it consisted of a couple of hotels, a few unprepossessing boarding houses, two shops, and that was about it. So I set off for Pemayangtse monastery. The road dropped downhill like a plumb-line, taking me with it. It would have dragged me to who knows what uncharted depths, had not a small providential voice encouraged me to arrest my descent by clinging on to a passer-by and asking him whether, by any remote chance, I was heading in the right direction. He responded by pointing cheerfully at the sky above. From this, I deduced that my present course had been ill-advised, and that I would have to retrace my steps. On such occasions, all too plentiful as they are, I try my best to be stoical.

When I'd returned to level ground and satisfied myself that I was now on the right track, I set off once more for the monastery. It was ideal walking weather. We were in cloud. It was cool. I put my reverses behind me and, before long, reached a fork in the road. No-one was around to ask, and I didn't want to be caught out twice. I debated whether I should flag down a car for instructions. The first one that approached was travelling too fast to be intercepted in safety. The second one wasn't. As it came closer, it started to look familiar. It was a white Mahindra Commander with West Bengal plates and a roof rack on top.

'That's my jeep,' I muttered to myself, and it was. I waved it down. Namgil was at the wheel with half-a-dozen stowaways in the back.

'Hello', I said, perusing the illicit cargo, 'doing a spot of moonlighting?' He nodded. When Namgil doesn't understand, he nods – rather like royalty the world over in fact.

'Which road Pemayangtse Monastery?' I asked. He told me. I smiled at the passengers and they smiled back. Namgil drove off, with a cheery wave, and a lack of concern that only royalty can muster.

The road leading up to the monastery was lined by a hundred yards of flags. Not chunky flags like the union jack but long oblong flags perhaps 10 inches by 1 inch, attached to a bamboo pole, and forever rippled by the wind. If you've seen any Japanese films, you will know what I mean. You see them all over Sikkim and they are how all flags should be. Most flags just flap. These flutter like leaves in a breeze. In a curious way it's rather spiritual.

From my limited experience of Buddhist monasteries, they all seem to have three floors. I started on the top, where there was an astonishingly intricate wooden structure depicting a heavenly palace. It was more lavish than a Carmen Miranda hat[BG]. It was constructed as a temple with six levels that I could count (although I have a feeling seven is more likely), and each level had further levels within it. Populating the levels, crowding them out in fact, were parrot people, dancing ladies, the Buddha in various forms, fornication, musicians, warriors, intricate little staircases, you name it. Apparently, it took one man five years to build it, which I'd have said was quick. I found the whole thing completely entrancing, which is all I'll say. If I were to wax too lyrical, my mother-in-law would read this and her enduring suspicions would be confirmed. 'Heaven save us', she'd splutter, snatching a despairing swig from her tumbler of neat gin, 'he's going to become a Buddhist.'

I sat on the steps outside for a while, taking the air and watching the monastery kids milling around below me. After a while their curiosity got the better of them and they came over and surrounded me. They were engaging but, to speak frankly,

BG   Carmen Miranda was the singer who wore a basket of fruit on her head.

grubby, the kind of boys my mother would have had stripped and in a hot tub before you could say 'carbolic'. Monastery kids is what they were. They lived in the monastic boarding house and wore the house colours, the burgundy tunic, or *shentab* as they told me. They were taught by the monks and had both a monastery name and a family name. I made this discovery because they wanted me to write down who they were – which I did. When I had faithfully transcribed the names of three brothers, as Karma Tashi, Karma Dseden and Sherab Dorshi, I looked at Sherab as if to say 'uh, how come you're not called Karma like your brothers?' Sherab was his monastery name, he explained. I assumed that they would all eventually become monks and I was going to get round to that after we had finished discussing their twin loves, cricket and karate, except that the lunch gong sounded, and they were gone.

The second capital of the kingdom of Sikkim before it moved to Gangtok in 1814 was Rabdentse, and its ruins were not far from Pemayangtse. In fact, I could see them from the monastery. I asked about the route and set off. My first attempt terminated in a shrub jungle, but I had high hopes of the second. I took the road to Geyzing, and then branched off along a footpath. A signpost pointed to the ruins. This had to be right but, somehow, I found myself approaching a farm-house where a girl was cutting vegetables. She stood her ground when she saw me – which I thought was greatly to her credit – and kindly pointed out a route that would have me back on track. It would take me through the family chicken yard and along a path. I followed her instructions precisely and came to a clearing from where I could once again see the ruins, except that now there was a deep valley and forested hill between me

241

and them. I couldn't believe she expected me to hack my way through all that, so I retraced my steps.

At some point, the inner workings of my internal compass must have overheated, because I found myself ducking through the undergrowth of a dense forest, towards an open area which had to be the Geyzing road. It wasn't. It was a clearing where a farmer and his wife were planting motoi. I don't suppose they'd had many European visitors, at least not making an entrance from this side of their estate, and they seemed a little surprised.

'Good afternoon', I said, 'Pelling'?

It seemed the safest bet. Was I going to trust myself to pronounce Rabdentse, or Pemayangste for that matter? Heaven only knows where they'd send me if they misunderstood. I might never be seen again. The man couldn't have been kinder. He showed me to a path that wound round his field, through his farmhouse, where I had a skirmish with his dog, and towards the Pelling Road. I reached it at a canter, the mongrel yapping at my heels. The Rabdentse ruins would have to wait, and if anyone asked if I'd seen them, I'd say yes. Well, I had. Twice.

By the time I'd made it back to the hotel, it had turned cold, and by the time darkness fell, it was freezing. I put on all the layers I had with me – shirt, sweater and my state-of-the-art gore-tex rain jacket – and attempted to read a book. In vain. The lamp gave out less light than an underfed glow worm, besides which I could feel my facial hair turning to ice. The book hasn't been written that can compete with that.

I would like to tell you how I passed the remainder of the evening, but I have no idea. Perhaps I slumped into the sort of coma familiar to those who trespass unprepared into the higher altitudes. Perhaps, on the other hand, not. Who can say? In any event, I woke next morning to shafts of sunlight stabbing through the curtains. I peered out squinty-eyed, and there was a day that was as clear as a bell, save for a couple of puffy white smudges adrift in an ocean of blue. And there was Kanchenjunga unveiled and immediate, parading herself in all her glory. And that folks is why you come to Pemayangtse. And to see the Rabdentse ruins.

20. DARJEELING

... more than just tea

You know what the Sikkimese and rich ladies in Range Rovers have in common? When you let them pass on a narrow lane, they both stick their noses in the air and drive past as if you don't exist. I thought this only happened in Cornwall, but no, it happens in Sikkim. Namgil was as bad as the rest of them. I wondered, for a while, if there was some secret sign language I was missing which might indicate acknowledgement – a Masonic raising of the eyebrow, a twitch of the left ear perhaps – but I'd been studying Namgil carefully over the last few days and hadn't detected a thing. In his case, I could forgive him. Centuries of royal breeding couldn't just be eradicated overnight.

We reached a town that wasn't on the map. This event coincided with a coughing noise coming from Namgil, which sounded like Jorethung. I assumed, perhaps wrongly, that these two occurrences – the arrival and the cough – were connected, and, this being so, Jorethung was most likely to be the town's name, rather than, say, a reference to the weather or simply a sound that Namgil made when he had a frog in his throat.

Jorethung, if such it was, summed up why this part of the world felt different. The streets were wide and shady, the vegetables for sale by the side of the road were laid out neatly, the jeeps were in good nick and, above all, there was a gap between one person and the next. It didn't look like the pavement outside Harrods on the first day of the sale or the final moments of an Auld Lang Syne embrace. It had a density appropriate for relaxed living. According to the Tourist Board, Sikkim as a whole has a population of 491,000 living in a total area of 7096 square kilometres, which works out, by my calculations, as 69 people per square kilometre. This, curiously, is almost exactly the same as in Scotland with 67, and considerably lower than those two hotbeds of overpopulation, England with 380 souls per square kilometre, and India with 315. The USA has an indecently sparse 29.

The roadside was once again littered with signs urging drivers to take care, but in this part of Sikkim they had a more philosophical leaning than the ones I'd seen earlier. It looked like a new man was on the job and I'd say he deserved a medal. I mean, how many punchy ways are there to say 'please drive carefully'? After such creative gems as, *'If married divorce speed'*, *'Drinking and driving can put a bad finish to the car'*, and *'Speed thrills but kills'*, he'd found himself (and who can blame him) reduced to, *'We love you less your speed,'* and *'Well done is better than well said'*; neither of which quite hit the mark. At this point, I think he realised that the bottom of the barrel had been scraped, and had moved on to dreaming up nourishing ideas for crash victims to mull over until such time as their next life came around. If the last thing you'd read before smashing into a rock face was, *'Universal responsibility is the only real source of happiness'*, you would at least have plenty to chew on during your travels through the ether. The same would apply to the simple, but thought-provoking, *'Bridges cross natural barriers'*, *'Let your policy be quality'*, and *'Work is worship.'* It was good stuff. Come for a drive and receive an education.

We drove down to the border and back into West Bengal, at which point I followed the advice of a helicopter pilot, who once told me that the prime requirement when flying is to look ahead for a field to come down in should an emergency occur. Let me say no more than that, on this leg of the journey, emergencies were occurring frequently. My interest in the countryside was entirely confined to whether it contained woodland dense enough to provide cover. Namgil pretended not to notice the low groaning noises coming from the passenger seat – which was majestically polite of him – but the downside was that he continued to hurl the Mahindra around the S bends as if all was well with the world. Which it wasn't.

The road up to Darjeeling climbed steeply enough to require first gear, the temperature gauge went to red and Namgil stopped to let the engine cool. I crawled out, green-faced. A large fish was being offered for sale by a man walking along the other side of the road and while, normally, I might have been keen to inspect it and engage the vendor in conversation, on this occasion I stared resolutely in the opposite direction. I tried to convince myself it was a river fish, since the nearest ocean was probably several thousand miles away, and ice was conspicuous by its absence. I did my best not to dwell on the impact a morsel of rotten piscean flesh would have on my intestines should I find myself eating it later that night. However, the things we dwell on and the things we don't are not always within our control.

When we reached Ghoom, unmistakeable evidence of the British Raj was pulling into the station. A toy train was chuffing along the narrow-gauge railway line (begun 1879), its little whistle blowing and everybody on board having fun. At least it looked fun, and I rather wished I was on it. It was the traditional method of reaching Darjeeling – well, traditional since the days the British settled in.

Originally, Dorje Ling as it was called, had been part of Sikkim. Then the Brits 'discovered' it, and decided it would be just the place for Bengal soldiers to recuperate after spending too long in the scorching heat of the plains.[92] So they added it to the empire in the 1830s, in the murky fashion that was not untypical of the way they acquired much of the rest of British India.

The Raja of Sikkim, one Tsugphud Namgyal, was 'persuaded' to hand it over, believing, not unreasonably, that land or money would come to him by way of compensation.[93] He was out of luck. The Governor General in Calcutta chose to look on it as a gift, in rather the same way that it would never occur to a mafia don, dining at an Italian restaurant, that his meal could be anything other than complimentary.

My Darjeeling hotel, when we finally reached it, was rather fancy. On another day I might have succumbed to the temptation of sitting quietly within easy reach of all its conveniences. Instead, I decided (courageously I thought) to take my chances with what ailed me, and explore. The hotel had an exit onto what was called the Mall. This was just the sort of road that the British would build, which is not surprising since they did build it. There were no shops. It was a promenade. It was for a stroll after tiffin, a place to take the airs after one overindulgence too many. And that broadly speaking was what the locals were doing. Strolling, chatting, not going anywhere in particular.

The Mall led to a large open square with men and women sitting on benches around the outside, watching a few hardy souls daring to walk across the middle. It reminded me, for an intimidating moment, of Mrs Varton's dancing class, a detention centre for 12-year-olds, whose parents regarded the foxtrot as one of life's essentials. No-one ventured onto the dance-floor there either, unless held by the ear and dragged. None of the boys anyway.

One side of the square looked out onto mountains and valleys that stretched into the mist and, on the other, were various buildings snatched indiscriminately from miscellaneous street corners of small town England: a modern concrete box with a satellite dish (selling Indian fast food), a building that might have housed a country railway station, and a rounded concrete structure, painted pink, with a bay window which, in England, would have been a seaside cafe, or one of those old cinemas that were once called 'the Roxy'. That was before they were converted into bingo halls. It was magnifique. Whether it was India, I wasn't so sure.

The railway station building housed the Oxford Book and Stationary Co, which was the best bookshop I'd seen in India thus far; the biggest anyway. It was the Blackwells of the East, and I bought three books. The Roxy next door was proudly displaying a sign announcing, 'No wine sale today. Dry day.'

But they were doing a special on Kalimpong lollipops and Gouda cheese. It also sold giant-size containers of Horlicks. In fact, it had devoted two whole shelves solely to this rather particular nutty milk drink.

Not everyone will be familiar with Horlicks these days, just as not everyone remembers Muffin the Mule and the Flowerpot Men, but I had fond memories of it. My mother used to make it for me when she felt I needed a good night's sleep, and it had become a warm and soothing part of the folklore of childhood. It wasn't that long ago that some stirring of my 'good parent' gene moved me to go out and buy a jar of the stuff for my own kids. I extolled its virtues. It was, I told them enthusiastically, an absolutely delicious bedtime drink which they'd love (OK, I oversold it a little), besides which – I added this as a clincher – its health benefits were unrivalled. The jar remains in our kitchen cupboard still, as a silent and reproachful memento of gentler days. But here there were two shelves of giant-sized Horlicks stocked, presumably, to meet the voracious, nay insatiable, demand of the good people of Darjeeling. When everything else has been expunged, Horlicks may be the most enduring legacy of the British Raj.

Back in the square, it suddenly dawned on me what was truly, deeply different about this place. There were no cars. This was India without hooting, without traffic jams and without bilious exhaust smoke. It was wonderful, and I took a deep breath to make sure I did the moment justice. An India with car-free cities would, truly, be something to contemplate.

I took the road that went down the hill and followed the whiff of baking bread coming from Glenary, the Master Baker. I couldn't remember baking smells in India before but it may be that, being lighter than exhaust, they lie on a higher level than olfactory senses can reach. Glenary's was a tea-room. Beyond the chocolate counter, and the pastries, was a dining area looking out to the Himalayas. Old ladies were clustered around wooden tables decked with red and white gingham tablecloths. They were drinking tea. This was Cheltenham at 7,000 feet.

Further down the road, the cars and the hooting and the fumes started again. It was like the last stop of the Vaporetta in Venice. There you are thinking that the Grand Canal and the Doges Palace are the real world and then the Vaporetta comes to the end of the line and you see cars. It's a shock, like someone slapping you across the face when you're dreaming. I wasn't ready to wake up, so I reversed course back up the hill, past the Hasty Tasty Indian fast-food joint, and popped into the kiosk next door to buy packets of tea. Not just any old stuff, but genuine Darjeeling tea from Darjeeling. This was ridiculously exciting.

The road to the right of the square led to a string of market stalls selling vegetables, meat festering in the sun, my old friend the fish (or one of his close relatives), and sundry street-side fry ups. My stomach wasn't up to this and I turned around and sauntered back along a low road which ran round to Observatory Point. It was a leafy, arboretum walk and I was sure the views would have been stunning had not the mist rolled up the hill and blanketed them out. It was still delightful, in that you could sense the vast Himalayas in front of you, but there was no disguising the fact that the visual impact was a notch or two lower. There is only so long you can gaze into an opaque wall of fog before you start talking to yourself. I went back to the hotel instead.

Two of the unmissable sights of the world are the Taj Mahal by moonlight and sunrise over Everest – as seen from Tiger Hill, Darjeeling. I hadn't timed the Taj very well, but I wasn't going to miss a glimpse of Everest waking up to a new day a hundred miles away. It meant a 4.30 start next morning. I'd just finished dinner in the company of some friendly Americans when the manager of the hotel sidled over with an expression that meant trouble.

'The Travel Agent has just rung. There is a strike at Siliguri starting at 6am. To reach Bagdogra airport, you have to leave tomorrow morning at 3am to be through Siliguri blockade before 6.' It was then 11pm.

'Come again' says I, who was still coming to terms with 4.30.

'You want wake-up call at 2.30?'

I took a moment to consider how to frame a reply. What I wanted was to sleep for a little longer than that, see the sun rise over Everest, come back for a leisurely breakfast and then head off to Bagdogra to catch a plane to Delhi. I enquired about alternatives.

'You could stay here and catch the next flight.'

'Sounds good, when's that?'

'Monday', he said smugly, 'if there is a seat.'

It was now Thursday. I decided I'd better kiss goodbye to Tiger Hill, and get up at 2.30.

Namgil was outside the hotel at 3am. Who told him, I don't know. It certainly wasn't me. He drove like the clappers down the mountain, past several dogs asleep in the road, past the toy train asleep in its sidings, and then swerved skilfully around a dog that had moved effortlessly from the sleeping stage to the dead stage. This is what happens when an animal stretches out on tarmac – which Indian dogs do routinely everywhere I've been – and takes a nap. It gets squashed. Why Indian canines haven't yet learnt this is a Darwinian mystery. In the end the laws of natural selection will throw up a species which knows that roads mean death. It's happened in Britain. How many times do you see a dog sleeping on a motorway? Never. Dogs with the it's-ok-to-sleep-on-motorways gene don't make it to the reproduction stage (which, if you're a dog, is quite a penalty). Dogs that know where not to nap may take longer to evolve in a gentle society like India, but they're bound to come.

We were through Siliguri while the blockading strikers were still in their beds, and at Bagdogra airport before dawn. The sun would now be about to rise over Everest and all those watching from Tiger Hill would soon be seeing the sight without which their lives would be incomplete. I, meanwhile, was outside a locked terminal building waiting for someone with a key to show up. Nor was it terrifically uplifting to reflect that my plane was due to leave at 2.15pm. Making the hugely optimistic assumption that it would be on time, there were ten hours to kill.

Namgil and I said our goodbyes. I thanked him for his careful driving. He graced me with a nod. I couldn't say for sure whether he was of royal lineage, but I do know this: should his countrymen one day require a supreme ruler, Namgil would do the job with aplomb. If asked, I would be honoured to write a reference.

By and by, more passengers arrived and the terminal building was opened. The old terminal building. The new one was still under construction. It was OK, but small and, as the sun started to do its work, hot and airless. It was mid-summer and we were no longer in the hills.

I would like to tell you that, among the ever-expanding band of strike-breakers, a party atmosphere gradually developed, a prison camp camaraderie, that united the various nations present into one joyful whole. Unfortunately not. After one hour, the strike-busters looked glum. After three, morose but trying hard to put a brave face on things. After five resigned. After eight, the war stories came out. One person had been eaten by leeches while trekking. Another had had his flight from Guwahati cancelled and had driven in a convoy through bandit country to get here. Later arrivals told us how they had talked their way past the Siliguri blockades. Then, a rather nervy lady, suffering more than most from the effects of the Black Hole of Bagdogra, treated us to the story of a Captain Anstruther, who was kept in a cage by his Chinese captors for five months in the 1840s. The cage measured 3'6" by 2'1". His legs were held in irons, and his hands were handcuffed to a ring round his neck. After offloading this, she relapsed into glum depression. The rest of us drifted back into our own thoughts.

As the hours slipped by, details of the strike began to emerge. There was a certain lack of consistency in the various stories doing the rounds, but all and sundry seemed to agree that it was the work of the CPM, the Communist Party (M for Marxist), which also happened to constitute the government of West Bengal. One of the comrades had been murdered, apparently, and everyone was out in sympathy.

Then again, maybe it wasn't murder. The only significant death I could find reported in the *Calcutta Telegraph*, was that of the Industry Minister, Bidyut Ganguly, but the paper appeared to regard this as probable suicide. The Minister – his 'lavish' expenditure on his daughter's wedding unexplained – had doused himself in kerosene, and set himself alight. What caught my eye, though, was the response of his government colleagues. It was a classic of content-free speech in its purest form, of which even our current Government would have been proud. The Deputy Chief Minister came up with the following, and I quote: 'I will not say anything beyond this, except that the death was ante-mortem in nature.' Those were the Minister's words and I would invite you to reflect for a moment on the concept of ante-mortem death. What could it be? Death, before death catches up with you? Picture the Grim Reaper with his scythe advancing towards you, and there you are running as fast as you can to stay ante-mortem. In the end you die of a heart attack, I suppose – the strain of remaining ante-mortem becoming just too much. A pretty nasty way to go but was it, I wondered, sufficient reason for all the man's fellow Marxists to come out on strike?

Being, by this time, confused, even by my own undemanding standards, I approached one of the soldiers manning the Terminal entrance for an explanation. All he would say was, 'This West Bengal. India politics gone crazy.' Then he shook his head from side to side like an alarmingly unstable pogo stick.

As the day wore on, I was finding it increasingly hard to ignore the uncomfortable fact that I didn't have a confirmed seat on the plane. I had a ticket, but this didn't necessarily equate with being allowed to board. At the back of my mind was the appalling thought that, even if the plane were to arrive and take off again, I might not be on it. 'We have spoken to the airline and ticket is OK' was how the local travel agency had described the situation when I had first bought the ticket.

'It's looking very promising' was how Ali, the local agency rep, had reported matters to me at ten o'clock that morning. By eleven, he was starting to avoid my glances, though still running around talking to the airline people. By twelve, there was neither hide nor hair of him to be seen. 'I'm sorry there isn't a seat' was starting to emerge as the front runner. However, if there's one thing that India has taught me, it's that it never pays to become unduly anxious. I put my fate in Ali's hands and did my best to sit quietly.

I had found myself a plastic chair a few yards from the airline desk. This had been chosen carefully on the grounds that it was next to a pillar, and thus would provide head support. This, in turn, had raised the possibility, and indeed the fact itself, of a quiet doze during the interminable hours of waiting. As a result, I had become rather attached to my chair and was quietly determined to hold onto it. Its downside, however, was about to be revealed.

A buzz swept around the terminal. Our plane had landed. This was followed, a while later, by an announcement. All those lucky passengers with confirmed seats took this as a signal to charge the check-in. The queue, such as it was, was in the shape of a python that has just swallowed a goat – a huge swelling at the front, with a thin straggly tail at the back. A large Indian gentleman, slowed down by three cardboard boxes which he was pushing, decided to attack the python from the side and, in the course of this manoeuvre, managed to get his bottom wedged between the undigested goat and my face. This was not pleasant, but since yet more people coming in from behind had removed his opportunity to retreat, we were stuck.

I was like a man standing on one of Jupiter's moons, who

looks up and all he can see in the sky above is the vast planet in front of him. So it was with my view of the man's posterior, stationed at a proximity closer than I would hold a book if reading it, closer indeed than my normal focal length. I was extremely tempted to give Jupiter a nudge, but couldn't quite see how I was to place my hand on either of the encircling orbs without running the risk of being misinterpreted. So there we were, conjoined for eternity. This was not turning into the best day of my life. The room was hot and humid, humanity was breathing into my face from the worst possible orifice, and I probably wasn't going to get on the flight anyway.

The goat was finally digested, not without considerable burping and belching, and the passengers passed through to the departure area. I stayed on my seat, awaiting the signal from the desk, a signal which did not come. I reviewed my options. 1) Go back to Darjeeling – if I could find a driver. 2) Spend the weekend in Siliguri, and thus become the first tourist ever to do so, or 3) top myself. And then, when hope had been all but extinguished, when all the passengers had their seatbelts securely fastened, as the plane was revving up its engines, Ali came through. He had secured me a seat. You may be relieved to hear that I didn't break down and sob with gratitude. Instead, I did the British thing. I gave him money.

I was searched four times between the airport building and the plane – about 100 yards – but I didn't object. I was aboard. Then to Delhi, where I collapsed senseless on a hotel bed, and caught the early train next morning for Chandigargh.

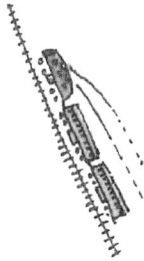

21. CHANDIGARH

… Who doesn't love concrete?

The train up to Chandigarh was the Shatabdi Express, which was on time, fast and comfortable. This came as quite a shock, not because I'd had any bad experiences of Indian railways – I hadn't – but because every Indian train that has ever appeared on British TV has been shown dawdling along at two miles an hour, with enough people clinging to its sides to populate Canada. Not the Shatabdi Express. It positively wooshed. I didn't inspect its exterior, but there was nothing to suggest it was occupied externally – no bodies flying past the window, no scratching noises coming through the roof. It wasn't that kind of train. This was executive travel. Sealed water bottles were complimentary. Breakfast was served by a man wearing sanitised plastic gloves of the sort favoured by dentists. In the next seat to me was an eminent (and chatty) ear, nose and throat surgeon. Time passed quickly.

Chandigarh would win an award for the most un-Indian

city in India. That's because it was designed by a Frenchman, the great Le Corbusier himself. Frenchmen as a rule need no encouragement when it comes to spending vast amounts of public money on grand projects, but Nehru, who was Prime Minister after Independence in 1947, didn't know this. Build me, he said, a new capital of the Punjab (the old one, Lahore, now being in Pakistan[BH]), and make it 'symbolic of the freedom of India… an expression of the nation's faith in the future.'[94]

He might as well have injected Le Corbusier with Nandrilone. The response was the planned city to end all planned cities. It didn't have districts like other cities. It had sectors representing human organs – a head, a heart, an intellect, lungs and even entrails. The entrails were where industry was sited; deep in the bowels, far away from all the higher function stuff, like government. Everything was regulated, even the dustbins.[95] If you wanted somewhere to put your rubbish, you had to have the government model, the one that was officially sanctioned for your type of house. Who else but a Frenchman could have dreamt up all that?

One of the things that became abundantly clear to me on the way in to the city, was that Chandigarh was not a place you could see on foot – unless you enjoyed yomping down the miles of boulevard that seemed to separate one sector from the next. So, after quickly checking into an all mod-cons hotel, I found myself a compliant taxi driver and set off. Quite which sectors

---

BH   At Independence, the North West and North East corners of old India were chopped off to create a Muslim homeland in Pakistan and what is now Bangladesh. The fault line went right through the Punjab. Somewhere between ten and fifteen million people took what they could carry and did their best to make sure they were on the right side of the border when the music stopped.

we visited, or where we were at any one time, I'm not sure I could tell you but I did know one thing: the abiding impression of Chandigarh was of concrete. Le Corbusier had insisted on it, and it was everywhere. The University was concrete. The Gandhi Bhavan, a rather fine building surrounded by water, was concrete. The Legislative Assembly, the High Court, the Secretariat, the houses: all concrete. Some disease must have struck architects in the fifties and sixties. A week after a concrete structure has gone up, it gives the impression of needing a good scrub. Forty years later, the overwhelming emotion it inspires is suicide. Just look at any British university campus built in the sixties.

The Fine Art Museum, stacked to the gunnels with ancient artefacts apparently, was, by some miracle, faced in red sandstone. This simple fact alone made me want to look around. Except it was closed. It was Saturday. It would also be closed on Sunday. Quite right, you can't let the working man see this kind of stuff. Close it over the weekends and open on Monday so that all those retired folks can have it to themselves.

The taxi driver, sensing disappointment, took me along to see Le Corbusier's sculpture, entitled Open Hand. The hand was vast (85 feet high) and stood at the end of a long and aimless road. It was pointing into the distance, like a gargantuan *'Toilets This Way'* sign for the truly desperate. The unfurled palm was a symbol of the Administration's motto, *'open to give, open to receive.'* My immediate assumption was that this was a 'let's-get-the-whole-thing-out-in-the-open' reference to the kickback culture, and rather laudable in its way. Le Corbusier, however, explained it as, 'Open to receive the newly created wealth, open to distribute it to its people and others. The Open Hand will

259

assert that the second era of the machine has begun: the era of harmony.'[96] That's how socialist planners in the 1950s liked to speak. I think they felt it justified all that concrete.

By now, the driver had settled into his role as tour guide, and was happy to motor back and forth across Chandigarh, pointing at things as we passed. By and by, as the miles clocked up and the smile on my man's face turned from broad to radiant, I started to wonder whether my first reaction to Chandigarh had not been a tad severe. There was much to admire. No traffic jams for a start. Clean air. No cows. A vast man-made lake with giant swans that turned out to be *pedalos*. Fun fairs, space, light and recreation. All good and important things, which were undoubtedly some compensation for that eerie feeling that this was Milton Keynes.

For no very good reason, I asked the taxi driver to take me to the town boundaries. And there they were: all those who couldn't afford Chandigarh prices, camping on the perimeter like the Tyrannosaurs in Jurassic Park, hungrily waiting for the electric fence to fuse. We were in a shanty town, unauthorised presumably, and complete with rubbish, acres of cows, and wrecks of broken down, rusted vehicles ready to be sent back to Siliguri. It could only be a matter of time. One day the power would fail and the masses would break through. Chandigarh would become like the rest of India: overcrowded, polluted, bustling and colourful. A place for all the people to live in. That wouldn't be so bad.

I looked out of the window of my hotel next morning. It was raining. I never thought I'd find myself looking at drizzle and thinking, 'oh good.' But I did. These were the pre-monsoon rains just beginning, and they were landing on the earth like water on a hot frying pan. Chandigarh can reach 45° degrees in the summer, after which a light shower is like a lingering sigh of relief.

I whiled away some of the morning by reading the matrimonial section of the Sunday Tribune[97]; North India's self-proclaimed premier newspaper. If, over my frugal breakfast of banana and tea, I was suddenly to be overwhelmed by the desire to add to my stock of wives, this was where I'd start shopping. It was the ultimate buyer's market: pages of advertisements by young women for husbands and not one by a man for a wife.

Listen to this: 'good-looking, smart, slim, intelligent, public school educated, graduate, 24 years old, 5'5" from an old, distinguished, affluent, cultured, well-connected and highly educated service family.' I mean, we're not talking riff-raff. There were hundreds more where this came from. How about 'beautiful, fair, slim, attractive 26/162/52 computer software engineer, from a well-educated but small status Garg family'? Sound good?[BI]

If, however, after surveying the list of endless possibilities, you were still not sure whether marriage was for you, you could always opt for the charms of a washing machine. There, in the middle of the page, in a position which no prospective husband could miss, was a boxed advertisement for the IFB, lowest water and electricity consumption, hot wash, tumble wash and spin drying. Its slogan: 'the best match your clothes can catch.' Hmm.

BI   Just a thought, but you might want to check out the mysterious numbers, 26/162/52. Is it: a. computer code, b. vital statistics, c. bookie's betting slip ref, d. none of the above.

The young women were organised in columns, arranged by caste: Brahmin, Rajput, Khatri, Jat, Jain and so on. The precise sub-category to which a person belongs is important to Indians, in a way that the average European finds impossible to understand. The Hindustan Times had a story[98], not an everyday one presumably, but one that revealed the resonance caste has, even today. In a village on the outskirts of Amritsar in the Punjab, two boys became friends, Kulbir, a high caste Jat Sikh, and Gurchuran, a low caste Balmiki. After a while Gurchuran fell in love with Kulbir's sister, Jasbir, and, knowing that the family would not agree to their marriage, the couple eloped. Kulbir sought them out, spent time with them and won their confidence. He and Gurchuran went shopping one day on a motorbike. Gurchuran was driving. Kulbir, sitting behind, drew out a pistol and shot him under the chin. They both fell off the bike, unsurprisingly, whereupon Kulbir reloaded and, at point blank range, shot the bleeding Gurchuran in the head.

Kulbir made no attempt to deny the crime – which, since he was still clinging to the smoking gun when apprehended, might have been a difficult trick to pull off. Instead, he spoke of his family's humiliation at this inter-caste marriage, adding, chillingly, that his sister, Jasbir, would be his next target. She had, he said, 'spoiled' the good name of his family. He wasn't to have the chance. Jasbir, unable to bear the death of her husband at the hands of her brother, set fire to herself and died of her burns in hospital. A sorry story, almost unintelligible to the western mind[BJ].

BJ   And yet … 'For never was a story of more woe / than this of Juliet and her Romeo.'

I decided to walk to the Rock Gardens, which had been recommended to me by the ENT surgeon on the train coming up. The rain had stopped. It was muggy, but not yet unbearable. I was staying in sector 10. My target was sector 1. Armed with a good map, and fortified further by the thought that this was a grid system with every street at right angles to the next and therefore impossible to get lost, I set out. Trees lined the pavement. The roads were wide and well made. Solid houses were set back from the road with their 'yard' in front. Cars were parked outside the front door. This could have been suburbia in Maryland except, of course, that the probability of being shot here was infinitely lower.

It was a strange feeling to be strolling in India without anything visibly Indian to look at, apart from the occasional bicycle rickshaw. There were no street names as far as I could tell. What there were instead were signs which said 305/1 or 1/24. At the time, these meant nothing at all to me, but I later discovered that they were references to Chandigarh's Orwellian 7V road system. V-1 (or voie-1, as Le Corbusier, being French, liked to call it) was a road that connected to national highways. V-2 roads were the major avenues of Chandigarh. V-3s were corridor streets for cars, and so on and so forth down to V-7 for pedestrians only. Le Corbusier was not a man who left things to chance. Nevertheless, I shouldn't grumble because I made it to the Rock Gardens without getting lost, and it's not often I can say that.

The man who designed the Rock Gardens, Nek Chand, was a road inspector in the early 1950s. His job was to supervise road building in Chandigargh. Instead of looking at the broken stones and discarded rubble of urban life, and saying,

'Beam me up Scotty,' he saw all this waste as, and I quote, 'a novel resource.' For fourteen years from 1958 to 1972, in the evenings and at weekends, he worked away, collecting his bits and pieces, carrying water to the site on his bicycle, and making his lovely sculptures. He did all this without a rupee of public support.

The Chandigarh authorities didn't know about it. Nor did his wife who, trusting woman that she was, thought he was busy with his official duties.[99] She has to be in the running for the 'wife of the century' award. 14 years of coming home late, away at weekends and she sits quietly at home thinking, 'Oh, I do wish they wouldn't work poor Nek so hard.' Mmm. Never once wondered about other possibilities? Never thought he might have taken up golf? When the knock on the door came and the man from the works department began his sentence with, 'You know how you thought Nek's been working late for us these last 14 years, well ...,' I imagine the good woman had to sit down.

The stone shelter occupied by Nek during his years of conjugal absence is part of the Garden. A notice says, 'This is the hut where from Mr Nek Chand made modest beginnings of his immortal masterpiece.' It is a masterpiece. I hope it will be immortal. Out of shattered sinks, ancient rocks, chunks of black stuff that looked like shiny coal (but didn't rub off on your fingers and leave smudge marks on your trousers), old pots, broken plugs, pink, blue, green and white pieces of tile – in fact, waste – have come images of castle walls, pebble mosaics, Greek temples, little pot men on a hillside watching as you pass, tiled ladies under a waterfall, villagers enjoying a picnic, spotted dogs, stone monkeys, peacocks, soldiers and much else you might happen across while out strolling through life's broad acres. It was a labyrinth and a great dreamy place, and if they were to remove the plastic bottles and old tissue paper from the miniature lakes, it would be even better. They might also do something about the heat, because by midday my temperature gauge was showing red, and by 1.30 my gasket was about to explode.

A large insect with a 1" bright red tail had taken a shine to me, and I decided that the moment to leave had come. Nature doesn't give nasty looking insects a bright red tail without a good reason. I headed for the exit, past a notice announcing that Nek Chand was available to speak to visitors, but 'it is a humble request to visitors to please contact the gatekeeper at the entrance.' Indians speak like that. I decided that Padam Shri Nek Chand had done enough for the world without having to speak to me, and proceeded on.

A bicycle rickshaw, somewhat feebly powered by an ageing driver, was just pulling in to the Garden entrance as I came out. Since he was the only form of transport available, I grabbed him. We had a slight problem initially in that he didn't respond when I mentioned the name of my hotel. Whether it was the heat I'm not sure, but I was unable to think of any way of indicating where I wished to be taken, other than by repeating the hotel name. These repetitive utterances had become sporadic, like the gasps of a fish on dry land that has given up hope of oxygen, when, inspirationally, I remembered I had a map. I pulled it out and gave him my interpretation of where the hotel was. Map reading skills are not something I usually proffer except in extremis, but on this occasion, I was rewarded with a nod that meant, 'jump in my son.' I did, quickly.

It was the time of day when this particular mad dog wanted to be inside air-conditioned walls at the earliest opportunity. Once we were under way, the rickshaw driver's aging legs managed to create a pleasant breeze. There was hardly any traffic, or exhaust smoke or indeed anything in the outside world to interrupt the calming quiet of being towed along behind a bicycle – except perhaps a nagging thought. There are some who would say (my oldest daughter among them) that allowing myself to be pedalled by a man in the autumn of his life was decadent and exploitative, and I should be ashamed. In an ideal world, they would, of course, be right. And part of me was ashamed. My ageing dynamo up front should be at home snuggling up to a nice cold refrigerator, and enjoying a quiet glass of something restorative – but, I regret to say, I fear it won't happen, not, at least, in this lifetime. Too much has to change to make not-hiring the man better than hiring him.

Let me encourage you to look at it this way. Bicycles don't pollute the environment. That's a plus. I was providing employment (that's a very important plus), and with what I was about to pay the honest pedaller in order to quieten my rumblings of conscience, (modest though it may have been by British standards), he would probably be able to take the rest of the week off. He certainly showed no sign of being unhappy with his end of the deal, and that, I concluded, in the way you do when little niggles have been swept under the carpet, was therefore that.

Back at the hotel, I picked up an old copy of the Tribune and read about a scam which had made politicians rich and Haryana roads potholed. It pains me to say this but India has its fair share of corruption; there's something dodgy going on most days[BK]. To the tourist, however, whose footsteps hardly break the outer crust, India doesn't feel this way. You don't imagine that you'll be walking along one day and suddenly be plunged, without trial, into the modern equivalent of the Black Hole of Calcutta. I don't anyway.

I put down the paper, went outside for a sweaty stroll, came back, picked up a book, couldn't settle and made plans to move on. Chandigarh was neat, clean, not at all polluted, and positively rolling in green grass and open spaces. It had everything you could want in fact, and everything that I wished other big Indian cities had, but it was a little light on colour. I was a tourist. I wanted colour. And cool. Shimla would be that.

[BK]   If in doubt, Chowdhury and Keane, *To Kill a Democracy*, (Oxford, 2021) provide chapter and verse: corruption, criminal politicians, cronyism, you name it.

22. SHIMLA

… A place in the country

The narrow gauge, single-line track, built by the British in 1903, starts outside Chandigarh, at a place called Kalka. The way to ride up to Shimla is in a First-Class carriage, so the guide books say, except there wasn't a first class. Not when I showed up, anyway. I went chair class. The precise meaning of this classification was not explained, but I did have a chair. Well, if I were being picky, a bench, but I wasn't complaining.

It was a grand way to proceed, particularly if you were one of those who believed that, as you journeyed down life's great highway, you should stop and smell the roses. This train went so slowly, you could have leant out and picked the roses. You could have jumped off the front end, gathered an armful of flowers, and hopped aboard the back as it ambled past. Even were you to be delayed while deciding which blooms to cut, you could always chase the train up the line and catch it at any of the innumerable stations en-route. This was very definitely a stopping train. It stopped to let passengers buy food, it stopped to unload water (it was the water train), and, on occasions, it stopped for no very obvious reason other than it liked stopping. This was travel at its most relaxed.

Whereas most trains move predominantly in a straight line, this one went mostly around corners. The engine spiralled upwards from Kalka at 2,100' to Shimla at 6,800', passing through 102 tunnels and over 869 bridges.[100] It was a magnificent feat of engineering. Shimla was built for rest and recreation and this was British commitment to the idea of a place in the country, at its finest. Some of the bridges were like Roman aqueducts and, on one of these, a young man was standing with his arms outstretched towards the hills, like a diver on the high board about to attempt the triple pike with tuck. Though I was some way away, he could only have been a westerner. When you see someone in the 'I'm-searching-for-cosmic-inspiration' pose, while standing above a drop of a few thousand feet and holding on to nothing at all, you may safely assume he has a white skin, almost certainly a beard and is wearing sandals. In the perverse way of the voyeur, I rather hoped for a flash of something hurtling earthwards, and to catch a muted scream carried in on the breeze. I would then turn to my fellow passengers with a shocked enquiry as to whether anyone else had heard <u>that</u>.

Unfortunately, (or perhaps not), we swung round a corner where there was no view at all. It had been obliterated by a forest of strange-looking pine trees with bare trunks, and upward pointing green arms perched on top like candelabra. The weedier specimens could only manage a U formation, and resembled the sort of cacti you see in real westerns – those that featured the Grand Canyon, as itself, and John Wayne as

John Wayne.

Everybody got off at a pretty little station called Barog to have their breakfast or, as the sign eloquently put it, to 'take eatables.' Well, almost everybody. I just got off. The guard allowed enough time to consume a five-course dinner and then gave his whistle a discreet toot. The train did likewise, only louder, and the passengers ambled back to their seats. After a while we moved off. We reached Solan and stopped once more. Every station was an opportunity to get up, walk around, meet friends, buy something from a kiosk, have a drink – and it couldn't have mattered less, except that there was a station every 15 minutes, and I was starting to notice the first signs of a western twitch. A little voice began to whisper in my ear. Its message was that it could see no reason why the guard didn't put that bloody whistle to his lips, and let's get this show back on the road. Solan was my worst moment. We waited half an hour. After that I was fine. I relapsed back into my usual torpor.

At Kanderghat, the carriage filled up. A young mother, in a pink sari and weighed down by an astonishing amount of jewellery, not to mention a well-padded baby, sat down opposite me. She had pendulous earrings, a discreet stud adorning her contoured nose, sundry necklaces, bracelets that started on her wrist and extended up to her elbow, and bangles on her ankles. The first thing she did, once she had made herself comfortable, was to part the curtain of ironmongery across her front and start breast feeding. Baby, who was a happy little fellow, sucked mightily. Then he stopped and gave his mother a twinkly-eyed stare. Mum smiled back amused and, with one hand, adjusted the fold of the towel in which he was wrapped. Lunch was then resumed. It was a touching scene. I instinctively reached for my water bottle and took a swig.

Sitting next to me was an old man who reminded me somewhat of a St Andrews character called Eck. While not homeless exactly, Eck used to spend his days wandering the streets of our proud old medieval town, entertaining the populace with fortissimo snatches of cracked Italian opera. His unique sound emerged from a voice box ravaged by a lifetime of cheap booze. Eck and my neighbour shared the same round, pocked face, the same pugnacious hunch of the shoulders and the same disinclination to waste time and money on laundry. One of Eck's more endearing traits, now I come to think of it, was that when he noticed a couple of well-dressed middle-aged ladies within earshot, he would stiffen like a man who suddenly knew his life's purpose was about to be fulfilled. He would set his feet apart, lean the top half of his body forward for balance, and then blast the good women with abuse such as you have never heard. This usually had them scuttling across the road, tutting, and glancing fearfully over their shoulders in case Eck was in pursuit. His Himalayan doppelganger wasn't in the same class, vocally. He merely stared at the vicinity of the barely exposed breast, as if non-plussed, and continued to do so intently until he got off two stations later. Mother and baby took this in their stride.

At Kathleeghat, we waited for a pipe to be rigged up to drain some of the water from the tank we were carrying. This took a while. Then we headed up the hill once more and I couldn't help noticing water spilling out of the tanker. It wasn't gushing, but it was more than trickling. A water tanker that leaks only a little on a six-hour journey is not ideal, but I didn't say anything. We had to be nearly there, surely. We came to a station called Summer Hill, and with a name like that, I knew we must be close. The clincher was that it had a notice, which read 'retiring rooms available.' Such a relic of Victorian Britain could only herald our imminent arrival at Shimla, formerly Simla, the number one British hill station, once described as the 'cradle of more insanity than any place within the limits of Hindustan.'[101] A suitable place, therefore, for the government of one fifth of mankind[102] to set up shop, which is what the Viceroy, the Commander-in-Chief and anybody who was anybody in the Raj did for half of every year between 1864 and Independence in 1947. Anything to escape the heat.

Shimla was built on several small spurs of the lower Himalayas, but it now rolls down the mountain like a landslide, and about as attractively. It was altogether bigger, more congested and noisier than I thought it would be but, like Darjeeling, it had a Mall, on which cars were not allowed. Strolling down it was an undiluted pleasure, which I would wholeheartedly recommend to anyone, especially if, at 6.30 pm, the temperature is a lovely 19.5°, as it was then.

The first thing I noticed about the Mall was that you couldn't go five yards without finding a shop selling Cadbury's chocolate, and not just Dairy Milk either, but the whole enchilada: Fruit and Nut, Roast Almond, big sizes, small sizes. You spot these things if you have a digestive system that spends half its time teetering on the brink of gastroenteritical collapse. A substance that is nutritious, filling and inert is worth more than mere words can express. I stocked up like a camel taking in water, bagging enough to keep me going until I reached my next oasis. Then, after I'd paid, I remembered one of chocolate's other properties that probably explained its absence from shops situated at sea level. At 40° – and it wouldn't be less than that down in the plains – chocolate escapes from its wrapper and flows down your trouser leg.

The Mall, and a lane called the Ridge which ran down into it, had the indelible markings that the Raj stamped on all its products. The Library was mock Tudor. The Church was Gothic. The General Post Office was timbered. There was a Gaiety Theatre which – and here I rely on the pictures in the entrance hall – had an auditorium in the manner of the ornate Victorian theatres back home. I wasn't allowed to look for myself. Members only. Domino's Pizza parlour (probably post-Raj) vied with Kwality Corner Fast Food. The shop window register was off the scale and there was a very good second hand, antiquarian bookshop, called Maria's, which took credit cards.

One of the several volumes weighing me down as I stepped out[103], had a whole chapter devoted to that same theatre which had barred my entrance, and I could tell you every play that was put on there, and who played what from the day of its birth until the writer abandoned his labours in 1925 – but I won't. You may be interested to know, however, that Rudyard Kipling acted there, as did his daughter, known only as Miss Kipling. It was not the manner of the author to sprinkle the Christian names of young ladies across his very proper pages.

Not that life in Shimla itself was at all proper, back then. Society was made up of the bees and the butterflies. The bees – the men of government and the army – ran the country. Their wives, and others up from the plains to recover their health, filled their days with riding, racing, shooting, dinners, balls, picnics, the gay social whirl, and frolic in all its various forms. According to The Times Correspondent in 1857, Shimla's butterflies were wracked by class distinction, they gambled dangerously, they waltzed from one ball to another and then sat around bitching about each other. The highlight of the day was the promenade around Jakhu hill (above the Mall), a route which led – the Gods of love being favourable – to the consummation of many a dalliance.[104]

The place where the Ridge runs into the Mall is known as Scandal Point, but the scandal to which it refers was not one between an officer and another man's wife, nor indeed between an Englishman and a woman from the Indian part of town. What would have been newsworthy about either of those? THE scandal was when Maharaja Bhupinder Singh had an association with one of the Viceroy's daughters, for which he was summarily banned from Shimla. There being no Court of Human Rights at the time, the Maharaja devised his own method of sticking two fingers in the air. He built Chail, his own Shimla, and since it had everything a Brit could want, including the world's highest cricket pitch, he found himself besieged by weekend visitors from Shimla, including the Viceroys.[105] Do we think this afforded him some wry satis-faction? We do.

I parked myself on a bench above the scene of the Maharaja's lapse, noticed that donkeys were for hire, which didn't tempt me, and that I could, if I so wished, purchase a Tibetan shawl. I decided, instead, to make inroads into my chocolate mountain, while listening to a brass band playing from a podium above the square. Its melody was clearly military, and was vaguely reminiscent of a tune I knew well – only I couldn't quite place it. Similar things, except in reverse, have happened to me after I've slaved away all day to prepare a meal for my loved ones only to have them look down at the offering, and then, with just the merest hint of compassion, utter the words, 'erm, what is it supposed to be?' Sometimes the word 'exactly' is tacked on to the end, which cuts even deeper. So, I had a great deal of sympathy for the band. They had probably been practising for weeks to give us a medley of old favourites which we would instantly recognise. I'm sure they imagined us tapping our feet and singing along, and I would dearly have loved to oblige, only it wasn't quite turning out as foot-tapping, sing-along music. The drums were being thrashed to within an inch of their lives, and out of the trumpets (which were carrying the tune) came intermittent squawks, of which an alarmed parrot would have been proud. The Brighouse and Rastrick they were not, but I thought they were terrific. As the great American sports writer Grantland Rice no doubt reflected after he'd spent all day preparing dinner, it's not the winning or the losing, but how you played the game.

I spent what was left of the evening hunkered down with the most readable part of my haul at Maria's: Rudyard Kipling's, *Plain Tales from the Hills*. The stories circled around and in Shimla, and Shimla revolved in turn around the redoubtable Mrs Hauksbee. I brought her with me to dinner. Over a plate of boiled rice, curried vegetable and something resembling vegetarian sausage, I read of her plans to prevent the young and impressionable Peythroppe from making a most unsuitable match. When, on the eve of the wedding, she had him kidnapped and taken to Rajasthan, I paid the bill and absent-mindedly dumped a few month's wages on the table as a tip. I was half way out the door before I realised what I'd done. I'd forgotten I was in India, but I could hardly walk back and hoover up the notes. Mrs Hauksbee would most definitely not have approved. I'd have been drummed out of the Brownies.

When I was back in my room, I thought I'd ring Creative Travel. Nobody would be there at this time of night, but I rang anyway on the off-chance. I wanted to find out if Deepak could track down Pappu and have him drive for me when I returned to Delhi. Someone picked up the phone. Not Deepak, but Rajeev, his boss. My admiration was boundless. I could see him all alone in a room black as night, except for a pool of light above a desk. He was hunched over it, for sure, a green visor over his eyes, doing the figures. I apologised for the disturbance. Actually, I felt very bad. This was no time to be ringing. However, I asked him if he thought he could find Pappu and Rajeev said he would be pleased to see what he could do. Indians are a wonderfully courteous people.

Next day, the hotel found me a driver and we went for a tour. Our first port of call was the Bishop Cotton School, one of India's finest educational establishments (for those with the money). It was founded by the Bishop of Calcutta (the eponymous Cotton) as a thanksgiving to God for delivering the British people from that most momentous of events, what the British called the Indian Mutiny of 1857. When the first reports of the uprising reached them, the people of Shimla, along with most of the white population of India, thought they were about to be murdered in their beds.[106] I imagine they were as surprised as anyone that they weren't.

India had a population in those days of 120 million or so[107], of which less than one hundred thousand were Brits. What kept the Union Jack flying, was an army that was nine parts Indian to one part British.[108] Once the sepoys in the Bengal army had decided that there were limits to what they were prepared to do for pay and pension – and this didn't include being converted to Christianity or using cartridges greased with the fat of prohibited animals – there wasn't a great deal standing in their way. They captured Delhi and much of the territory between Varanasi and Rajasthan without too much trouble, by which time it must have looked as if the game was up. Had most of the Princes of India, the Sikhs, the Rajputs and sundry others not decided that they had more to gain than to lose by keeping the British in power, that would have been that. The fat lady would have sung.

The Mutiny, which is better labelled as The Uprising, was just about the fiercest, bloodiest war fought on Indian soil in modern times.[109] Neither side behaved well, and that's putting it mildly. Mass murder was the order of the day.[110] The sepoys butchered the women and children at Cawnpore, and the British rounded up anybody guilty by association and forced them to lick the blood from the floor with their tongues. Then they made them swallow beef (if Hindu) or pork (if Muslim) and, after that, they hanged them.

The British Press crackled with images of what that the Manchester Guardian called 'outrages fouler than our pens can describe'[111], and the Queen's soldiers pursued vengeance with a self-righteous and blood-curdling enthusiasm not normally associated with the British at war. That not all the stories were true, nor all those hanged or blown from cannon guilty, was neither here nor there. One of the enduring images of the Mutiny was the graphic picture, published in the *Illustrated London News,* of a Miss Wheeler pointing a pistol at her head as fiendish sepoys approached. The caption read, *Death before*

Dishonour. Miss Wheeler was later found to have opted for dishonour before death. Sensible woman. She was discovered living with her Muslim abductor.[112]

One of the fascinating things about the Raj – I think so anyway – is how it managed to be both well-intentioned and appalling all at the same time. Many, particularly those in the Indian Civil Service, came to India with the aspiration to do good works; better trains and drains, better schools, better management of forests, the upholding of the rule of law, incorruptible administration, that sort of thing[113]. Many others came for the sole purpose of making money. Here's a story which gives something of the flavour of the push and pull between the best and the worst in India. I found it in one of the books[114] I'd bought at Maria's though I didn't notice the little treasure I was carrying around until I was back home. It's a generally appalling story but it has some mitigation at the end.

In 1862, the date of this story, India was deluged by the arrival of large numbers of non-officials, tea-planters and the like, who were racially arrogant, there for the money and not much liked by the Government.[115] Among their number was a man called Rudd who was asked to buy a sheep for the household of his boss, Mr Jellicoe. Rudd duly selected one from the flock of a shepherd called Fazil. Unfortunately, the sheep was 'in lamb' and so Fazil politely asked him to pick another. Rudd took no notice and merely carried off mother and contents, with her owner following unhappily after. The story rambles on but the upshot was that Fazil appealed to Jellicoe, who returned the sheep and reprimanded Rudd. Thus, thwarted and rebuked, Rudd pelted Fazil with stones, kicked him in the loins and shot him in the back as he was running away. Rudd was brought to trial for shooting an Indian, a man who, let it be remembered, had done nothing more than express a view about the disposal of his own property. Faced with overwhelming evidence against him, both Indian and British, Rudd was convicted of wilful murder. And there, you might have thought the matter would rest. Not so.

The voice of the planters at that time, the *Bengal Hurkaru*, appealed for clemency. 'Marvellous indeed', it crooned, 'is the instinct of mercy.' This from a journal which had bayed for Indian blood during the Uprising. Faced with the hanging of an Englishman, however, it demanded reprieve, and vast numbers of signatures were gathered urging that the sentence be commuted. I am happy to report that it wasn't. Lord Elgin, the Viceroy, held his nerve and, 'despite the earnest prayers of more than 3,000 people', Rudd became one of very few Englishmen to swing. A later Viceroy, Curzon, (1899-1905) deplored what he saw as the 'usual conspiracies' to prevent the white man from facing justice. These 'usual conspiracies' were, he said, 'a black and permanent blot upon the British name.' Indeed so.

Whether, once the stramash over the Uprising was over, all these goings-on in the plains made much difference to the lives of Mrs Hauksbee and her companions in Shimla, I rather doubt. Not if Kipling is any guide. Even today, if a Martian landed at the Bishop Cotton School, (where, let me remind you, your scribe now found himself), he could be forgiven for thinking the Raj was still with us. The inmates wore uniform, and said 'Good Morning Sir' as they went past. The Dining room was panelled like an Oxford College. Long tables and benches, with a top table at right angles, filled the room. Lists of school elevens ran along the walls. House shields sported improving Latin inscriptions and the houses had names like Curzon or Ibbetson. Curzon had been Viceroy, Ibbetson, Lieutenant Governor of Bengal. Apparently, the Central School in Shimla, which was a state school costing one rupee a month, had houses called Nehru, Shuba (after Chandra Bose who fought for the Japanese in World War II), Tagore, the poet and Gandhi. That was the other team: the nationalists.

Having breezed in off the street, I thought I should ask permission to look around and perhaps poke my head into one of the classrooms. I muttered something to that effect to a young teacher who happened to be passing, and he immediately whisked me away to the Head Master's study. This was several levels higher up the pecking order than I had intended to go. I was wearing a cap, a scruffy T-shirt, and trousers that I'd had on for so long that little puffs of dust issued forth every time I rubbed against something. When I sat down, the effect was similar to dropping a bag of flour. I found myself in the inner sanctum, holding my cap in front of me, like a supplicant, and edging onto a chair as circumspectly as possible. The Head Master looked me up and down with a disdain that I couldn't help but agree was entirely appropriate. He listened to my request and, perhaps because not many tourists dropped by on a regular basis, felt it was safe to grant it. Then, as I left his office, he added: 'But if there is a lesson going on, I trust you will not create a disturbance.' Force of habit from long ago all but overpowered me, and I came very close to blurting out the old formula, 'Who me, Sir?' I didn't. I got a grip of myself and remembered I was no longer ten years old.

After a pleasant ramble around the school, during which I

took great care to disturb nothing and nobody, we went up Jakhu hill. By car. It was walkable, but if truth be told I was feeling weary and washed out. I thought I might look inside the nearby temple of Hanuman, the monkey god, but was diverted by the legions of red-faced monkeys outside. They were curling forwards, their heads in their hands, dozing, or were just lying flat like a dog that's slept in the road once too often. One of them had learned how to turn on a tap and drink the water, which, I'd say, took brains. If he married well, his offspring could probably make a start on calculus. My driver, who had walked up with me, was rather matter of fact about the whole scene. 'That Ridge,' he said, pointing at the view in a general kind of way. 'This monkey,' he said looking at a monkey. 'This monkey shit,' he said looking at monkey shit. Hard to know what to say to that.

From there, we went up past some extremely dense forest. I think it was called Wild Flower Hill Ridge, which sounds unlikely I know, but the S-bends were taking their toll and I wasn't altogether with it. There was an outdoor zoo at the top, which boasted a snow leopard, except that it was either visiting relatives or out to lunch. It certainly wasn't in residence. I did see a yak, though, in the nearby village. It had been combed and prettified, and its long hair fell fetchingly over its eyes. It reminded me rather of the comedian Les Dawson[BL] with four flat feet and a saddle. Its owner was hauling it along by a rein that went through its nostrils, and it didn't look entirely chuffed.

BL   Who was Les Dawson, I hear you ask? He was an English comedian who liked to make mother-in-law jokes of the sort that would not be allowed today. What did he look like? Hmm ... a bit like a yak with two feet.

Later that evening, while taking a gentle constitutional along the Mall, I came to the conclusion that it was definitely time I went home. I was starting to adopt local customs. I found myself half way through a spit before managing to bring out my handkerchief in the nick of time. Suppose I did that in St Andrews – forgot myself and gobbed. It didn't bear thinking about. Mind you, let me make it clear that I have not dropped litter. Not yet. I have carried banana skins and empty water bottles for miles in search of a litter bin, almost never found one, and so stuffed the lot in my haversack. When re-discovered days later, and still no nearer a litter bin, the rotting banana skins have presented an ethical dilemma, on which it would be all too easy to slip. Do you hang onto them, allowing them to decompose in the midst of your clothing, or do you chuck them in the street like everybody else? Not an easy one, that, unless you can find a moment when no-one is watching.

I went back to the bench on which I'd heard the band play so memorably, and took a long last lingering view out over the Himalayas – not something those of us from Northern Europe see too many times. A Scandinavian couple was standing next to me. The man pointed out a spot on the horizon and uttered the word that had my ears cocking like an excited spaniel. 'Kanchenjunga,' he murmured. No, surely not. It couldn't be visible from here, could it? Since I had last seen it, I'd driven to Bagdogra, taken a two-hour flight to Delhi, a three-hour train journey to Chandigarh, and at least another six to Shimla. Heavens, if that was Kanchenjunga again, she sure did get around.

A reflection on British justice in India ...
who was it for?

The question was a recurring one. Lord Ripon, (Viceroy 1880-1884) posed the rhetorical question as to whether India was to be ruled 'for the benefit of the Indian people of all races, classes and creeds' or 'in the sole interest of a small body of Europeans?' The top brass thought one thing, the white planters, mill owners etc thought another. The Ilbert bill of 1883, which would have allowed properly qualified Indian magistrates to conduct trials of whites, was howled down by 'the (white) mob shaking their fists in the face of the whole native population.' This was a 'white mutiny' and its contemptuous message was not lost on Indian magistrates and educated Indians generally. Ripon weakened, the Ilbert Bill was emasculated and two years later, in 1885, the first meeting of the Indian National Congress was held. As Niall Ferguson says, 'It is not too much to see the White Mutiny as the fount and origin of ... alienation from British rule.' [116]

And, while we're at it, what right did Britain think it had to be governing India (or anywhere else for that matter) in the first place?

The right to govern was not a question much asked by the East India Company. It was a private company which came to India to make money through trade. That it ended up also making law, it would have regarded as circumstantial. The question was more to the fore after 1858 when India was governed directly from London.

The question of the right to govern is difficult. Ethical questions always are (which is why autocratic states prefer to avoid them). The answer given by Arthur Balfour, the widely experienced British statesman, to the House of Commons in 1910 boiled down to this: that India was better off under a benign government, such as the British, than under one of its own.

This is, of course, highly problematical. As to the many reasons why, there is no one better to be your guide than Edward Said. He has much to say about Balfour, and matters arising, in his book, 'Orientalism.'[117]

23. BACK TO DELHI (AGAIN)

… Pappu, Gandhi and farewell

The journey back was uneventful, and I can heap no higher praise on it than that. The Shatabdi express pulled into Delhi station on time. That was two out of two. The doors were flung open, and I was immediately reminded of the meaning of the word 'hot'. The word does not have the sense in which it is typically used in Scotland. There it denotes, 'pleasantly warm'. For the benefit of my Scottish friends, let me say that when it is pleasantly warm, you are not able to tandoori a chicken merely by holding it up by its back legs. Nor are you able to have a steam bath, simply by throwing water on the ground. When it's hot, Delhi-hot, you can do both of these things. This is particularly true when in Delhi's station, which was a madhouse populated by millions. Maybe billions. All those gyrating human bodies weren't cooling the place down, I can tell you that.

One tip I would pass on to you at Indian stations is this;

always take a porter. It's the best 50 rupees you'll ever spend. Even if it's 100 rupees, it's good value. Apart from anything else, a porter will help you find the exit and, believe me, you don't want to be blundering about hauling your luggage, looking for one. Not when the temperature would make a Martian melt. I grabbed my porter while I was halfway out of the train, and I stuck to him like a wet T-shirt – as did mine to me.

I didn't expect Pappu to be there. I had a vague recollection that, at this time of year, when sensible tourists stayed at home, he was laid off, and probably back in Haryana. So I came out of the station not thinking much about anything, and there he was, smiling that curiously toothy smile of his. He was a sight for sore eyes. 'Apke se he' I said, the words suddenly popping out of left field after all that time unused in Nepali country. 'Tik he,' he replied. It was as if I'd never been away. Rinki and Tinku were good. His wife was good. The village was still standing. Nobody, or so I deduced, had yet reached the condom passage in Porterhouse Blue. My cred was still intact.

Pappu ushered me to the car. It was my old friend, the Ambassador, spotless as ever. We pushed our way out of the station and swerved hair-raisingly into oncoming traffic. I was back. It felt good. First stop was what I now thought of as 'my Club'. I collected my key from the same kindly man who'd been there last time, and walked round the place three times before accidentally stumbling across 'my cottage'. Pappu followed behind in the car, like Security shadowing a President who has decided to stretch his legs. Quite what he thought this circumnavigation was all about, I've no idea.

My time in India was running out and I still hadn't seen anything of India's greatest citizen since Ashoka. This had to be remedied. Pappu drove me round to Birla house where Gandhi had spent his last days. It was closing in half an hour, but a young man on the door let me in, provided I was quick. I took the exhibits at a gallop. Gandhi in England training to be a lawyer. Gandhi in South Africa chucked out of a first-class carriage. Gandhi receiving an admiring letter from Tolstoy of all people. Who would have imagined that? His investigation of General Dyer and the massacre at Amritsar, his bonfire of foreign cloth, his crusade against untouchability, his meeting with King George V in London in 1931 wearing only a dhoti, the Quit India campaign which led to Independence in 1947. His whole life flashed before me like a video on fast forward. It was surprisingly knackering. You know what Gandhi left behind when he died? Two spoons, two forks, one knife, one cleaver, one stick, one stone, glasses, glasses case, and a fob watch. Not much considering. Then I was gently ushered off the premises.

Only as far as the gardens, though, since these didn't have gates that shut. It was in these gardens, in the late afternoon of January 30th, 1948, that Gandhi was assassinated. He had come out of his room to join the people in prayer. The path he trod, the very footprints, have been preserved. He was shot three times in the chest by a Hindu named Ghotse who, so it was said, held him responsible for the break-up of India. I don't know why exactly, but the steps of his last walk, like a fossilised witness, were as moving a memorial as could be. Gandhi had once said, 'If I am to die by the bullet of a man, I must do so smiling.' Nearby were recorded the words of Albert Einstein; "Generations to come, it may be, will scarce believe that such a one as this ever in flesh and blood walked upon this earth."

Since the museum was now shut, Pappu suggested that the Raj Ghat, where Gandhi was cremated, was not to be missed. Actually, what he said was, 'this place Mahatma Gandhi Sanardi all travel agency compulsory looking all tourists coming Delhi.' Now this sentence may look awkward – and I'd have added a comma or two if I could have made up my mind where to put them – but the thing was, when uttered by Pappu, it was entirely comprehensible. Don't ask me how, but it was. He'd clearly been working on his English. I gave him a nod of encouragement and off we went. An eternal flame on a simple marble platform marked Gandhi's last resting place. Hindus were praying beside it. We didn't linger. At six in the evening, it was hotter than 6pm, even in India, had any right to be. Pappu taught me a new phrase: *bahut gharmia*, *very hot*. This was a worthy addition, and I practised it with a flick of first finger across the forehead, as if removing beads of sweat. Except they weren't beads. They were torrents.

Pappu took me to the Club. I rang the kind man, who'd organized my accommodation there, to report in after my travels. He told me he'd played golf that day. I could hardly believe him. He did allow that it had been a degree or two above what you'd normally understand by bahut gharmia, but what, he asked, was the alternative? Not to play? Put like that, I could see his point. Nonetheless, it was heroic.

I went over to the dining room, still marvelling, and enjoyed the cheapest (edible) meal in India, (with only a minor panic when the banana fritter arrived and I discovered it was cold). Tomorrow would be my last day in India. I transferred to the bar feeling somewhat maudlin.

The next morning started slowly with tea, and two slices of

toast wrapped (curiously) in greaseproof paper. I unwrapped them and nibbled half-heartedly, until Pappu collected me for a last lingering look at the sights. It was definitely time to go. Delhi was starting to look elegant. I think it probably is. Wide streets, trees, imperial architecture, old ruins. The fact was that things which appalled me when I first came, didn't now. I hardly noticed them. People hang from buses. Do they? I suppose they do, now you come to mention it. Children beg in the streets and tap your car window as you are waiting at traffic lights. Yes, if you say so. People thrust postcards up your nostril to make you buy. Yes, and your point? It was high time I left. A little longer and Pappu's driving would appear sedate.

At the airport, I gave Pappu a small parcel of improving books for his village. In English. We said our goodbyes. As I turned to go, I sneezed. Pappu said, 'God is bless you.'

The plane had newspapers. 'At 12.32 GMT yesterday', I read, 'India's billionth person was born.' A baby called Hope.

AN EXTREMELY BRIEF HISTORY OF INDIA.

Clump One – Hindu and Buddhist beginnings (to 1001 CE)

In the beginning was the Great Flood. (*No civilization worth its salt can start without a Great Flood.*) The Indian equivalent of Noah was Manu, a simple man who was kind to a little fish. When the Flood was imminent, the little fish, which was by then a big fish, gave Manu the appropriate instructions; 'Build a boat', it said.

Around 2500 BCE, came Harappa and Mohenjo-Daro, large cities in the Sindh and Punjab regions of what is now Pakistan. These were built of brick, laid out on a grid system and had good drainage – but no-one has yet deciphered their linguistic remains.

Next up were the Aryans in c.1500 BCE. Where they came from is unclear, as is how they interacted with the Harappans. Unlike the Harappans, however, they left nothing for archaeologists to get their trowels into but they more than compensated for this with their language (Sanskrit), their gods (the Hindu pantheon) and their abundant literature. The Vedas were theirs as were the Upanishads and two of the world's great epics, the Ramayana and the Mahabharata.

History is misty but, through the fog of that ancient millennium, agriculture became more intensive, cities re-appeared and development moved east and south. Kingdoms and dynasties emerged; most noticeably Magadha and Maurya.

The Magadha kingdom around Pataliputra (Patna) was where, sometime in the 6th or 5th century BCE – hard to see through all that mist – the Buddha achieved enlightenment. Buddhism prospered. Ashoka (268-231 BCE), the third ruler of the Mauryan dynasty, converted to Buddhism and spread the word of enlightened thinking (of Dharma) throughout India and beyond. The Mauryan empire ran from Afghanistan and probably Nepal down to the south of India, an extent of dominion greater than that achieved by the Mughals and comparable to that of the British.

After Ashoka, and for the next 500 years (at a time when the Romans were in full swing in Europe), the fog descends once more. The Mauryan dynasty disintegrated while others, this time in smaller regional blocs, came and went. The best of the cultural highlights occurred in the 2nd century BCE with the appearance of Vatsyayana's Kama Sutra and Patanjali's seminal writings on yoga.

Fast forward then to c.300 - 500 CE and the golden age of the Guptas; golden because of its achievements in literature and art as much as for the somewhat gentle (though extensive) empire over which the Guptas ruled. The Guptas (the King-of-kings) were less hands-on than Ashoka, presiding over a number of vassal states who were left largely to their own devices. Buddhism once again prospered alongside Brahmanism (Hinduism) and dharma was once again pursued. Artistic totems emerged such as the rock carving at Mathura and the cave paintings at Ajanta. In poetry and drama, Kalidasa, acclaimed as the Indian Shakespeare, was pre-eminent.

The next few hundred years of comings and goings are fragmented, confusing and, if not omitted from this *Extremely Brief History*, the history won't be extremely brief, or even brief. Suffice it to say that, by the 11th century CE, if you didn't have the bad luck to be killed on the battlefield, India was probably one of the world's more pleasant places to live. Its economy was as sophisticated as any, its manufacturing was skilled, its roads were safe, the ports and markets were bustling and capital was rolling in[118]. There was, however, a gathering cloud.

Clump Two – Islamic invasions (1001 - 1526)

Islamic invaders had pecked at India's north-western frontier in the 8th century but, from 1001 CE, Northern India was plundered by a succession of Muslim invaders from Afghanistan and the Turkic tribes thereabouts. After the Rajputs (from Rajastan) had been routed at the battle of Tarain in 1192, there was nothing much to hold up the Muslim advance. They came for plunder; if you are from impoverished areas in Afghanistan, like Ghazni or Ghor, expeditions have to be self-financing, and these certainly were. Temples were looted and destroyed on a scale rarely witnessed, blood was spilled by the tanker-load, and gold and treasures were piled up to the rafters and carted off.

More permanent (but equally destructive) occupation of the land around Delhi by dynasties from Afghanistan, or the

Turkic tribes roundabout, began with Mohammed of Ghor in 1194. His Ghorid dynasty was followed by the 'Slave' dynasty (1206-1290), then the Khaljis (1290-1320), the Tughluqs (1320-1413), the Saiyyids (1414-1451) and the Lodis (1451-1526).

Clump Three – the Great Mughals, also Muslim (1526-1707)

Things settled down, relatively speaking, with the arrival of Babur, the first of the six Great Mughals (so called because of Babur's Mongol descent). After Babur, came Humayun, Akbar, Jahangir, Shah Jehan and Aurangzeb who ruled, collectively, from 1526-1707. Their Empire may have been heavily militarised, and just about everyone but themselves may have been squeezed to the last drop[119], but treasures weren't carted off to foreign lands and you can't argue with their public works programme; just check out the Taj Mahal. One of the family's more conspicuous weaknesses was its gargantuan appetite for luxury in all its forms, for opium, alcohol and for fratricide.

The best of the Great Mughals was Akbar (r. 1556-1605) who was interested in, and tolerant of, other religions. He allowed Hindus into the imperial civil service and both married Hindu women himself or married them to his sons. The worst was Aurangzeb (r.1658-1707), an unflinching Muslim who forbade the building of new Hindu temples, who taxed Hindus for being Hindus (ostensibly in return for military protection by the Faithful) and who drained the empire by relentless campaigning in the south. He succeeded in alienating the Sikhs in the Punjab, the Rajputs in Rajasthan and the Marathas (led by the charismatic Shivaji) in the Deccan.

By the time of Aurangzeb's death in 1707, India was in ruins. Its administration was shot through with corruption, its lands were ravaged by famine, and the extreme profligacy of its tiny elite was no longer sustainable by its overburdened population[120]– all of which paved the way for yet more foreign invaders.

Clump Four – The British (mid 1700s -1947)

In the early 18th century, the British, the Dutch, the Danes, the Portuguese and the French all founded companies to compete for trade with India. The British East India Company came out on top. It started small but was soon able to establish Calcutta as an attractive place to do business. As a result, it was bankrolled by Indian bankers and was able to use its military capability to make itself an attractive partner to a number of Indian States (different States at different times.) In 1765, it manoeuvred itself into a position where it was granted the right to make laws and levy taxes in India's richest state, Bengal. This was an extraordinary situation for a private company to be in, and one which the EIC didn't hesitate to exploit.

The East India Company was *Part One* of the British Conquest. Remembering that this is an extremely brief history, let me pick a word which best characterizes its governance: *greed*. Macauley, in his essay on the impeachment of Warren Hastings in 1787,[121] described the governance of the East India Company as 'English power … unaccompanied by English morality.'

The consequence of this untrammelled greed was most clearly demonstrated in 1770 when, with Bengal laid bare by drought and appalling famine, the Company rigorously continued to insist on its taxes being paid. William Dalrymple has called this 'one of the greatest failures of corporate responsibility in history.'[122]

The Indian Uprising of 1857 led, in 1858, to the British Government taking over the administration of India. It ruled until Independence in 1947. This is *Part Two* of the British Conquest. Under direct British rule, government administrators developed a reputation for incorruptibility[123], while government engineers built railways, drains and all that – but as to whether, taken in the round, the British Empire was good or bad for India, opinion is divided.

For the defence, some like Niall Ferguson[124] have argued that Britain gave India an international language (English), facilitated international trade and provided a blueprint for the institutions that underpin a liberal democracy: an elected parliament, common law and a free press. For the prosecution, some such as Shashi Tharoor[125] have lambasted the British Raj for its ruthless appropriation of Indian resources, for causing famine, for the ruin of millions, for the destruction of thriving industries, for the denial of opportunities to compete, for its racial arrogance and for its suppression of India's capacity to forge its own path.

The former Prime Minister of India, Manmohan Singh, took a more measured view of Britain's legacy. Speaking in July 2005, he said, "*Our notions of the rule of law, of a Constitutional government, of a free press, of a professional civil service, of modern universities and research laboratories have all been fashioned in the crucible where an age-old civilization of India met the dominant Empire of the day. These are all elements which we still value and cherish. Our judiciary, our legal system, our bureaucracy and our police are all great institutions, derived from British-Indian administration and they have served our country exceedingly well. The idea of India as enshrined in our Constitution, with its emphasis on the principles of secularism, democracy, the rule of law and, above all, the equality of all human beings irrespective of caste, community, language or ethnicity, has deep roots in India's ancient culture and civilization. However, it is undeniable that the founding fathers of our Republic were also greatly influenced by the ideas associated with the age of enlightenment in Europe. Our Constitution remains a testimony to the enduring interplay between what is essentially Indian and what is very British in our intellectual heritage.*[126]

And then, lest we forget, there's cricket. Born in England it may have been, but now India's great love, played across the sub-continent wherever there is a spare patch of grass or concrete. A small thing, perhaps, in the great scale of things but a source of much pleasure, unity and camaraderie nonetheless.

Clump Five – Independence, 1947.

At Independence in 1947, India split. The largely Muslim state of Pakistan was formed. Somewhere between 200,000 and 3m people died in the Hindu-Muslim violence which followed. Between 1946 and 1951, some six million Muslims emigrated to Pakistan and some nine million Hindus and Sikhs moved in the opposite direction. It was calamitous.

But … let's not end this *Extremely Brief History* with calamity. Instead, let's end with the words which rang out across the world and resonate still; the words of India's first Prime

Minister, Jawaharlal Nehru, as he addressed India's Constituent Assembly just before the midnight hour of Independence, August 14, 1947.

"Long years ago we made a tryst with destiny, and now the time comes when we shall redeem our pledge, not wholly or in full measure, but very substantially. At the stroke of the midnight hour, when the world sleeps, India will awake to life and freedom. A moment comes, which comes but rarely in history, when we step out from the old to the new, when an age ends, and when the soul of a nation, long suppressed, finds utterance...

... The ambition of the greatest man of our generation has been to wipe every tear from every eye. That may be beyond us, but so long as there are tears and suffering, so long our work will not be over. And, so, we have to labour and to work, and work hard, to give reality to our dreams. Those dreams are for India, but they are also for the world."

The speech lasts four minutes on YouTube and, in it, there is much to savour.

REFERENCES

[1]   Stanley Wolpert, *A New History of India*, (Oxford University press, New York, 1997), p.155.

[2]   Bamber Gascoigne, *The Great Mughals*, (Constable, London, 1998), p245.

[3]   William Dalrymple, *The Anarchy*, (Bloomsbury 2020), p.14.

[4]   Gascoigne, op. cit., p.12

[5]   HAR Gibb (trans.), *The Travels of Ibn Battuta AD 1325-1354*, vol. III, (Cambridge University press, Cambridge, 1971), pp. 677, 711.

[6]   Ibn Battuta, op. cit., p.708.

[7]   Ibn Battuta, op. cit., p.623

[8]   Erich Von Daniken, *Chariots of the Gods*, (Souvenir Press, London, 1996), p.92

[9]   Feuerstein, Kak & Frawley, *In Search of the Cradle of Civilization,* (Quest Books, 1995,) p.45.

[10]   John Keay, *India, a History*, (Harper Collins, 2000), p27.

[11]   *India, Lonely Planet Guide*, (Lonely Planet Publications, 1999), p 468

[12]   Wolpert op. cit., p.39.

[13]   Stephanie Jamison, *Sacrificed Wife, Sacrificer's Wife*, (Oxford University Press, New York, 1996), pp 65-72.

[14]   Wolpert, op. cit., p.62

[15]   DC Sircar, *Inscriptions of Asoka*, (Publications Division,

Ministry of Information and Broadcasting, Government of India, 1998), Major Rock Edict, XIII, p.42

[16] DC Sirkar, op. cit., pp25-62.

[17] Roy Craven, *Indian Art,* (Thames & Hudson, 1997), p.40.

[18] Wolpert, op. cit., pp108-9.

[19] Craven, op. cit., pp.188-9.

[20] Roy Craven, op. cit., pp. 140, 188.

[21] Stanley Breedon and Belinda Wright, *Through the Tigers Eyes,* (Ten Speed Press, Berkeley, California, 1996), pp 127-33.

[22] Julian Pettifer, BBC World, 6/8/00.

[23] Gascoigne, op. cit., p.86

[24] Abu-L-Fazl, *The Akbar Nama, vol. II,* (Atlantic Publishers, reprinted 1989), pp 416-17.

[25] Breedon and Wright, op. cit., p.168.

[26] Breedon and Wright, op. cit., p.168.

[27] Breedon and Wright, op. cit., p. 169.

[28] P.G. Wodehouse, *Mr Mulliner Speaking,* (from Jeremy Paxman, The English, p.176).

[29] Abul Fazl, The Akbar Nama, vol. III, p.1220

[30] Louis de Bernières, *Captain Corelli's Mandolin,* (Minerva, London, 1995), p.179.

[31] Gascoigne, op. cit., p.181.

[32] Nicollao Manucci, *Storia Do Mogor 1653-1708,* trans. William Irvine, (John Murray, London, 1906), vol. 1, p.197.

[33] Manucci, op. cit. vol. 1, p194.

[34] Manucci, op. cit., vol. 1 p. 217 (see also Bernier).

[35] Manucci, op. cit., vol 1, pp 359-60.

36   Manucci, op. cit., p. 360.

37   Manucci, op. cit., vol. 1, p. 339 and p. 382

38   Dalrymple, op.cit., p.72

39   Formerly Rajputana, home of the Rajputs

40   Ralph Fitch, from *Early Travels in India 1583-1619*, ed. William Foster, (Oxford University Press, 1921), pp.17-18.

41   Craven, op. cit., p.201.

42   Gascoigne, op. cit., p 99, 107-8

43   Gascoigne, op. cit., pp.81-2.

44   Catherine Asher, The New Cambridge History of India I.4, Architecture of Mughal India, (Cambridge University press, 1992), p.54.

45   Alexander Rogers (trans.) and Henry Beveridge (ed.), *Memoirs of Jahangir*, (Atlantic Publishers, New Delhi, 1989) vol.I, p. 255.

46   Andrew Robinson, *Maharaja*, (Thames & Hudson, London, 1988), p.90.

47   Gayatri Devi, *A Princess Remembers, The Memoirs of the Maharani of Jaipur*, (Tarang Paperbacks, New Delhi, 1994), pp.96, 98.

48   Gauba, op. cit., p. 179.

49   Robinson, op. cit., p.7.

50   Charles Allen and Sharada Dwivedi, *Lives of the Indian Princes*, (Eshwar, Mumbai, 1986), pp. 80-1.

51   Allen, Dwivedi, op. cit., p. 184.

52   Allen, Dwivedi, op. cit., p.269, 277.

53   Allen, Dwivedi, op. cit., p.15.

54   William Crooke (ed.), *Tod's Annals and Antiquities of Rajasthan, Vol II*, (Oxford University Press, 1920), p.949.

55 Devendra Handa, *Osian, History, Archaeology, Art and Architecture*, (Sundeep Prakashan, 1984), p.4.

56 Handa, op. cit. p12.

5   Handa, op.cit., p.16

58 L.N.Khatri, *Jaisalmer, Folklore, History and Architecture*, (Morchang Publication, 1997), p.58.

59 Robinson, op. cit., p127.

60 Khatri, op. cit., p.41.

61 Feuerstein, Kak and Frawley, op. cit., p.129.

62 Gascoigne, op. cit., p.143.

63 Breedon and Wright, op. cit., p.50.

64 Francois Bernier, *Travels in the Mogul Empire, AD 1656-1668*, trans. Archibald Constable, (Westminster 1891), pp 39-40.

65 Tirtankar Roy, *Review of Inglorious Empire*, Cambridge Review of International Affairs, (31/1/2018).

66 Dalrymple, op cit., p.240

67 Nigel Biggar, *Colonialism a Moral Reckoning*, (William Collins, 2023), p.287.

68 David Gilmour, *The British in India*, (Penguin 2018), pp 167-169

69 Roy, op.cit.

7⁰ R.C. Majumdar, (general editor), *The History and Culture of the Indian People: vol. VII, The Mughal Empire*, (Bharatiya Vidya Bhavan, Mumbai, 1984), p.339.

71 R.C.Majumdar, op. cit., p.336-340.

72 Tod's Annals, op. cit., volume 1, p. 368.

73 Prahlad Singh, *Stone Observatories of India*, (Holiday Publications, Jaipur, 1997), p.15.

74 Rudyard Kipling, *From Sea to Sea, vol 1*, (MacMillan,

London, 1910), p.10.

[75] Kipling, op. cit., p.19.

[76] Gascoigne, op. cit., p.76

[77] R.C.Majumdar, op. cit., p.101.

[78] The Travels of Peter Mundy 1608-1667, Vol II, (Hakluyt Society, 1914), p.90, 108.

[79] *Daily Telegraph*, 11 March 2000, Dr Richard Dawood.

[80] James, op. cit., pp 30-32.

[81] Dalrymple, op. cit., p.74.

[82] Dalrymple, op. cit., p.34.

[83] Dalrymple, op. cit., p.121.

[84] Dalrymple, op. cit., p.219.

[85] Dalrymple, op. cit., p.52.

[86] Dalrymple, op. cit., p.257.

[87] Dalrymple, op. cit., p.322.

[88] Breedon and Wright, op. cit., pp 29-31.

[89] Born Tsa-chu, Nepal, 1914.

[90] Keay, op. cit., p. 429

[91] AKJ Singh, *Himalayan Triangle*, (The British Library, 1988), and Alistair Lamb, *British India and Tibet 1766-1910*, (Routledge & Kegan Paul, 1986) – both throughout.

[92] Lamb, op. cit., p.69-70.

[93] AKJ Singh, op. cit, pp. 179-180.

[94] Ravi Kalia, *Chandigarh, the Making of an Indian City*, (Oxford University Press, 1999), p.21

[95] Kalia, op. cit., p.124

[96] Kalia, op. cit., p.117

[97] *Sunday Tribune*, 7 May 2000.

[98] *Hindustan Times*, 1 December 1999.

[99] M.S. Aulakh, *The Rock Garden*, (Tagore Publishers, Ludhiana,1986), pp19-20.

[100] Gillian Wright, *Hill Stations of India*, (Penguin, London, 1998), p.105

[101] Sir Penderel Moon, *The British Conquest and Dominion of India*, (Duckworth, 1989) p.497.

[102] Gillian Wright, op. cit., p.94.

[103] Edward J Buck, *Simla, Past and Present*, (The Times Press, Mumbai, 1925)

[104] Buck, op. cit., p.208.

[105] Allen and Dwivedi, op. cit., p.127.

[106] Buck, op. cit., pp 76-77.

[107] James, op. cit., p.66.

[108] Keay, op. cit., p.445.

[109] Wolpert, op. cit., p238.

[110] James, op. cit., pp 251-3.

[111] James, op. cit., p.283.

[112] James, op. cit., p.287.

[113] David Gilmour, op.cit, p.161 onwards.

[114] G.O.Trevelyan, *The Competition Wallah*, (Macmillan, London, 1866), pp 272-281.

[115] Moon, op. cit., pp.771-2.

[116] Niall Ferguson, *Empire*, (Penguin, 2003), pp 202-205.

[117] Edward W Said, *Orientalism*, (Penguin Classics 2019), pp 31-49.

[118] Keay, op. cit, p188.

[119] Abraham Eraly, *the Mughal World, India's Tainted Paradise*, (Phoenix 2008), pp.165-181.

[120] Eraly, op cit, pp. 380-381

[121] Thomas Babington Macauley, Critical and Historical

Essays, (JM Dent, 1907, vol 1,) p.556.

[122] William Dalrymple, op cit., p.219.

[123] Gilmour, op cit, p. 40.

[124] Niall Ferguson, *Empire – How Britain made the Modern World*, (Penguin 2003).

[125] Shashi Tharoor, *Inglorious Empire – what the British did to India*, (Penguin, 2017).

[126] Biggar, op cit., pp283-284.

ACKNOWLEDGEMENTS

My first trip to India was life changing in many ways and I'm extremely grateful to all those who guided my footsteps in one way or another. Particular thanks to Indevir and Veena Juneja, Geoffrey Sprot, Chris Hardwicke, Amar Singh, Brij Mohan Thapar and Deepak Modgill.

Thanks too to those who ferried me on the journey or who fed me tasty morsels of information as I went along, notably Shibu, Satya Gupta, Dhanajay Singh, Raj Kashoor, Rajjan, Madhu Sudan, Promswar and Namgill. Most particularly, I'd like to thank Pappu who, after many hours on the road, I came to regard as a friend.

The encyclopaedic cover of this book is the work of Jurek Pütter. His wonderfully artistic condensation of Northern India into the requirements of a travel book is a thing to be treasured. Subsequent design magic was also wonderfully worked by Dan Forde.

I'm grateful to the excellent library and print facilities at the University of St Andrews, and grateful too to those who have been kind enough either to read the text and make comments, or to offer help in miscellaneous other ways. These include Rachel and James Gallagher, Helen and Colin Hastings, Jonathan Tobert, Robin Vicary, Chris Given-Wilson, Alec Crawford, Bill Zachs, Roger McStravick, Howard Goldfinger, Julio, Anna and Katerina. Special thanks to Andrew for his astute remarks, to Natasha for her encouragement, and to Madeleine who, as ever, was always happy to bring her writer's eye to bear.

Printed in Dunstable, United Kingdom

73688469R00180